P9-DVH-528

Better Homes and Gardens®
Fish and Seafood Cook Book

BETTER HOMES AND GARDENS BOOKS
NEW YORK • DES MOINES

Feature Pompano en Papillote wrapped in the traditional brown paper package in your dinner menu. The delicate pompano fillets covered with a rich crab meat sauce are revealed by slashing the tops of the packages open.

BETTER HOMES AND GARDENS BOOKS

Editorial Director: Don Dooley
Managing Editor: Malcolm E. Robinson   Art Director: John Berg
Food Editor: Nancy Morton
Senior Food Editor: Joyce Trollope
Associate Editor: Nancy Byal
Assistant Editors: Sandra Wood, Lorene Mundhenke,
Pat Olson, Sharyl Steffens
Copy Editor: Lawrence Clayton
Designers: Arthur Riser, Julie Zesch, Harijs Priekulis

© Meredith Corporation, 1971. All Rights Reserved.
Printed in the United States of America.
Second Printing.
Library of Congress Catalog Card Number: 76-132433
SBN:696-00494-1

CONTENTS

Better Homes and Gardens
TEST KITCHEN

Our seal assures you that every recipe in the *Fish and Seafood Cook Book* is endorsed by the Better Homes and Gardens Test Kitchen. Each recipe is tested for appeal, practicality, and deliciousness.

Whether you're an experienced chef who has prepared many gourmet meals or a beginning homemaker who is starting to experiment with seafood cookery, you will find here all you need to know—about basic preparation, menu planning, what to look for when buying fish, and what to do with the fish once you have it in your kitchen.

You'll find many hints and actual menu plans to help you prepare tasty seafood combinations—menus that emphasize the most delicate of flavors, others that bring out the full flavor of fish and shellfish—all designed to please and to satisfy both family and guests.

In this section, you'll also come across questions that you should ask yourself before you make any purchase. What to look for when buying canned, fresh, or frozen fish. How much to plan for one or many servings. How to recognize a fresh fish. You'll understand all these things if you familiarize yourself with market forms, characteristics of seafood, and with how much you need to buy.

Also included for the fisherman in the family are drawings to help make cleaning, skinning, and filleting the catch as uncomplicated as possible. You won't find any secrets about catching fish or where the fish are biting—that's left up to the skill of the fisherman. But you will find many basic recipe ideas for frying, broiling, poaching, steaming, baking, and barbecuing. The Barbecued Fish as pictured here is a good example of fish cooked over a campfire.

Seafood Basics

PLANNING THE MENU

"What's for dinner?"—that eternal question homemakers face daily can be solved more easily if you include fish and shellfish in your menus. These foods will add nutrition, variety, and flavor to any meal of the day.

The nutritional value of fish is particularly important to homemakers concerned with giving their families well-balanced meals. Fish is a rich source of high-quality protein, and supplies minerals, such as iron, iodine, calcium, phosphorus, copper, and potassium. Most fish also contain some of the B vitamins. Because fish have little sodium and because many fish are low in fat and comparatively low in calories (see chart on page 14 for fat/lean classification and calorie count), fish is an excellent menu item to use when planning menus for low-sodium or low-calorie diets.

Because there are so many species of fish and shellfish (over 240), you can use this food to add variety to your dinner table. Not all species of fish are abundant and many are seasonal, but there is always a plentiful supply of fresh, frozen, and canned fish from which to choose in fish markets and supermarkets.

You can also add sparkle to your menu by serving fish in a variety of ways. A different kind of fish, fish steaks, shellfish in the shell, or a whole, stuffed fish, for instance, can add appetite appeal to a meal.

When deciding how to present this delicious and nutritious food, consider the characteristics that make fish so appealing: fish has a delicate flavor that blends well with most foods; its tender texture is complemented by the crispness of a salad, relish, or vegetable; it is also versatile and can appear in other dishes besides the entrée—as a tempting appetizer, mouth-watering soup, crisp salad, or appetite-filling sandwich. In fact, fish is light enough that you can serve it as the main course, and add an appetizer and a luscious dessert without making the menu too filling. It also cooks quickly, so it's a boon when time is short. However, do remember to balance the fish menu with mildly flavored foods that will not overpower the delicious, yet delicate flavor of fish.

All of these features taken into account make possible many different, delicious menus that are as enjoyable to cook as they are to eat.

Menu

COMPANY SPECIAL

Vegetable Juice   Crackers

Rice-Stuffed Pike Fillets

Buttered Broccoli

Molded Strawberry Salad   Relishes

Cream Puffs

Milk   Coffee

RICE-STUFFED PIKE FILLETS

Use 2 pounds fresh or frozen pike fillets. Thaw frozen fish. Skin and cut into 6 strips. Sprinkle with salt and pepper. In saucepan cook 2 tablespoons chopped onion and ⅓ cup uncooked long-grain rice in 2 tablespoons butter till browned, 5 to 8 minutes, stirring frequently. Add 1 cup water, 1½ teaspoons lemon juice, 1 chicken bouillon cube, and ⅛ teaspoon salt. Bring to a boil; stir to blend.

Cover and cook over low heat till liquid is absorbed and rice is fluffy, 20 to 25 minutes. Stir in one 3-ounce can chopped mushrooms, drained. Spread mixture on fillets. Roll fillets and place, seam side down, in greased baking dish. Brush 2 tablespoons melted butter over fish. Bake at 350° for 25 to 30 minutes.

Meanwhile, in saucepan melt 2 tablespoons butter; blend in 2 tablespoons all-purpose flour. Dissolve 1 chicken bouillon cube in ½ cup boiling water; add bouillon and ½ cup milk to saucepan. Cook and stir till bubbly. Pour sauce over fish in serving dish. Sprinkle with toasted almonds and paprika. Serves 6.

Make the meal special—

Plan on serving this menu often. The flavors of Rice-Stuffed Pike Fillets—browned rice wrapped inside fillets and covered with creamy sauce—are accented by broccoli spears and a molded strawberry salad. →

PATIO PARTY
Tomato Juice Cocktail
Lobster Luncheon Salad
Crescent Rolls
Butter Curls
Strawberry Chiffon Pie
Iced Tea   Coffee

FAMILY FAVORITE
Hot Bouillon   Crackers
Potato-Coated Fish
Buttered Peas   Baked Potatoes
Tossed Salad
Pudding   Sugar Cookies
Milk   Coffee

CRAB IN AVOCADO BOATS

3 tablespoons butter or margarine
2 tablespoons all-purpose flour
½ teaspoon salt
²/₃ cup milk
1 tablespoon lemon juice
1 7½-ounce can crab meat, drained,
    flaked, and cartilage removed
3 large avocados, halved and seeded
¼ cup fine dry bread crumbs
¼ teaspoon dried marjoram leaves,
    crushed

In saucepan melt *2 tablespoons* butter; blend in flour and salt. Add milk all at once. Cook and stir till thickened and bubbly. Add lemon juice; fold in crab meat. Arrange unpeeled avocado halves in shallow baking dish; spoon crab mixture atop. Melt remaining butter; toss with bread crumbs and marjoram. Sprinkle over avocados. Bake at 350° just till warm, about 10 minutes. Makes 6 servings.

LOBSTER LUNCHEON SALAD

1 8¾-ounce can pineapple tidbits
1 5-ounce can lobster, drained
1 cup halved seedless green grapes
4 ounces natural Swiss cheese, cut in
    strips (1 cup)
1 cup dairy sour cream
    Bibb lettuce
1 small head lettuce, shredded (4 cups)

Drain pineapple, reserving ¼ cup syrup. Break lobster into pieces. Toss together pineapple, lobster, grapes, and cheese. Chill. Combine sour cream and reserved pineapple syrup; chill. Just before serving, line salad bowl with Bibb lettuce; add shredded lettuce and top with lobster mixture. Spoon some dressing over salad. Pass remaining dressing. Serves 6.

POTATO-COATED FISH

4 fresh or frozen pan-dressed catfish
    or other fish (about ½ pound each)
1 beaten egg
1 cup instant mashed potato flakes
1 envelope onion salad dressing mix
    Salad oil

Thaw frozen fish. Season fish with salt and pepper. Combine egg and 1 tablespoon water. Combine potato flakes and dressing mix. Dip fish into egg mixture, then roll in potato mixture; repeat. Brown fish in hot salad oil on one side for 4 to 5 minutes. Turn carefully; brown on second side till fish is brown and flakes easily when tested with a fork, 4 to 5 minutes. Drain on paper toweling. Makes 4 servings.

SUMMERTIME DINNER
Ham Canapés
Crab in Avocado Boats
Vegetable Salad
Popovers   Butter
Baked Alaska
Tea   White Wine   Coffee

SNAPPER WITH CASHEWS

     2 pounds fresh or frozen red snapper
        steaks or other fish steaks
     6 tablespoons butter, melted
     2 cups soft bread crumbs (3 slices)
     ¼ cup chopped cashew nuts
     ½ teaspoon seasoned salt
        Dash pepper

Thaw frozen fish. Cut fish into 6 portions. Sprinkle with salt and arrange in greased 9x9x2-inch baking pan. Drizzle *2 tablespoons* butter over fish. Combine crumbs, nuts, seasoned salt, and pepper; add remaining melted butter. Sprinkle crumb mixture over fish. Bake at 350° till fish flakes easily when tested with a fork, 25 to 30 minutes. Makes 6 servings.

SEAFOOD-SAUCED WAFFLES

     ¼ cup chopped green pepper
     ¼ cup finely chopped onion
     2 tablespoons butter or margarine
     1 10½-ounce can condensed cream of
        mushroom soup
     ½ cup milk
        Few drops yellow food coloring
     2 5-ounce cans shrimp, drained and
        split lengthwise or lobster, drained
        and cut in pieces
    12 squares hot waffles

In saucepan cook green pepper and onion in butter till tender. Stir in soup, milk, and food coloring. Bring to boiling, stirring occasionally. Add shrimp or lobster; heat through. Serve over hot waffles. Makes 6 servings.

Menu

DINNER IN A JIFFY
Snapper with Cashews
Buttered Corn
Blender Coleslaw
Rolls   Butter
Chocolate Cake
Milk   Tea

Menu

WEEKEND BRUNCH
Bloody Mary Cocktail
Seafood-Sauced Waffles
Asparagus Spears
Radish Roses
Chilled Fruit Cup
Coffee   Tea

Menu

POTLUCK SOCIAL
Salmon-Noodle Bake
Green Beans   Carrot Sticks
Molded Fruit Salad
Bread   Butter
Brownies
Milk   Tea   Coffee

SALMON-NOODLE BAKE

     ⅓ cup diced green pepper
     3 tablespoons butter, melted
     1 10½-ounce can condensed cream of
        celery soup
     ½ cup milk
     6 ounces sharp process American
        cheese, shredded (1½ cups)
     1 16-ounce can salmon, drained and
        flaked
     4 ounces medium noodles, cooked
     ¼ cup sliced ripe olives
     1 cup soft bread crumbs

In saucepan cook green pepper in *2 tablespoons* butter till tender. Add soup and milk; heat till bubbly, stirring constantly. Add cheese; stir till melted. Stir in salmon, drained noodles, and olives. Turn into 1½-quart casserole. Combine crumbs and remaining butter. Sprinkle atop casserole. Bake, uncovered, at 350° for 30 to 35 minutes. Makes 6 servings.

BUYING, CLEANING, AND STORING SEAFOOD

What to look for when buying fish and shellfish is just as important as how to clean, store, and cook your seafood for the dinner table.

Buying Fish

Purchase fresh fish in several forms—either whole or cut into fillets, steaks, or chunks. When buying a fresh, whole fish, look for these desirable characteristics: the flesh of the fish should be elastic, yet firm; the eyes should be bright, clear, and bulging; the gills should be red, if not already removed; and the inside of the fish should be bright pink or red. Avoid fish that has a strong odor and a dull, slimy skin. If the scales and fins have not been removed, ask to have this done for you at the store.

Or buy fresh fish that has been cut into steaks, fillets, or chunks. You won't be able to check normal exterior signs—eyes and gills—but these cuts should also be firm and have a fresh appearance—not dried out around edges —and there should be little fish odor.

Frozen fish is another popular market form, making fish available for everyone to enjoy. When buying frozen fish, look for tightly sealed and wrapped fish that is solidly frozen without frost on inside or outside of package.

Canned fish is also an appealing form of seafood. Several different types of fish are processed in this manner. Some fish are packed according to the size of pieces, while others are packed by species or in flavored sauces.

Use should determine the form of canned fish you buy. For example, tuna is available in various-sized pieces. Use fancy or solid pack when appearance is important; chunk-style for casseroles; grated or flaked for sandwich spreads. Other fish, such as salmon, are packed according to species. The deeper red species, such as chinook and sockeye, break into larger flakes for salads, while pink and chum are best for loaves because they break into smaller flakes. Other fish, such as sardines and herring, are available packed in variously flavored sauces.

Buying Shellfish

Although there are not as many varieties of shellfish on the market, most types can be purchased in several different forms. Shellfish are marketed fresh—live, partially prepared, or cooked ready for eating—and they are available frozen and canned ready to use.

When choosing fresh, live shellfish, it is important that they show signs of life. Be sure that crabs and lobsters actively move their legs. Oysters and hard-shell clams, on the other hand, should close their shells tightly when gently tapped. Avoid buying those with gaping shells that do not close when tapped.

Partially prepared, fresh shellfish include those shellfish that have been removed from their shells and packed in a clear liquid ready to be cooked or eaten as is. Scallops, oysters, clams, and mussels are in this group. Shrimps and prawns generally are partially prepared because the heads have been removed before they reach the market.

Fresh-cooked shellfish, ready to eat when purchased, include whole crabs, lobsters, or shrimp as well as meat from these shellfish. All fresh, cooked types of shellfish should be purchased from the market's refrigerated case.

Frozen shellfish is also available—cooked, uncooked, in and out of the shell. Packages should be tightly wrapped with no frost. When buying shellfish in transparent bags, there should be no sign of freezer burn on the seafood.

Shellfish can also be purchased in cans. Whole shellfish, lumps of meat, minced meat, and smoked meat are all widely distributed. These shellfish may be vacuum-packed without liquid or liquid-packed in a brine or juice.

Bounty of the lakes and seas

Fish include freshwater whitefish, saltwater halibut, →
and red snapper. Shellfish are (left to right) oysters,
cooked (red) and uncooked (gray) blue crab, cooked
lobster and Dungeness crab, and clams.

CLEANING AND FILLETING FISH

There are several methods that you can use to clean, fillet, and skin fish (this is especially appropriate to anglers). These drawings incorporate one way to accomplish these tasks. The main idea is to save as much meat as possible while keeping the process simple.

A few points to keep in mind: have a well-sharpened knife, especially for the filleting and skinning processes, and clean the fish the same day it is caught, while it is fresh.

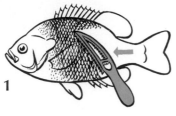

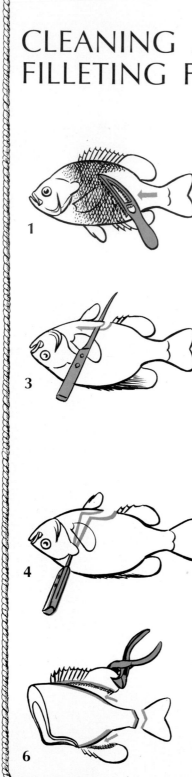

1. To pan-dress a small fish, first remove scales. Using a knife or scraper, work toward the head end.

2. Using a sharp knife, make a parallel cut ¼ to ½ inch deep along both sides of dorsal and anal fins.

3. Hold fish with back resting on table. Make cut just behind vent and slip knife forward under skin.

4. Keep cutting to pectoral fin. Lay fish on side. Make deep cut behind pectoral fin. Repeat on other side.

5. Pull head upward, breaking backbone. Then, pull off head, pectoral and pelvic fins, and remove entrails.

6. With pliers, pull off dorsal and anal fins, using a forward motion towards head end. Remove the tail.

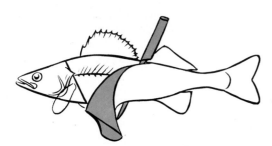

To fillet a dressed fish, *hold fish by head and insert a sharp knife into fish diagonally behind head and pectoral fin. Be sure blade is on top of backbone and rib cage. Slide knife along rib cage freeing meat from bones until tail is reached. Do not cut through skin at tail. Skin fillet; repeat other side.*

To skin the fillet *while it is still attached at the tail, place fillet on table, skin side down. Holding onto the tail, move knife in a sawing motion while pulling on skin. Repeat on other side of fish.*

KNOW YOUR VOCABULARY

Fish can be purchased in various market forms as fresh or frozen products. This list describes the more common forms of fish.

Whole or round: Fish as it comes from the water. Before cooking you must scale and eviscerate it (remove internal organs).

Drawn: Fish that has been eviscerated.

Dressed or pan-dressed: Fish that has been eviscerated and scaled. The head, tail, and fins are usually removed. Pan-dressed refers to the smaller-sized fish. (1)

Fillets: Pieces of fish cut lengthwise from sides of fish away from backbone. It is generally a boneless cut. When cut from one side of fish, it is a single fillet. (2)

Steaks: Cross-section slices from a large, dressed fish. Slices are ⅝ to 1 inch thick with a cross-section of backbone. (3)

Butterfly fillet: A piece of fish cut from both sides of the same fish and held together by uncut meat and skin from underside.

Chunks: Cross-section pieces cut from a large, dressed fish. The only bone present is a cross-section of the backbone.

Portions: Pieces of fish cut from blocks of frozen fish that are bone-free. Portions are available uncooked or partially cooked, both having a bread coating.

Sticks: Pieces of fish cut from a frozen block that are breaded and partially cooked.

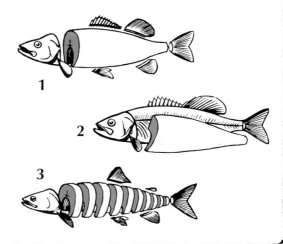

Fish Facts

Knowing market forms, whether the fish is a fat (contains more than 5 percent fat) or lean variety, and calorie counts aid shopping, meal planning, and choosing the best cooking method. Calorie counts are for an uncooked 3½-ounce portion unless otherwise indicated.

FRESHWATER FISH	COMMON MARKET FORMS	FAT/LEAN	CALORIES
Carp	whole, dressed	lean	115
Catfish	whole, dressed	lean	103
Lake Herring	whole, drawn, fillets	lean	96
Lake Trout	drawn, dressed, fillets	fat	241
Pike	whole, dressed, fillets	lean	93
Rainbow Trout	drawn, dressed	fat	195
Smelt (4 or 5 medium)	whole, dressed	lean	98
Whitefish (1 piece 3x3x⅞″)	whole, drawn, dressed, fillets	fat	155
Yellow Perch (1 medium)	whole, fillets	lean	91

SALTWATER FISH	COMMON MARKET FORMS	FAT/LEAN	CALORIES
Cod (1 piece 3x3x¾″)	drawn, dressed, steaks, fillets	lean	78
Eel (1 serving)	whole, dressed	fat	233
Flounder or Sole (1 piece 3x3x⅜″)	whole, fillets	lean	68
Haddock (1 fillet)	drawn, fillets	lean	79
Hake	whole, drawn, dressed, fillets	lean	74
Halibut (1 piece 3x2x1″)	drawn, dressed, steaks, fillets, chunks	lean	100
Herring (Atlantic)	whole, canned	fat	176
Mackerel	whole, drawn, steaks, canned	fat	191
Mullet	whole	lean	146
Pollock	drawn, dressed, steaks, fillets	lean	95
Pompano (1 piece 3x3x¾″)	whole, fillets	fat	166
Red Snapper	drawn, steaks, fillets	lean	93
Salmon (Chinook)	whole, dressed, steaks, fillets, canned	fat	222
Sea Bass	whole, drawn, steaks, fillets	lean	96
Striped Bass or Rockfish	whole, drawn, fillets, steaks	lean	97
Swordfish (1 piece 3x3x¾″)	dressed, steaks	lean	118
Tuna	whole, drawn, dressed, canned	fat	145
Whiting	whole, drawn, dressed, fillets	lean	74

How Much to Serve

The following amounts are for one average entrée serving. Less is needed if served with a rich sauce or as an appetizer.

FISH:

whole	12 ounces
dressed or pan-dressed	8 ounces
fillets, steaks, portions	5 ounces
sticks	4 ounces

CLAM:

in shells as appetizer	6
in shells as entrée	15 to 20
shucked	½ to ¾ cup

CRAB:

whole blue crab	2 to 4
whole Dungeness crab	½ to 1
crab meat	4 ounces

LOBSTER:

whole	1 pound
tail	8 ounces
meat	4 ounces

OYSTER:

in shells as appetizer	6
shucked	½ to ¾ cup

SCALLOP: 4 to 5 ounces

SHRIMP OR PRAWN:

in shells	6 large
shelled	4 ounces

Seafood Substitutions

To substitute one form of a seafood for another, refer to the lists below. The amounts under each type are about equal.

FISH:
1 pound fish fillets or steaks, cooked
2 cups flaked fish

CLAM:
18 clams in shells
1 pint shucked clams
2 7½-ounce cans minced clams

CRAB:
8 to 10 ounces king crab legs in shell
1 6-ounce package frozen crab meat
1 7½-ounce can crab meat
1 cup cooked and flaked crab meat

LOBSTER:
1 1-pound lobster or 1 8-ounce tail
4 to 5 ounces cooked lobster meat
1 cup cooked meat
1 5-ounce can lobster

OYSTER:
24 oysters in shells
1 pint shucked oysters

SHRIMP:
12 ounces raw shrimp in shells
7 or 8 ounces raw, shelled shrimp
1 4½- or 5-ounce can shrimp
1 cup cooked, shelled shrimp

Storing and Freezing Seafood

Because fresh fish and shellfish are perishable, from the time the seafood is caught or purchased until it is used, it should be kept iced or refrigerated. For longer storage, seafood items should be kept solidly frozen.

1. Store fresh fish tightly wrapped in moisture-vaporproof material or in airtight containers in refrigerator. Use within a day or two.

2. To freeze fish cuts, dip steaks or fillets in a solution of ⅔ cup salt to 1 gallon water for 30 seconds. Then, tightly seal in freezer paper or in a freezer container. Keep packages small — family-sized portions make ideal packages. Separate individual servings with two pieces of waxed paper for easy separation, or wrap portions individually. Seal and label with contents, weight or servings, and date. Turn freezer control to lowest setting; freeze fish quickly. Store at −10° or below. Do not freeze fish longer than six months. Slightly longer storage is permissible at very low temperatures, but prolonged storage affects flavor, texture, and color.

3. Cooked fish should be stored in a covered container. It can be kept in the refrigerator up to three or four days.

4. Shellfish is handled a bit differently, although proper wrapping and storage techniques are followed. Live shellfish should be cooked immediately and the cooked meat used as soon as possible. Keep shellfish refrigerated.

5. The different varieties of shellfish require different freezing techniques. Shuck oysters, clams, and scallops before freezing. Pack in freezer containers, leaving a ½-inch headspace. Crabs and lobsters should be cooked before freezing. Then chill, remove meat from shells, package, and freeze. Use the frozen cooked meat within one month. Uncooked shrimp may be frozen in shells or shelled. Use most frozen shellfish within three months.

COOKING PRIMER FOR FISH AND SHELLFISH

There really are no well-guarded secrets about the best way to prepare seafood. If you're not sure of the proper cooking techniques, a few basic hints and recipes should help you get your sea legs in the art of cooking fish.

Preparing Fish

Many cooks are surprised when they discover that fish is one of the easiest and quickest foods to prepare. Fish is moist, tender, delicately flavored, and easy to digest when cooked properly. It is a highly versatile food and is used in the preparation of a large number of recipes —from appetizers and salads to main dishes.

Most varieties of fish can be successfully substituted for one another in recipe preparation. Fresh or frozen fish, likewise, can be substituted if the frozen fish is thawed before use or if extra cooking time is allowed when using frozen fish. The most satisfactory way to thaw fish is in the refrigerator in the original wrapping. Plan on a one-pound package taking about 24 hours to thaw. Or for speedy thawing, place wrapped packages under cold, running water. Only one or two hours is needed to thaw a one-pound package using this method. Use thawed fish within a day.

A few additional points to keep in mind: For best quality, do not let fish thaw at room temperature or in warm water. Do not refreeze thawed fish. Do not thaw frozen fish portions or fish sticks before cooking.

Once the fish is ready to cook, you must consider the variety. Fat fish can successfully be broiled or baked because the fat in the fish helps keep it from drying out during cooking. Lean fish, on the other hand, generally are poached, fried, or steamed, but they, too, can be baked or broiled if basted with some type of melted shortening. Or prepare the lean fish in a sauce to keep it moist. These are general guidelines.

Almost any fish can be cooked by any method if allowances are made for the fat content of the fish during cooking.

During cooking, the flesh of the fish will change from the translucent look before it is cooked to an opaque, whitish appearance, and the juices will become milky. When cooked, the fish will flake apart easily when tested with a fork, and bones, if present, will separate easily from the meat. Handle the fish gently during cooking as it flakes apart.

POACHED FISH

Use 2 to 3 pounds fresh or frozen fish fillets or steaks. Thaw frozen fish. Place in greased 10-inch skillet. Add boiling water to cover. Add 1 small onion, quartered, and 2 teaspoons salt. Or substitute Court Bouillon (see page 21). Simmer, covered, till fish flakes easily when tested with a fork, 5 to 10 minutes. Carefully remove fish. Use as a main dish with sauce or in recipes using cooked fish. One pound fillets makes 2 cups cooked, flaked fish.

STEAMED FISH

Use 1 pound fresh or frozen fish fillets or steaks, or one 3-pound dressed fish. Thaw frozen fish. Bring 2 cups water to boiling in 10-inch skillet or fish poacher with tight fitting cover. Sprinkle fish with 1 teaspoon salt. Place fish on a greased rack in pan so that fish does not touch water. Cover pan tightly and steam till fish flakes easily when tested with a fork—fillets, 3 to 4 minutes; steaks, 6 to 8 minutes; dressed, 20 to 25 minutes. Carefully remove fish. Use as a main dish with sauce or in recipes using cooked, flaked fish as an ingredient.

A recipe with many uses

Add a basic technique to your recipe repertoire. →
Prepare Steamed Fish to be served hot with lemon or a sauce, or remove skin from cooked fish, glaze, then chill it for an attractive buffet dish.

PANFRIED FISH

Accompany this basic recipe with citrus wedges or a favorite sauce —

Use 2 pounds fresh or frozen fish fillets, steaks, or pan-dressed fish. Thaw frozen fish. Cut fillets or steaks into 6 portions. Combine 1 beaten egg and 2 tablespoons water. Mix ¾ cup fine saltine cracker crumbs *or* ¾ cup cornmeal with ½ teaspoon salt and dash pepper. Dip fish into egg mixture; then roll in crumbs. Heat small amount of shortening in skillet; add fish in single layer.

Fry at moderate heat till browned on one side, 4 to 5 minutes. Turn and brown other side till fish flakes easily when tested with a fork, about 4 to 5 minutes longer. Drain on paper toweling. Makes 6 servings for fillets and steaks; 4 servings for pan-dressed fish.

OVEN-FRIED FISH

Use 2 pounds fresh or frozen fish fillets or steaks. Thaw frozen fish. Cut into 6 portions. Dip in ½ cup milk; roll in mixture of 1 cup fine dry bread crumbs and 1 teaspoon salt. Place in single layer, skin side down, in greased baking pan. Drizzle with mixture of ¼ cup melted butter and ½ teaspoon lemon juice. Bake at 500° till fish browns and flakes easily when tested with a fork, 10 to 15 minutes. Serves 6.

Test fish for doneness with a fork. Place fork, tines down, in the fish at a 45 degree angle and turn clockwise. When it flakes easily, the fish is cooked.

DEEP-FAT FRIED FISH

Use 2 pounds fresh or frozen fish fillets, steaks, or pan-dressed fish. Thaw frozen fish. Cut into 6 portions. Combine 1 beaten egg and 2 tablespoons water. Combine 1¼ cups fine saltine cracker crumbs and dash pepper. Dip fish into egg, then roll in crumbs. Place in a single layer in fryer basket. Fry in deep, hot fat (350°) till browned and fish flakes easily when tested with a fork, 3 to 5 minutes. Drain on paper toweling. Makes 6 servings for fillets and steaks; 4 servings for pan-dressed fish.

BROILED FILLETS AND STEAKS

Use 2 pounds fresh or frozen fish fillets or steaks. Thaw frozen fish. Cut into 6 portions. Place fish in a single layer on greased rack of broiler pan or in greased baking pan. Tuck under any thin edges. Melt 2 tablespoons butter. Brush *half* the butter over fish. Season fish with 1 teaspoon salt and dash pepper. Broil about 4 inches from heat till fish flakes easily when tested with a fork, 10 to 15 minutes. Brush fish with remaining melted butter once during cooking. Makes 6 servings.

BROILED DRESSED FISH

Use one 2-pound fresh or frozen dressed fish. Thaw frozen fish. Remove head, if desired. Rinse and dry fish. Place fish on greased rack of broiler pan or in greased baking pan. Melt 3 tablespoons butter. Brush fish, inside and outside, with some of the butter and season with 1 teaspoon salt and dash pepper. Broil about 4 inches from heat for 5 to 8 minutes. Turn and brush with melted butter. Broil till fish flakes easily when tested with a fork, 5 to 8 minutes longer. Makes 4 servings.

BAKED FILLETS AND STEAKS

Use 2 pounds fresh or frozen fish fillets or steaks. Thaw frozen fish. Cut into 6 portions. Place fish in single layer, skin side down, in greased baking pan. Tuck under thin edges. Brush with 3 tablespoons melted butter. Sprinkle with 1 teaspoon salt and dash pepper. Bake, uncovered, at 350° till fish flakes easily when tested with fork, 15 to 20 minutes. Serves 6.

BAKED DRESSED FISH

Use six 8-ounce fresh or frozen pan-dressed fish or one 3-pound fresh or frozen dressed fish. Thaw frozen fish. Remove heads, if desired. Rinse and dry fish. Place in a single layer in greased baking pan. Brush fish, inside and outside, with ¼ cup melted butter and season with 1½ teaspoons salt and ⅛ teaspoon pepper. Bake, covered, at 350° till fish flakes easily when tested with a fork, 25 to 30 minutes for pan-dressed fish, and 45 to 60 minutes for dressed fish. Serves 6.

BARBECUED FISH

This recipe is pictured on page 4 —

Use 1½ pounds fresh or frozen fish fillets or steaks, or 4 pan-dressed fish (about 8 ounces each). Thaw frozen fish. (For pan-dressed fish, wrap tails in greased foil. Season insides.) Cut fillets or steaks into 4 portions.

Combine ½ cup salad oil, 1 tablespoon Worcestershire sauce, ½ teaspoon onion salt, and ⅛ teaspoon pepper. Place fish in a well-greased wire broiler basket. Brush with sauce. Grill over *medium-hot* coals 5 to 8 minutes. Brush with mixture, turn, and brush second side. Grill till fish flakes easily when tested with a fork, about 5 to 8 minutes longer. Serve with lemon wedges. Makes 4 servings.

Preparing Shellfish

The key to deliciously prepared shellfish is to cook it only until done. Additional cooking tends to toughen the meat and dry it out. When shellfish is frozen, it can be thawed, like fish, in the refrigerator. Or, if desired, shellfish can be cooked while it is still frozen, but additional cooking time must be allowed.

Some people enjoy eating raw oysters, clams, and scallops. These shellfish are considered gourmet fare when eaten raw because the muscles are very tender and flavorful. To prepare them for eating raw, open the shells and cut the muscle free. The meat is best when served very cold. To accomplish this, place the muscle in half of the shell on a bed of cracked ice. Accompany these raw delicacies with lemon or lime juice, prepared horseradish, or freshly ground pepper for a flavor treat.

A more common way to enjoy shellfish, however, is cooked—steamed, boiled, broiled, baked, or fried. When done, the muscle of the mollusk-type shellfish, such as oysters, mussels, and clams, will curl around the edges. Or, if cooked in the shells, the shell will open when properly done. Any clams or oysters that do not open their shell during cooking should be discarded and not eaten. This indicates that it was not alive before cooking. It is important that shellfish, such as clams, oysters, crabs, and lobster be alive when cooked, especially for boiling and steaming. To dispel any qualms you may have, the shellfish will be killed instantly and humanely when it is plunged into the kettle of boiling water.

There is also a special way to tell when shellfish, such as lobster and shrimp, are done. They turn a bright pink or red color when properly cooked. After cooking, the shellfish can be served with a sauce or melted butter, or the meat can be removed from the shells for use in other dishes using cooked seafood.

BOILED SHRIMP

In saucepan combine 6 cups water, 2 tablespoons salt, 2 tablespoons vinegar, 2 bay leaves, 1 teaspoon mixed pickling spices, and 2 branches celery; bring to boiling. Add 2 pounds fresh or frozen shrimp in shells or shelled. Heat to boiling; reduce heat and simmer till shrimp turn pink, 1 to 3 minutes. Drain. If cooked in shell, peel shrimp; remove black vein.

Note: Vinegar and spices may be omitted when using shrimp for highly seasoned dishes.

BROILED SHRIMP

Use 2 pounds fresh or frozen jumbo shrimp in shells. Thaw frozen shrimp. Remove shells and vein. Combine ¼ cup melted butter and 2 tablespoons lemon juice. Add dash bottled hot pepper sauce. Brush mixture on shrimp.

To broil in the range, place shrimp on a well-greased broiler rack and broil 6 to 8 inches from heat. To broil on an outdoor grill, place shrimp on grill (a piece of wire screen will prevent shrimp from falling through). Grill over *hot* coals. Broil 5 to 8 minutes, turning shrimp and brushing with butter mixture once or twice during cooking. Season the cooked shrimp lightly with salt. Makes 6 servings.

Working over container, *open hard-shelled clams by holding the clam in one hand (hinged side against palm) and inserting knife blade between the halves.*

Hold the shell firmly *and cut around the opening. Twist the knife up slightly to pry the shell open. With your thumb, pull the top half of the shell up.*

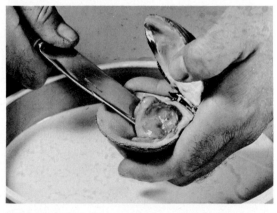

Cut muscle free *from two halves of shell. Reserve the deep half for serving on the half shell or put muscle and juice in a container for use in the shucked form.*

FRENCH-FRIED SHRIMP

  2 pounds fresh or frozen shrimp in
    shells
  1 cup sifted all-purpose flour
  ½ teaspoon sugar
  ½ teaspoon salt
  1 slightly beaten egg
  1 cup ice water
  2 tablespoons salad oil
    Shortening

Thaw frozen shrimp. In a bowl combine flour, sugar, salt, egg, water, and salad oil. Beat till smooth. Remove shells from shrimp, leaving last section and tail intact. Butterfly shrimp by cutting almost through center back without cutting tail end; remove black vein. Dry shrimp well. Dip shrimp into batter. Fry in deep, hot fat (375°) till golden. Drain on paper toweling. Serve with cocktail sauce.

STEAMED CLAMS

Thoroughly wash soft-shelled clams in shells.* Place clams on rack in a kettle with 1 cup hot water. Cover pan tightly and steam just till shells open, about 5 minutes. Discard any that do not open. Serve in shells with melted butter or drain and remove the meat from shells. When eating clams in shells, allow about 15 to 20 clams per person as a main dish.
   *Clams you dig from the sand need special cleaning. Cover the clams with salt water (⅓ cup salt to 1 gallon cold water); let stand 15 minutes; rinse. Repeat twice. Then steam.

How to Shuck Oysters

Shucking or opening oysters is done much in the same manner as for clams. After the oyster is washed and thoroughly rinsed in cold water, open it with an oyster knife or other blunt-tipped knife. It's easier to open the oyster if the thin end of the shell has been broken off with a hammer. Then, holding the oyster firmly on a table with the flat shell up, insert the knife between the halves. Cut around the opening close to the flat upper shell and pry the top shell off. Loosen the muscle from the bottom shell. If serving on the half shell, use the deeper, bottom half. Remove any bits of shell which may cling to the muscle.

BROILED OYSTERS

Open 36 oysters in shells. With knife remove oysters; drain. Wash shells thoroughly. Place each oyster in deep half of shell. Arrange shells on bed of coarse rock salt (ice cream salt) in shallow pan. Sprinkle each with table salt and pepper. Broil 4 to 5 inches from the heat till edges of oyster begin to curl, about 3 minutes. Serve with lemon. Serves 6.

POACHED OYSTERS

2 cups water
1 teaspoon salt
1 pint shucked oysters, drained

In saucepan bring water and salt to a simmer. Add oysters; simmer (do not boil) till oysters begin to curl around the edges and become plump and firm, 1 to 4 minutes, depending on size of oysters. Drain oysters and chill. Serve in any way that raw oysters would be used, such as on the half shell for an appetizer.

DEEP-FAT FRIED OYSTERS

Drain shucked oysters. Dry with paper toweling. Roll oysters in all-purpose flour seasoned with salt and pepper. Dip into a mixture of 1 beaten egg and 1 tablespoon water, then roll in fine dry bread crumbs. Fry in deep, hot fat (375°) till golden, about 2 minutes. Drain on paper toweling. Serve hot fried oysters with Tartar Sauce or other sauce, if desired.

BROILED SCALLOPS

Use 2 pounds fresh or frozen scallops. Thaw frozen scallops. Place scallops in a shallow baking pan. Sprinkle with salt, pepper, and paprika. Dot with butter or margarine. Broil 3 inches from heat till the scallops are lightly browned, about 6 to 9 minutes. Serve with lemon wedges or Tartar Sauce and garnish with parsley, if desired. Makes 6 servings.

DEEP-FAT FRIED SCALLOPS

Use fresh or frozen scallops. Thaw frozen scallops. Dry with paper toweling. Roll scallops in all-purpose flour seasoned with salt and pepper. Dip into a mixture of 1 beaten egg and 1 tablespoon water, then roll in fine dry bread crumbs. Fry in deep, hot fat (375°) till golden, about 2 minutes. Drain on paper toweling. Serve hot with lemon or lime wedges.

PANFRIED SCALLOPS

1 pound fresh or frozen scallops
2 tablespoons all-purpose flour
½ teaspoon salt
Dash pepper
¼ cup butter or margarine

Thaw frozen scallops. Dry scallops with paper toweling. Combine flour, salt, and pepper. Dip scallops in seasoned flour to coat. Melt the butter or margarine in skillet. Cook scallops in butter over medium heat, turning occasionally, till browned and opaque in appearance, about 5 to 8 minutes. Serve with lemon wedges, if desired. Makes 3 or 4 servings.

BOILED SCALLOPS

Use 2 pounds fresh or frozen scallops. Thaw frozen scallops. In saucepan bring 1 quart water and 2 teaspoons salt to a boil. Add scallops; return to boiling. Reduce heat; simmer 1 minute. Drain scallops. Serve hot with lemon juice or chill and use in salads. Serves 6.

COURT BOUILLON

In large saucepan combine 3 quarts water; ½ cup vinegar; 1 onion, sliced; 1 lemon, sliced; 1 cup sliced celery; 1 cup sliced carrot; 1 tablespoon salt, 6 whole cloves; 3 bay leaves; and 3 peppercorns. Bring to boiling. Simmer the mixture, covered, 30 minutes. Add seafood and cook according to timing in recipe.

BOILED WHOLE LOBSTER

Choose active live lobsters. Plunge headfirst into enough boiling, salted water or Court Bouillon (see page 21) to cover. Bring to boiling; reduce heat and simmer till done, 20 minutes. Remove. Place on back. With sharp knife, cut in half lengthwise. Discard all organs in body section near head except red coral roe (in females only) and brownish green liver. Remove black vein that runs to tip of tail. Crack claws. Serve with butter. Or remove meat and use in recipes calling for cooked lobster. Allow a 1-pound lobster for each serving.

BROILED WHOLE LOBSTER

Choose active live lobsters. Plunge headfirst into enough boiling, salted water to cover. Cook 2 minutes. Remove. Place lobster on back on cutting board. With sharp knife, split lengthwise from head to tail. Cut off head, if desired. Using scissors, snip out under shell membrane on tail section. Discard all organs in body section except red coral roe (in females only) and brownish green liver. Remove black vein. Crack large claws of the lobster.

Place lobster on broiler pan, shell side up; broil about 5 inches from heat 7 minutes. Turn; flatten lobster open to expose meat. Brush with 1 tablespoon melted butter. Season with salt and pepper. Broil 7 to 8 minutes longer. Serve with melted butter and lemon wedges. Allow a 1-pound lobster for each serving.

BAKED STUFFED WHOLE LOBSTER

Plunge 2 live lobsters (about 1 pound each) headfirst into enough boiling, salted water to cover. Cook 2 minutes. Remove from water; place lobster on back on cutting board. With sharp knife, split lengthwise from head down to base of abdomen. Spread body open and discard all organs in body section except brownish green liver and red coral roe. Remove black vein. Crack large claws.

Combine 1 cup soft bread crumbs, 3 tablespoons melted butter, 2 tablespoons grated Parmesan cheese, and 1 teaspoon grated onion. Spoon into body cavities. Place lobsters, shell side down, in shallow baking pan. Bake at 350° till lightly browned and meat is cooked, 30 to 35 minutes. Pass melted butter. Serves 2.

Snip along each side *of the thin undershell on boiled lobster tails. Remove the undershell to expose the meat for serving or for taking out the meat.*

Grasp the tail *with one hand and insert index finger of the other hand between shell and meat. Pull the shell away from the meat, thus separating the two.*

BOILED LOBSTER TAILS

Drop frozen lobster tails into enough boiling, salted water to cover. Bring to boiling. Reduce heat and simmer the 3-ounce tails, 3 to 4 minutes; 6-ounce tails, 8 minutes; and 8-ounce tails, 11 minutes. Drain. Prepare the tails to serve (see pictures). Accompany with melted butter and lemon or use the meat in recipes calling for cooked lobster.

Lift lobsters *by taking hold of them just behind the eyes. This is the easiest way to pick up the lively creatures for plunging into the pot headfirst.*

Butterfly lobster tails *for broiling. Cut through center of hard top shell and meat, but do not cut undershell. Spread tails open so meat is on top.*

BROILED LOBSTER TAILS

Partially thaw lobster tails. Using knife, butterfly tails (see picture). Place on broiler pan, shell side down. Dash few drops bottled hot pepper sauce into melted butter; brush over meat. Broil 4 inches from heat till meat loses its translucency and can be flaked with a fork, about 17 minutes for 6- to 8-ounce tail. Loosen meat; serve with butter and lemon.

BOILED DUNGENESS CRAB

Wash and scrub live Dungeness crabs. In large kettle bring to boiling enough salted water to completely cover crabs. (Use 1 tablespoon salt per quart of water.) Plunge crabs into water. Cover; bring to boiling. Reduce heat; simmer, allowing 8 minutes per pound. Drain.

When cool enough to handle, remove meat as follows: Pull off top shell. Remove all the spongy parts—gills, stomach, and intestines. Rinse. Remove small apron-shaped piece on bottom of crab and the projecting mouth parts opposite this piece. Break body in half. Break off legs and claws; break legs into segments.

Crack claws and legs. Remove meat from claws, legs, and body with a knife or small fork. Remove all cartilage from meat. Serve hot or cold with melted butter or use in recipes calling for cooked crab. Allow ½ crab per serving.

BOILED HARD-SHELL CRAB

Wash and scrub live hard-shell blue crabs. Bring enough salted water to boiling in a large kettle to completely cover the crabs. Plunge live crabs into the water. Cover and return to boiling. Reduce heat and simmer 15 minutes. Drain. When cool enough to handle, remove the meat in the same way as for the Dungeness crab, except after the spongy parts are discarded, remove the semitransparent membrane covering the meat in the body. Also discard the small appendages since these will contain little, if any, meat. The large claws, however, will contain some meat. Remove meat with fingers, nutpick, small fork, or knife. Allow about 3 to 4 blue crabs for each serving.

FRIED SOFT-SHELL BLUE CRAB

Sprinkle 8 cleaned soft-shell blue crabs with salt. Roll in a mixture of ½ cup fine saltine cracker crumbs and 1 tablespoon all-purpose flour. Dip in a mixture of 1 slightly beaten egg and ½ cup milk; roll in crumbs and flour again. Heat a small amount of salad oil in a skillet. Fry crabs in hot fat 3 to 5 minutes on each side, depending on size of crabs. Drain. Serve with lemon wedges. Makes 4 servings.

To Deep-Fat Fry: Fry coated crabs in deep, hot fat (350°) till golden, about 4 minutes. Drain thoroughly on paper toweling.

Set the atmosphere for your dinner at the start of the meal by serving one of these prized appetizers. You'll be amazed at how versatile fish and seafood can be and at the endless variety of ideas available—from creamy pâtés to tiny canapés.

Create an exotic mood with hors d'oeuvres that are served after the guests are seated around the dinner table. Present an appetizer in a glass icer surrounded with crushed ice or serve the first course in a lettuce-lined seafood shell. Your guests are sure to take notice of your culinary skill and lavish you with well-deserved praise.

Or serve the appetizer before your guests are seated at the table. Choose dips and spreads which can be eaten while guests mingle, relax, and get acquainted before sitting down for the meal. Accompany these with vegetable dippers and crackers.

But you're not limited to serving appetizers as the first course of any meal. An assortment will make a complete meal at open-house buffets, parties, or receptions. In fact, some favorites such as the well-known steamed clams double as a main course when the size of the serving is slightly increased.

Don't reserve appetizers just for company meals. The family will also be delighted when they are served a special appetizer. Why not start out tonight with one of the seafood cocktails pictured here—Crab-Fruit Cocktail, Lobster Appetizer, Clam-Vermouth Drink, Tuna-Celery Cocktail, or Crab Claw Appetizer— served with sauce in a cup.

Appetizers

SEAWORTHY COCKTAILS AND HORS D'OEUVRES

OYSTERS ROCKEFELLER

24 oysters in shells*
2 tablespoons snipped parsley
1 tablespoon chopped onion
1 tablespoon butter, melted
  Paprika
1 cup cooked chopped spinach
¼ cup fine dry bread crumbs
½ cup butter or margarine

Open oysters (see page 20). With knife, remove oysters from shells; drain oysters. Wash shells. Place each oyster in deep half of shell.

Combine parsley, onion, and 1 tablespoon melted butter; spread over oysters. Sprinkle with a little salt, pepper, and paprika. Top each with 2 teaspoons spinach, then ½ teaspoon bread crumbs. Dot each with about 1 teaspoon butter. Arrange shells on bed of rock salt in a shallow pan. Bake at 450° till browned, about 10 minutes. Makes 8 servings.

*Or buy shucked oysters and use small baking shells instead of the oyster shells.

CLAMS CASINO

24 small hard-shell clams in shells*
¼ cup butter or margarine, softened
¼ cup chopped green onion
¼ cup chopped green pepper
¼ cup finely chopped celery
2 tablespoons chopped canned pimiento
1 teaspoon lemon juice
4 slices bacon, crisp-cooked and
   crumbled

Open clams (see page 20). With knife, remove clams from the shells. Wash shells. Place each clam in deep half of the shell. Sprinkle clams lightly with table salt. Blend together remaining ingredients. Top each clam with a scant tablespoon of mixture. Arrange half-shells on bed of rock salt in a shallow pan. Bake at 425° for 10 to 12 minutes. Makes 8 servings.

*Or substitute oysters in shells.

OYSTERS BIENVILLE

18 oysters in shells
½ cup chopped green onion
1 clove garlic, minced
2 tablespoons butter or margarine
2 tablespoons all-purpose flour
⅔ cup chicken broth
1 egg yolk
⅓ cup dry white wine
1 3-ounce can sliced mushrooms, drained
2 tablespoons snipped parsley
  Dash bottled hot pepper sauce
½ tablespoon butter or margarine
½ cup soft bread crumbs (1 slice)
2 tablespoons grated Parmesan cheese

Open oysters (see page 20). With knife, remove oysters. Wash shells. Place each oyster in deep half of the shell. Arrange shells on bed of rock salt in a shallow pan; set aside.

Cook green onion and garlic in 2 tablespoons butter till tender but not brown. Blend in flour and ¼ teaspoon salt. Add chicken broth all at once. Cook and stir till mixture thickens and bubbles. Beat egg yolk and wine together. Add a little of the hot mixture to egg and wine; return to hot mixture. Stir in mushrooms, parsley, and hot pepper sauce. Cook over low heat, stirring till mixture almost boils.

In small saucepan melt ½ tablespoon butter; add soft bread crumbs and toss to coat. Stir in Parmesan cheese. Heat oysters at 400° for 5 minutes. Top each oyster with 1 tablespoon of the sauce mixture. Sprinkle 1 teaspoon bread-Parmesan mixture atop each oyster. Bake till heated through and crumbs are lightly browned, about 10 to 12 minutes longer. Serves 6.

Treasury of appetizers

*Choose a favorite from this trio. Each is as elegant →
and distinctive as its name—Oysters Rockefeller
topped with spinach, Oysters Bienville with wine and
mushrooms, and Clams Casino with bright peppers.*

TUNA-CELERY COCKTAIL

Find this appetizer as well as several other cocktails on this page pictured on page 24 —

½ cup catsup
1 tablespoon lemon juice
1½ teaspoons prepared horseradish
½ teaspoon Worcestershire sauce
¼ teaspoon grated onion
¼ teaspoon salt
Dash bottled hot pepper sauce
Lettuce
¾ cup sliced celery
1 6½- or 7-ounce can tuna, chilled, drained, and flaked

Combine catsup, lemon juice, horseradish, Worcestershire sauce, onion, salt, and hot pepper sauce. Mix well and chill thoroughly.

Line 6 cocktail glasses with lettuce. Toss celery and tuna together; divide mixture between the glasses. Spoon about 1 tablespoon sauce over each serving. Makes 6 servings.

CRAB-FRUIT COCKTAIL

½ cup mayonnaise or salad dressing
1½ teaspoons lemon juice
1 teaspoon vinegar
1 teaspoon chopped chives
Dash salt
1 7½-ounce can crab meat or 6 ounces cooked crab meat, chilled
1 tablespoon lemon juice
1 13½-ounce can pineapple tidbits (juice packed), chilled and drained
Lettuce

Combine mayonnaise, 1½ teaspoons lemon juice, vinegar, chives, and salt; chill thoroughly. Just before serving, break crab meat into chunks and remove any cartilage. Sprinkle crab meat with 1 tablespoon lemon juice. Arrange crab and pineapple tidbits in 8 lettuce-lined cocktail glasses. Spoon chilled dressing atop each. If desired, sprinkle with additional chopped chives. Makes 8 servings.

LOBSTER APPETIZER

½ cup chili sauce
¼ cup dry sherry
6 drops bottled hot pepper sauce
1 5-ounce can lobster, chilled and broken into chunks (about 1 cup)
Lettuce

Combine chili sauce, sherry, and hot pepper sauce; chill thoroughly. Arrange lobster pieces in lettuce-lined icers or cocktail glasses. Spoon chilled sauce atop each. Makes 4 servings.

CRAB CLAW APPETIZER

1 cup dairy sour cream
3 tablespoons drained, prepared horseradish
Dash paprika
Cocktail crab claws, cooked and chilled
Lettuce

Combine sour cream, horseradish, ¼ teaspoon salt, and paprika. Chill. For each serving, arrange about 6 crab claws on a lettuce-lined plate. Serve with a small cup of horseradish sauce. If desired, sprinkle paprika atop sauce. Makes enough sauce for 6 appetizers.

CLAM-VERMOUTH DRINK

1 16-ounce can clam-tomato juice cocktail
¼ cup dry vermouth
2 teaspoons lemon juice
4 drops bottled hot pepper sauce

Combine all ingredients; chill thoroughly. Serve in 4-ounce glasses as an appetizer. If desired, serve hot. Garnish with a lemon slice, if desired. Makes 4 servings.

BLOODY MARY À LA CLAM

For each serving combine in a cocktail shaker 2 jiggers tomato juice (3 ounces), 1 jigger vodka (1½ ounces), juice from half a lemon, dash Worcestershire sauce, celery salt, pepper, and clam juice to taste. Add chopped ice; shake. Strain into 6-ounce cocktail glass.

SHRIMP REMOULADE APPETIZER

An appetizer that doubles as a main-dish salad when shrimp are served in an avocado half—

- 2 pounds fresh or frozen medium shrimp in shells
- ¼ cup tarragon vinegar
- 2 tablespoons horseradish mustard
- 1 tablespoon catsup
- 1½ teaspoons paprika
- ½ teaspoon salt
- ¼ teaspoon cayenne pepper
- • • •
- ½ cup salad oil
- ¼ cup finely chopped celery
- ¼ cup snipped green onion
- Shredded lettuce

Add shrimp to boiling, salted water. Reduce heat and simmer shrimp for 1 to 3 minutes. Drain; remove shell and black vein.

In small bowl combine vinegar, mustard, catsup, paprika, salt, and cayenne. Slowly add the salad oil, beating constantly. Stir in the celery and green onion. Pour sauce over the cooked shrimp. Marinate shrimp in the refrigerator 4 to 5 hours. Spoon shrimp and a little sauce over a bed of shredded lettuce in individual seafood shells or in cocktail glasses. Makes 10 appetizer servings.

SHRIMP COCKTAIL

Keep any extra sauce in the refrigerator—

- ¾ cup chili sauce
- 2 to 4 tablespoons lemon juice
- 1 to 2 tablespoons prepared horseradish
- 2 teaspoons Worcestershire sauce
- ½ teaspoon grated onion
- Dash bottled hot pepper sauce
- Salt
- Shelled cooked shrimp, chilled
- Lettuce

Combine chili sauce, lemon juice, horseradish, Worcestershire sauce, onion, and hot pepper sauce. Mix well; add salt to taste. Chill.

Arrange 4 shelled, cooked shrimp in each lettuce-lined cocktail glass. Spoon about 2 tablespoons chilled cocktail sauce atop each. Makes enough sauce for 8 to 10 cocktails.

ANTIPASTO TRAY

Place one can chilled tuna in lettuce cup in center of large plate. Arrange cheese wedges, pepperoni slices, olives, radish roses, pickled peppers, honeydew balls with prosciutto ham, cherry tomatoes, marinated artichoke hearts, and anchovy fillets around the tuna.

SMOKED OYSTER PUFFS

- 1 3¼-ounce can smoked oysters
- 16 slices party rye bread
- ¼ cup mayonnaise or salad dressing
- 2 tablespoons sliced green onion
- 8 slices process Swiss cheese (8 ounces)

Drain oysters; set aside. Toast bread on both sides. Combine mayonnaise and green onion. Spread on one side of toast slices. Cut out rounds of cheese to fit toast. Place a smoked oyster on each bread round, then top with cheese round, covering mayonnaise. Broil 3 to 4 inches from heat till cheese is puffy and golden, 1 to 2 minutes. Makes 16 appetizers.

SALMON CANAPÉS

Make appetizers special by removing crusts—

- 12 slices bread, toasted
- 1 7¾-ounce can salmon, drained and flaked
- ⅓ cup mayonnaise or salad dressing
- 2 tablespoons chopped ripe olives
- 1 tablespoon snipped parsley
- 1 teaspoon finely chopped onion
- 1 teaspoon prepared mustard
- ¼ teaspoon Worcestershire sauce

Cut each slice of toast diagonally, forming four triangles. Combine remaining ingredients and spread about 1 teaspoon on each toast triangle. Broil 3 to 4 inches from heat till hot, about 1 minute. Garnish with additional olive slices, if desired. Makes 48 appetizers.

Make these appetizers ahead *by stuffing the seasoned crab meat into mushroom crowns. Before serving, heat Crab-Stuffed Mushrooms till piping hot.*

CRAB-STUFFED MUSHROOMS

    3 dozen large whole fresh mushrooms
    1 7½-ounce can crab meat, drained,
       flaked, and cartilage removed
    1 tablespoon snipped parsley
    1 tablespoon chopped canned pimiento
    1 teaspoon chopped capers
             • • •
    ¼ teaspoon dry mustard
    ½ cup mayonnaise or salad dressing

Wash and dry mushrooms. With a sharp knife remove stems from mushrooms. (Save stems for use in another recipe.) Combine crab meat, parsley, pimiento, and capers. Blend dry mustard into mayonnaise; toss with crab mixture. Fill each mushroom crown with about 2 tablespoons crab mixture. Bake at 375° till hot, about 8 to 10 minutes. Makes 36 appetizers.

ELEGANT OYSTER APPETIZER

Turn anchovies out of two 2-ounce cans anchovy fillets; drain. Separate fillets carefully. Cut 8 slices bacon crosswise in thirds. Partially cook bacon; drain. Drain 24 shucked oysters. Wrap fillet around oyster, then wrap with bacon; fasten with a wooden pick. Broil over *medium* coals, turning the appetizers several times till bacon is crisp. Makes 24 appetizers.

CRAB-DEVILED EGGS

    12 hard-cooked eggs
    ½ cup mayonnaise or salad dressing
    2 tablespoons finely chopped onion
    1 tablespoon prepared mustard
    ¼ teaspoon salt
    ⅛ teaspoon pepper
    1 7½-ounce can crab meat, drained,
       flaked, and cartilage removed

Cut each egg in half lengthwise. Carefully remove and sieve yolks or mash till smooth. Combine with mayonnaise, onion, mustard, salt, and pepper. Mix well. Add the crab to egg mixture, reserving a few pieces for garnish, if desired. Fill egg whites with yolk mixture. Chill. Garnish each egg half with a tiny sprig of parsley, if desired. Makes 24 appetizers.

PICKLED SHRIMP

    ½ cup salad oil
    ½ cup lime juice
    2 tablespoons vinegar
    1 tablespoon snipped chives
    1½ teaspoons salt
    ½ teaspoon dried dillweed
    3 drops bottled hot pepper sauce
    2 teaspoons capers
             • • •
    2 pounds shelled shrimp, cooked

Combine oil, lime juice, vinegar, chives, salt, dill, hot pepper sauce, and capers. Add shrimp; toss. Chill several hours, stirring occasionally. Drain and serve with wooden picks.

ANGELS ON HORSEBACK

    8 slices bacon
    16 shucked oysters
    4 slices bread, toasted and buttered
       Lemon wedges

Cut bacon in half crosswise. Partially cook bacon; drain. Wrap one piece of bacon around each oyster; secure with wooden picks. Place oysters on rack in shallow baking pan. Bake at 450° till bacon is crisp, 10 minutes. Cut each toast slice diagonally into 4 triangles. Place one oyster on each triangle. Serve hot with lemon wedges. Makes 16 appetizers.

CRAB-POTATO NIBBLERS

　　1 teaspoon instant minced onion
　　　Packaged instant mashed potatoes
　　　(enough for 2 servings)
1¼ teaspoons Worcestershire sauce
　⅛ teaspoon garlic powder
　　　Dash white pepper
　　1 7½-ounce crab meat, drained, flaked,
　　　and cartilage removed

　　　　　• • •

　　1 slightly beaten egg
　½ cup fine dry bread crumbs

Add instant onion to water called for when preparing potatoes according to package directions, and use *2 tablespoons less milk* than directions specify. Stir in Worcestershire sauce, garlic powder, and pepper. Add crab meat. Shape mixture into bite-sized balls. Dip into beaten egg, then roll in crumbs. Fry in deep, hot fat (375°) till golden brown, about 1 minute. Drain. Makes 36 appetizers.

CAVIAR-STUFFED EGGS

　6 hard-cooked eggs
　2 tablespoons butter or margarine
　1 2-ounce jar black caviar
　　(3 tablespoons)
　　Dash pepper

Cut each egg in half lengthwise. Carefully remove and sieve egg yolks. Blend in butter; carefully stir in caviar and pepper. Fill egg whites with yolk mixture; chill. Garnish with parsley, if desired. Makes 12 appetizers.

STUFFED SHRIMP APPETIZERS

24 medium shelled shrimp, cooked
　1 3-ounce package cream cheese,
　　softened
　1 ounce blue cheese, crumbled (¼ cup)
　　Dash garlic salt
　½ cup finely snipped parsley

Chill shrimp. Split shrimp part way down along vein side. Blend together cream cheese, blue cheese, and garlic salt. Using pastry tube, generously stuff cheese into groove split along back of shrimp. Lightly roll shrimp, cheese side down, in parsley. Makes 24 appetizers.

Discover a short-cut *when serving hot appetizers. Begin with instant products, then add crab meat and seasonings to flavor Crab-Potato Nibblers.*

ANCHOVY-STUFFED CELERY

Thoroughly blend together ¼ cup dairy sour cream, 2 tablespoons mayonnaise or salad dressing, 1 teaspoon anchovy paste, ¼ teaspoon dried dillweed, and ¼ teaspoon onion powder. Stuff mixture into diagonally cut celery sections. Chill thoroughly before arranging on serving plate. Makes about ⅓ cup filling.

Add a colorful garnish *to Stuffed Shrimp Appetizers. Roll chilled shrimp that has been split and stuffed with a cheese mixture in a bed of snipped parsley.*

Menu

OPEN-HOUSE BUFFET
Artichoke-Shrimp Flower
Swedish Meatballs in Chafing Dish
Cheese Ball   Crackers
Antipasto Tray
Pickled Mushrooms
Fruit Punch   Cocktails

Invite your friends for an open house to celebrate the holiday season, to christen a new home, or to meet a guest or new in-law.

This buffet menu leaves both hostess and guests free to circulate during the party. The recipes can be prepared early in the day, so you'll be able to mingle with the guests rather than taking care of last-minute details. The foods are eaten with the fingers or wooden picks, thus enabling guests to carry their plates and nibble the food as they circulate. Preparation and clean-up afterwards are also simplified because individual seating arrangements and silverware are not necessary.

Try these recipes ahead of time for practice. Then, decide on your guest list, set the date for the open house, make any advance preparations, and finally, enjoy the party.

ARTICHOKE-SHRIMP FLOWER

    1 artichoke
    1 3-ounce package cream cheese,
        softened
    2 teaspoons chili sauce
 ¼ teaspoon prepared horseradish
    1 4½-ounce can shrimp, chilled and
        drained

Wash artichoke; cut off 1 inch of top, the stem, and tips of leaves. Brush cut edges with lemon juice. Cook in small amount of boiling, salted water till leaf pulls out, about 30 minutes. Drain, chill, and pull off leaves. Combine cream cheese, chili sauce, and horseradish; mix well. Spread a small amount of mixture at base of leaf; top each leaf with a shrimp. Arrange sunburst fashion on a plate.

SCALLOPS À LA JIMMY

Use this recipe from Jimmy's Harborside Restaurant in Boston as an appetizer or double the amount for an entrée—

    1 pound fresh or frozen scallops
 ¼ cup butter or margarine, melted
 ⅓ cup fine soft bread crumbs
 ⅛ teaspoon garlic salt
 ⅛ teaspoon dry mustard
 ⅛ teaspoon paprika
    2 tablespoons dry sherry
        Lemon wedges

Thaw frozen scallops. Slice large scallops in half horizontally. Pour *2 tablespoons* of the butter in a shallow baking pan; arrange scallops in single layer. Combine bread crumbs, garlic salt, dry mustard, paprika, and remaining butter; sprinkle over scallops. Broil 4 inches from heat till lightly browned, for 6 to 8 minutes. Drizzle wine over scallops; serve hot with lemon wedges. Makes 6 to 8 servings.

MUSHROOM MORNAY APPETIZERS

Buy ready-made tart shells or make your own—

    1 3-ounce can sliced mushrooms, drained
 12 small baked tart shells
    1 7½-ounce can crab meat, drained,
        flaked, and cartilage removed
    2 teaspoons lemon juice
    3 tablespoons butter or margarine
    3 tablespoons all-purpose flour
 ¼ teaspoon salt
 1½ cups milk
    2 slightly beaten egg yolks
    4 ounces sharp process American
        cheese, shredded (1 cup)
    2 tablespoons dry sherry

Divide mushrooms among tart shells; top with crab meat and sprinkle with lemon juice. Melt butter in small saucepan; blend in flour and salt. Add milk all at once; cook and stir till mixture thickens and bubbles. Add small amount hot mixture to egg yolks; return to hot mixture and cook 1 minute. Remove from heat; stir in ¾ *cup* of the cheese and the sherry. Pour sauce over crab in tart shells. Sprinkle with remaining cheese. Bake at 350° for 20 to 25 minutes. Serve warm. Makes 12 appetizers.

CLAM CANAPÉS

1 7½-ounce can minced clams, drained
⅓ cup shredded Swiss cheese
1 tablespoon chopped green onion
¼ cup mayonnaise or salad dressing
Dash bottled hot pepper sauce

• • •

24 melba toast rounds
Parsley or paprika

Combine clams, cheese, green onion, mayonnaise, and hot pepper sauce. Spread about 2 teaspoons evenly over each toast round. Broil 3 inches from heat till cheese melts, about 2 to 4 minutes. Garnish with parsley or paprika. Serve immediately. Makes 20 to 24 appetizers.

SMOKED EEL CANAPÉS

6 thin slices party pumpernickel
Butter or margarine
12 thin slices skinned smoked eel or
other dry smoked fish (about one
4-ounce fish)
¼ cup dairy sour cream
1 teaspoon finely chopped onion
Capers, drained

Spread bread slices with butter or margarine; cut each slice in half. Lay one slice fish atop each half. Combine sour cream and onion. Spoon a dollop over smoked fish; garnish with capers. Makes 12 appetizers.

ANTIPASTO ROLL-UPS

2 6-ounce packages sliced mozzarella
cheese (8 slices)
1 8-ounce package sliced salami
(21 slices)
1 6½- or 7-ounce can tuna, drained
and flaked
1 hard-cooked egg, chopped
⅓ cup mayonnaise or salad dressing
1 teaspoon lemon juice

Cut each cheese slice into thirds. Arrange a piece of cheese on each slice of salami. Combine tuna, egg, mayonnaise, and lemon juice. Spread about 1 tablespoon mixture over cheese. Roll up, securing with wooden picks. Chill till serving time. Makes about 20 appetizers.

SALMON LORRAINE

Prepare one 9-inch pastry shell, crimping edges high. Prick pastry lightly. Bake at 450° till lightly browned, about 7 minutes. Remove from oven; reduce oven temperature to 325°.

In medium saucepan gradually blend 1½ cups milk into one 3-ounce envelope cream of potato soup mix, 1 teaspoon dry mustard, and dash pepper. Cook and stir till thickened and bubbly. Press mixture through sieve; discard any remaining potato chunks. Stir in ½ cup light cream. Combine 3 slightly beaten eggs; 4 ounces process Swiss cheese, shredded (1 cup); and 2 tablespoons finely chopped green onion with tops. Blend soup mixture into cheese mixture. Set aside while preparing salmon layer.

Drain one 7¾-ounce can salmon. Remove skin and any large bones. Flake well. Combine salmon and 3 tablespoons soft bread crumbs. Sprinkle evenly in partially baked pastry shell. Carefully pour in soup mixture. Bake at 325° till knife inserted off-center comes out clean, 50 to 60 minutes. Let stand 10 minutes. Cut into tiny wedges; serve warm. Serves 12.

OYSTER-STUFFED TOMATOES

Wash cherry tomatoes and cut a slit in each one. Fill with canned smoked oysters. Cut very large oysters in two or three pieces.

SHRIMP-STUFFED CELERY

1 4½-ounce can shrimp, drained
and finely chopped
1 3-ounce package cream cheese
2 tablespoons mayonnaise or
salad dressing
1 tablespoon finely chopped onion
1 tablespoon minced parsley
1 tablespoon finely chopped green
pepper
1 tablespoon finely chopped celery
1 tablespoon finely chopped green olives
Dash bottled hot pepper sauce
Dash Worcestershire sauce
Dash salt and pepper
Celery

Combine all ingredients except the celery. Stuff mixture into diagonally cut celery sections. Chill. Makes 1 cup filling.

PARTY-LAUNCHING SPREADS AND DIPS

TUNA-CHEESE LOG

Keep second log refrigerated until needed—

>   2 3-ounce packages cream cheese,
>   softened
>   1 ounce blue cheese, crumbled (¼ cup)
>   2 tablespoons finely chopped celery
>   1 tablespoon finely chopped onion
>   1 tablespoon mayonnaise
>   Few drops bottled hot pepper sauce
>   1 6½- or 7-ounce can tuna, drained
>   and flaked
>   ½ cup chopped pecans

In small mixer bowl beat together the cream cheese and blue cheese. Stir in the celery, onion, mayonnaise, hot pepper sauce, and tuna. Shape the mixture into two 5-inch rolls, 1½ inches in diameter. Chill several hours or overnight. Before serving, roll in chopped pecans. Serve with crackers. Makes 2 rolls.

EGG AND CAVIAR SPREAD

>   8 hard-cooked eggs
>   ¼ cup butter or margarine, softened
>   1 8-ounce carton French onion dairy
>   sour cream dip
> 1½ teaspoons prepared mustard
>   ½ teaspoon salt
>   ⅛ teaspoon pepper
>   2 tablespoons finely chopped celery
>   1 4-ounce jar black or red caviar
>   (½ cup)
>   1 tablespoon snipped parsley

Peel and chop the eggs very finely. Beat together with softened butter or margarine, ¼ *cup* of the sour cream dip, mustard, salt, and pepper. Stir in the celery. Spread egg mixture on a flat serving platter, shaping a layer about 1 inch thick. Chill till firm. To serve, spread remaining sour cream dip over top. Top with caviar and snipped parsley. Serve with assorted crackers. Makes about 2½ cups spread.

TUNA PÂTÉ

>   1 8-ounce package cream cheese,
>   softened
>   2 tablespoons chili sauce
>   2 tablespoons snipped parsley
>   1 teaspoon instant minced onion
>   ½ teaspoon bottled hot pepper sauce
>   2 6½- or 7-ounce cans tuna, drained
>   and flaked

Blend together the cream cheese, chili sauce, parsley, minced onion, and bottled hot pepper sauce. Add the tuna and mix well. Pack the mixture into a 4-cup mold. Chill at least 3 hours. Unmold and serve with crackers or crisp vegetables. Makes about 4 cups spread.

POTTED SHRIMP AND CHEESE

Trim this spread with tiny fluffs of parsley or a bouquet of watercress—

>   1 4½-ounce can shrimp, drained
>   4 ounces natural Cheddar cheese,
>   shredded (1 cup)
>   ¼ cup butter or margarine
>   1 tablespoon milk
>   Dash cayenne pepper

Finely chop shrimp. Have cheese at room temperature. In small mixer bowl beat cheese, butter, milk, and cayenne till fluffy. Blend in shrimp. Press mixture into 10-ounce custard cup. Chill. Unmold onto serving plate. Let set at room temperature 10 minutes. Serve with assorted crackers. Makes 1⅓ cups spread.

Pâté and lorraine adapt to seafoods

Offer a choice of Tuna Pâté or Salmon Lorraine (see → page 33). The pâté is spread on crisp celery sticks or crackers for eating out-of-hand, while the lorraine is served on plates, and is eaten with a fork.

CRAB AND CRACKERS

1 tablespoon lemon juice or dry sherry
1 7½-ounce can crab meat, drained,
   flaked, and cartilage removed
½ cup dairy sour cream
¼ cup mayonnaise or salad dressing
¼ teaspoon salt
   Paprika

In small bowl sprinkle lemon juice or sherry over crab meat. Let stand 10 to 15 minutes. Blend in sour cream, mayonnaise or salad dressing, and salt. Chill at least 2 hours. To serve, spoon 1 teaspoon of the mixture onto a cracker; sprinkle with paprika. Makes 1½ cups.

COD SPREAD

1 8-ounce package cream cheese,
   softened
4 teaspoons lemon juice
8 ounces cod fillets or other fish fillets,
   cooked and flaked (about 1 cup)
2 teaspoons grated onion
1 teaspoon prepared horseradish
⅛ teaspoon paprika

In small mixer bowl beat cream cheese and lemon juice; beat in cod, onion, horseradish, and paprika till fluffy. Sprinkle with additional paprika, if desired. Serve with crackers or toast thins. Makes 1¾ cups spread.

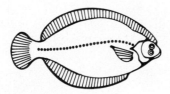

HALIBUT SPREAD

12 ounces halibut steaks, or other fish
    steaks, cooked and flaked (about 1½
    cups)
1 cup dairy sour cream
1 envelope green onion dip mix
1 teaspoon Worcestershire sauce

Combine halibut with dairy sour cream, dip mix, and Worcestershire sauce. Chill thoroughly to blend flavors. Serve with assorted crisp crackers. Makes 1⅔ cups spread.

CLAM SPREAD

1 7½-ounce can minced clams
1 clove garlic
1 8-ounce package cream cheese,
   softened
1 teaspoon lemon juice
1 teaspoon Worcestershire sauce
½ cup finely chopped, unpeeled
   cucumber
   Snipped parsley

Drain clams, reserving 1 tablespoon liquid. Rub mixing bowl with cut clove of garlic. In bowl blend cheese, lemon juice, Worcestershire sauce, ¼ teaspoon salt, dash pepper, cucumber, clams, and reserved clam liquid. Chill. Turn into a serving bowl; sprinkle with parsley. Serve with crackers. Makes 1½ cups.

SARDINE APPETIZER SPREAD

1 3¾-ounce can sardines in oil, drained
¼ cup butter or margarine, softened
2 tablespoons finely chopped green onion
2 tablespoons chili sauce
1 tablespoon lemon juice
¼ teaspoon dry mustard
   Few drops bottled hot pepper sauce

Mash the sardines with a fork. Combine with butter or margarine, onion, chili sauce, lemon juice, mustard, and hot pepper sauce. Blend thoroughly. Chill. Let stand at room temperature a few minutes before serving. Serve with crisp rye wafers. Makes ¾ cup spread.

SMOKED OYSTER SPREAD

1 3⅔-ounce can smoked oysters or
   mussels
1 tablespoon snipped green onion
1 tablespoon mayonnaise
2 teaspoons catsup
¼ teaspoon celery salt
   Dash Worcestershire sauce

Drain oysters or mussels; grind or chop very fine, making about ¾ cup. Add onion, mayonnaise, catsup, celery salt, and Worcestershire; mix thoroughly. Chill. Serve in a small bowl accompanied with crackers. If desired, garnish with snipped green onion tops. Makes ⅓ cup.

SALMON PARTY BALL

1 16-ounce can salmon
1 8-ounce package cream cheese,
    softened
1 tablespoon lemon juice
2 teaspoons grated onion
1 teaspoon prepared horseradish
¼ teaspoon liquid smoke
½ cup chopped pecans
3 tablespoons snipped parsley

Drain and flake salmon, removing bones and skin. Combine salmon, cheese, lemon juice, onion, horseradish, ¼ teaspoon salt, and liquid smoke; mix. Chill several hours. Combine pecans and parsley. Shape salmon mixture into ball; roll in nut mixture. Chill. Serve with crackers. Makes 3 cups spread.

STUFFED CHEESE BALL

1 whole baby Gouda or Edam cheese
    (about 8 ounces)
½ cup dairy sour cream
1 7½-ounce can minced clams, drained
2 tablespoons milk
1 tablespoon snipped parsley
⅛ teaspoon onion powder

Bring cheese to room temperature. Using a sawtooth cut, remove top of cheese. Carefully scoop out cheese, leaving a thin shell. Whip cheese and sour cream with electric mixer till smooth; blend in clams, milk, parsley, and onion powder. Mound whipped mixture high in red cheese shell, reserving remainder to refill as used. Chill thoroughly. Sprinkle with additional snipped parsley, if desired. Serve with assorted crackers. Makes 1½ cups spread.

CRAB AND CHEESE SPREAD

1 6-ounce package smoky cheese spread
1 3-ounce can deviled crab spread
¼ cup chopped pimiento-stuffed green
    olives
2 teaspoons milk

Combine all ingredients in a bowl. Blend thoroughly with electric mixer. Spread mixture on melba toast or unsalted crackers or stuff mixture into celery sections. Makes 1¼ cups.

Adding a hint of smoke *to complement the flavor and rolling in chopped nuts to contrast with the soft texture makes Salmon Party Ball a superb combination.*

OYSTER PÂTÉ

1 pint shucked oysters
2 tablespoons butter or margarine
¼ cup mayonnaise or salad dressing
2 tablespoons butter or margarine
1 tablespoon lemon juice
2 teaspoons finely chopped onion
½ teaspoon dry mustard
¼ teaspoon bottled hot pepper sauce
1 teaspoon unflavored gelatin
2 tablespoons cold water
1 hard-cooked egg, chopped

Drain oysters. Cook oysters, covered, in 2 tablespoons butter over medium heat till edges curl, about 2 minutes. Drain. In blender container combine mayonnaise, 2 tablespoons butter, lemon juice, onion, ½ teaspoon salt, mustard, and hot pepper sauce. Blend.

Soften gelatin in cold water. Dissolve over hot water. Stir into oyster mixture. Turn into a small mold. Chill several hours. Unmold carefully. Garnish with chopped hard-cooked egg. Serve with crackers. Makes 1¼ cups.

SHRIMP-DILL PÂTÉ

  ½ cup cold tomato juice
  2 envelopes unflavored gelatin
  1 cup boiling tomato juice
  2 cups dairy sour cream
  1 tablespoon dried dillweed
  2 tablespoons lemon juice
  ½ teaspoon salt
  ½ teaspoon Worcestershire sauce
  1 4½-ounce can shrimp, drained

Add ½ cup cold tomato juice and gelatin to blender container; cover and blend on low speed till gelatin is softened. Add boiling tomato juice; blend on low speed till gelatin dissolves. (If gelatin granules cling to side of container, stop blender and use rubber spatula to push into liquid.) Turn blender to high; add remaining ingredients, except shrimp. Continue blending till mixture is smooth. Stop blender and add shrimp. Turn blender on and off several times, just till shrimp are chopped. Pour into 5-cup mold or bowl. Chill till firm, about 4 hours. Unmold onto serving plate and accompany with crackers or party rye bread.

CRAB DIP

  1 8-ounce package cream cheese, softened
  ¼ cup mayonnaise or salad dressing
  3 tablespoons milk
  ¼ teaspoon salt
  ¼ teaspoon bottled hot pepper sauce
  ⅛ teaspoon garlic powder
  1 7½-ounce can crab meat, drained, finely chopped, and cartilage removed

In small mixer bowl beat together cream cheese, mayonnaise or salad dressing, milk, salt, hot pepper sauce, and garlic powder till smooth. Stir in crab. Chill. Serve with crisp vegetable dippers or chips. Makes 2 cups dip.

Quick way to chop shrimp

← *Making Shrimp-Dill Pâté in an electric blender will produce a creamy spread with a minimum of work. The gelatin mixture is blended in a few seconds and shrimp are chopped with several flicks of the switch.*

SHRIMP FONDUE

  1 10-ounce can frozen condensed cream of shrimp soup
  ¼ cup milk
  4 ounces process American cheese, shredded (1 cup)
  1 tablespoon lemon juice or dry sherry
  Toasted bread triangles, relishes, or crackers

Thaw soup; remove shrimp and chop. In saucepan combine soup, chopped shrimp, and milk; heat till bubbly. Add cheese and lemon juice or sherry; stir till cheese melts. Transfer to small chafing dish or fondue pot; keep warm. Dip toast triangles, crisp relishes, or crackers into the hot mixture. Makes 1¾ cups dip.

CHILI-MAYONNAISE DIP

  1½ pounds shelled cooked shrimp
  ⅓ cup chili sauce
  2 tablespoons creamy French salad dressing
  ½ teaspoon chili powder
  4 drops bottled hot pepper sauce
  • • •
  ½ cup dairy sour cream
  ⅓ cup mayonnaise or salad dressing

Chill shrimp. In blender container combine chili sauce, French salad dressing, chili powder, and hot pepper sauce; blend 30 seconds (or beat with electric or rotary beater till well blended). Stir together sour cream and mayonnaise. Fold in chili sauce mixture. Chill. Serve shrimp with dip. Makes 1 cup dip.

SMOKED-FISH DIP

  1 4-ounce smoked fish
  1 to 2 tablespoons milk
  1 3-ounce package cream cheese, softened
  1 tablespoon snipped parsley
  Dash garlic powder

Remove skin and bones from smoked fish; chop finely (need about ⅓ cup chopped fish). In bowl gradually add milk to cheese; blend till smooth. Stir in fish, parsley, and garlic powder. Chill. Serve with crackers. Makes ⅔ cup.

Keep this spread hot *throughout the party by placing it over a candle warmer or an electric hot tray. The delicate flavor of Hot Crab Cocktail Spread on crackers or chips will be a highlight of the evening.*

HOT CRAB COCKTAIL SPREAD

In a bowl thoroughly combine one 8-ounce package cream cheese with 1 tablespoon milk and 2 teaspoons Worcestershire sauce. To cream cheese mixture add one 7½-ounce can crab meat, drained, flaked, and cartilage removed, and 2 tablespoons chopped green onion; blend well. Turn mixture into a greased 8-inch pie plate or small, shallow baking dish. Top with 2 tablespoons toasted slivered almonds. Bake at 350° till heated through, about 15 minutes. Keep cocktail spread warm. Serve with assorted crackers. Makes about 2 cups.

HERRING DIP

This dip appeals to sophisticated tastes —

8 ounces pickled herring pieces or fillets
½ cup dairy sour cream
2 to 3 tablespoons milk

Drain the herring; chop finely or mash (should yield about ¾ cup). In a bowl combine herring and sour cream. Add enough milk to make of dipping consistency. Chill thoroughly. Serve with assorted crackers. Makes about 1¼ cups.

CLAM-GUACAMOLE DUNK

Clams add variety to this Mexican favorite—

  2 avocados, seeded and peeled
  1 7½-ounce can minced clams, drained
  1 tablespoon chopped, mild green chilies
  1 tablespoon chopped canned pimiento
  1 tablespoon lemon juice
  1 teaspoon grated onion

Sieve avocados or mash with fork till smooth. Stir in clams, chilies, pimiento, lemon juice, onion, and ¼ teaspoon salt; add additional salt to taste. Chill. Serve with crackers or crisp vegetable dippers. Makes 1⅓ cups dip.

ANCHOVY DIP

  1 8-ounce package cream cheese, softened
  ¼ cup mayonnaise or salad dressing
  2 tablespoons anchovy paste
  1 tablespoon milk
  1 tablespoon sliced green onion
  1 teaspoon lemon juice
    Dash garlic powder
    Few drops bottled hot pepper sauce

Beat cream cheese and mayonnaise together till well blended. Add anchovy paste, milk, green onion, lemon juice, garlic powder, and hot pepper sauce. Blend well. Chill. Serve with vegetable dippers. Makes 1⅓ cups dip.

AVOCADO-CRAB DIP

  1 large avocado, seeded, peeled, and cubed
  1 tablespoon lemon juice
  1 tablespoon grated onion
  1 teaspoon Worcestershire sauce
  1 8-ounce package cream cheese, softened
  ¼ cup dairy sour cream
  1 7½-ounce can crab meat, drained, flaked, and cartilage removed

In blender container or small bowl combine avocado, lemon juice, onion, and Worcestershire. Blend or beat till smooth. Add cream cheese, sour cream, and ¼ teaspoon salt; blend well. Stir in crab; chill. Serve with crackers.

CLAM-AVOCADO DIP

  1 7½-ounce can minced clams
  1 avocado, seeded and peeled
  2 tablespoons catsup
  1 teaspoon instant minced onion
  1 teaspoon lemon juice
  ¼ teaspoon prepared horseradish
  ¼ teaspoon Worcestershire sauce
    Dash salt

Drain clams, reserving liquid. Sieve avocado or mash with fork till smooth. Combine clams, avocado, catsup, instant minced onion, lemon juice, horseradish, Worcestershire sauce, and salt. If necessary, add some reserved clam liquid to make of dipping consistency. Chill thoroughly. Serve with crisp assorted crackers or celery sticks. Makes 1 cup dip.

CAVIAR DIP WITH ARTICHOKE

  1 artichoke
  ½ cup mayonnaise or salad dressing
  1 2-ounce jar black caviar
  2 teaspoons lemon juice
  ¼ teaspoon dry mustard
  ¼ teaspoon Worcestershire sauce

Wash artichoke, cut off 1 inch of top, the stem, and tips of leaves. Pull off any loose leaves. Brush cut edges with lemon juice. Cook in small amount of boiling, salted water till leaves pull out easily, about 30 minutes. Drain the artichoke, then chill thoroughly.

Meanwhile, combine mayonnaise, caviar (reserve 1 teaspoon caviar for garnish, if desired), lemon juice, dry mustard, and Worcestershire sauce. Chill. Arrange artichoke and bowl of dressing on serving tray. Dip caviar mixture with artichoke leaves. Makes ¾ cup.

SHRIMP-CUCUMBER DUNK

Cut 1 medium unpeeled cucumber lengthwise; remove seeds. Shred enough to make 1 cup; drain. In small mixer bowl combine shredded cucumber with 1 cup cottage cheese, 2 tablespoons finely chopped onion, 2 teaspoons vinegar, and ½ teaspoon prepared horseradish. Beat mixture till smooth. Stir in one 4½-ounce can shrimp, drained and coarsely chopped. Serve with crackers. Makes about 2 cups dip.

Looking for some classic or modern-day soup and chowder recipes to add to your repertoire? The assortment is varied. You can choose from old-standards, such as clam chowder and oyster stew, to modernized soups, so quick and easy to prepare. Are you getting hungry? Better hurry out to the kitchen and get that kettle of soup cooking.

Before you begin, however, plan the rest of the menu, too. If the soup or chowder is planned for the main course, choose one that is hearty. A big, steaming bowlful will be appreciated with a crusty piece of bread or an assortment of crisp crackers, especially on a cold, blustery day. Then, dress up the soup. A handful of tiny oyster crackers is a natural with seafood chowders. Finally, team the soup with a cold, crisp salad or assorted relishes and dessert—perhaps a fresh fruit.

Soup can also be planned as the first course. In this case, choose a less hearty soup that will stimulate rather than dull the appetite. Small bowls or cups of soup are in order if served as the beginning course so that the remaining parts of the meal can be enjoyed.

Many of the soups included in this chapter are quick to prepare, while a few take a bit of doing, but all are well worth any extra effort. A good example is the soup pictured here—Bouillabaisse. This French-inspired soup incorporates lobster, snapper, cod, scallops, and clams. When you sample this dish, you'll agree that the time spent in the kitchen is time put to good use.

Soups and Chowders

BOUILLABAISSE

This soup is pictured on page 42 —

　　1 pound frozen lobster tails
　　1 pound fresh or frozen red snapper
　　　fillets or sole fillets
　　1 pound fresh or frozen cod fillets or
　　　haddock fillets
　12 ounces fresh or frozen scallops
　12 clams in shells
　　2 large onions, chopped
　1/3 cup olive oil
　　4 cups coarsely chopped tomato
　　1 clove garlic, minced
　　2 sprigs parsley
　　1 bay leaf
　　1 teaspoon dried thyme leaves, crushed
　1/4 teaspoon saffron, crushed
　　French bread

Thaw frozen shellfish and fish. When lobster is partially thawed, split in half lengthwise; cut in half crosswise if necessary to make 6 to 8 portions. Cut fish fillets into 2-inch pieces. Cut large scallops in half. Wash clams well. In large saucepan cook onion in oil till tender but not brown. Add 6 cups water or fish stock, tomato, garlic, parsley, bay leaf, thyme, saffron, 1 tablespoon salt, and dash freshly ground pepper. Simmer, covered, 30 minutes. Strain the seasoned stock into a large kettle. Discard the vegetables and herbs.

　Bring the strained stock to boiling; add lobster and fish; cook 5 minutes. Add scallops and clams; boil till clams open, about 5 minutes. Serve with French bread. Serves 6 to 8.

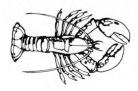

LOBSTER AND CORN STEW

Melt 2 tablespoons butter or margarine in a 2-quart saucepan. Add 1/4 cup chopped onion and 2 tablespoons chopped green pepper; cook till tender but not brown. Add one 17-ounce can whole kernel corn (undrained); one 5-ounce can lobster, drained and flaked; 1 cup light cream; 1 cup milk; 1/2 teaspoon salt; and dash white pepper. Heat through. Serves 4 or 5.

CIOPPINO (ITALIAN FISH STEW)

　　2 pounds fresh or frozen haddock fillets
　　　or halibut fillets, thawed
　　8 ounces fresh or frozen shelled shrimp
　1/2 cup chopped green pepper
　1/4 cup finely chopped onion
　　2 cloves garlic, minced
　1/4 cup olive oil or salad oil
　　1 28-ounce can tomatoes, cut up
　　1 15-ounce can tomato sauce
　1 1/2 cups water
　1/3 cup snipped parsley
　　1 teaspoon salt
　1/2 teaspoon dried oregano leaves, crushed
　1/2 teaspoon dried basil leaves, crushed
　　　Dash pepper
　　1 cup dry red wine
　24 clams in shells *or* 2 7 1/2-ounce cans
　　　minced clams, drained
　　1 pound frozen lobster tails, partially
　　　thawed

Thaw frozen fillets and shrimp. In Dutch oven cook green pepper, onion, and garlic in oil till tender but not brown. Add tomatoes, tomato sauce, water, parsley, salt, oregano, basil, and pepper. Cover; bring to boiling. Reduce heat; simmer 20 minutes. Add wine; continue simmering, covered, 10 minutes.

　Meanwhile wash clams in shells. Cut lobster, including shell, into serving-sized pieces. Cut fillets into pieces, removing bones if necessary. Add lobster to broth; simmer, covered, 5 minutes. Add fish and shrimp; simmer 5 additional minutes. Add clams in shells or canned clams; continue simmering, covered, till shells open, about 5 minutes, or till canned clams are heated through. Discard any clams in shells that have not opened during cooking. Serve in soup bowls. Makes 8 servings.

CLAM-TOMATO BROTH

　　1 32-ounce bottle clam-tomato juice *or*
　　　1 12-ounce bottle clam juice plus
　　　1 1/2 cups tomato juice
　　1 tablespoon lemon juice
　1/4 teaspoon garlic salt
　1/4 teaspoon onion powder

In saucepan combine all ingredients and dash pepper. Bring to boiling. Reduce heat; simmer 5 minutes. Serve hot or chilled. Serves 4 to 6.

ZUIDER ZEE'S SHRIMP GUMBO

Serve this dish just like it's made in Zuider Zee restaurants throughout the Midwest and Southwest—

> ¾ **cup chopped celery**
> ¾ **cup chopped green pepper**
> ½ **cup chopped green onion**
> 1 **tablespoon snipped parsley**
> 3 **tablespoons butter or margarine**
> • • •
> 1 **10½-ounce can condensed cream of mushroom soup**
> 1 **15½-ounce can okra, undrained**
> 1 **16-ounce can tomatoes, cut up**
> 2 **cups cooked rice**
> 12 **ounces fresh or frozen shelled shrimp, cooked, or 2 4½-ounce cans shrimp, drained and cut up**
> ½ **cup water**
> ½ **teaspoon salt**
> **Dash pepper**
> **Dash cayenne pepper**
> 1 **teaspoon filé**

In large saucepan cook celery, green pepper, green onion, and parsley in butter till tender. Blend in soup, okra and liquid, tomatoes, rice, shrimp, water, salt, pepper, and cayenne pepper. Heat to boiling; remove from heat and stir in filé (never cook filé). Serve piping hot. Makes 6 to 8 servings.

LOBSTER STEW

> ¼ **cup butter or margarine**
> 2 **6-ounce lobster tails, cooked, shelled, and cut in bite-sized pieces**
> 2 **cups light cream**
> 1 **cup milk**
> 1 **teaspoon salt**
> ¼ **teaspoon Worcestershire sauce**
> **Dash bottled hot pepper sauce**

In large saucepan melt butter; add lobster and cook about 5 minutes. Add cream, milk, salt, dash pepper, Worcestershire, and hot pepper sauce; heat to scalding. Remove from heat; cover and let stand 15 minutes to blend flavors. If necessary, reheat to serving temperature. Ladle into soup dishes. If desired, float a dot of butter atop each serving and sprinkle with paprika. Makes 4 servings.

HOT SCALLOP CHOWDER

> 1 **pound fresh or frozen scallops**
> 2 **cups boiling water**
> 1 **teaspoon salt**
> • • •
> 1 **10½-ounce can condensed cream of chicken soup**
> 1 **10½-ounce can condensed cream of potato soup**
> 1½ **cups milk**
> 1 **cup light cream**
> 2 **teaspoons snipped chives**

Thaw frozen scallops. Rinse and chop coarsely. Place in boiling salted water. Return to boil; reduce heat and simmer 1 minute. Drain. Combine soups and milk in blender container or mixer bowl. Blend or beat till smooth. Pour into saucepan; stir in cream and chives. Heat just to boiling, stirring occasionally. Add scallops; heat through. Pour into soup bowls; garnish with snipped chives, if desired. Serves 6.

COD CHOWDER

> 1 **pound fresh or frozen cod fillets**
> 2 **cups diced, peeled potatoes**
> ½ **cup chopped celery**
> ⅓ **cup chopped onion**
> 2 **tablespoons chopped canned pimiento**
> 1½ **teaspoons salt**
> 2 **cups milk**
> 1 **tablespoon all-purpose flour**
> 3 **slices bacon, crisp-cooked and crumbled**
> 1 **tablespoon butter or margarine**

Thaw frozen fillets. Skin fillets, if necessary; cut into ½-inch pieces. In 3-quart saucepan combine 2 cups water, potatoes, celery, onion, pimiento, and salt. Bring to boiling; cover and simmer 10 minutes. Add fish and simmer, covered, till fish and potatoes are done, about 5 minutes. Add 1¾ *cups* milk. Blend remaining milk with flour. Stir into chowder. Heat to boiling, stirring occasionally. Stir in bacon and butter or margarine. Makes 6 servings.

CLAM CHOWDER AU VIN

2 cups diced, peeled potatoes
½ cup chopped onion
½ cup chopped celery
¼ teaspoon salt
1 cup water
1 10¾-ounce can condensed Manhattan-
    style clam chowder
1 cup milk
1 7½-ounce can minced clams, drained
3 tablespoons dry white wine
½ cup whipping cream

In large saucepan combine first five ingredients. Cook, covered, till potatoes are tender, about 10 minutes; mash slightly. Add chowder, milk, clams, and wine. Heat but do not boil. Whip cream; stir into chowder. Season with salt and pepper. Sprinkle with snipped parsley, if desired. Makes 4 servings.

Add an elegant soup to the dinner menu. Clam Chowder au Vin is a Manhattan-style chowder accented with wine and whipped cream.

GLOUCESTER HOUSE CHOWDER

Tantalize chowder fans with the flavor of New England clam chowder made like the soup served at Gloucester House in New York City—

2 pints shucked clams
¼ cup finely diced salt pork
    (1½ ounces)
½ cup chopped onion
½ cup diced celery
1 cup diced potato (1 medium)
    • • •
1½ cups light cream
    Salt
    Pepper

Drain clams, reserving liquid. Add enough water to clam juice to make 1½ cups. Chop clams; set aside. In large saucepan fry salt pork till lightly browned. Add clam juice, onion, celery, and potatoes. Simmer, covered, till vegetables are tender, about 15 minutes. Add clams; cook 3 to 5 minutes. Add cream and continue cooking till mixture is hot. Season to taste. Makes 6 to 8 servings.

CLAM AND HALIBUT CHOWDER

Combine shellfish and fish with colorful slices of carrot and celery for a superb chowder—

3 medium carrots, bias-sliced
½ cup bias-sliced celery
½ cup water
¼ cup chopped onion
    • • •
2 10¼-ounce cans frozen, condensed,
    New England-style clam chowder,
    thawed, or 2 10½-ounce cans
    condensed, New England-style clam
    chowder
2 cups milk
1 pound halibut fillets, cooked and
    broken into chunks (about 2 cups)
2 tablespoons chopped canned pimiento
2 tablespoons snipped parsley

In 2-quart saucepan combine carrot, celery, water, and chopped onion. Cook, covered, till tender, about 12 to 15 minutes. Add clam chowder, milk, cooked halibut, and chopped pimiento. Heat through. Sprinkle with snipped parsley before serving. Makes 4 servings.

NEW ENGLAND CLAM CHOWDER

  2 dozen medium quahog clams or 2
        7½-ounce cans clams or 1 pint
        shucked clams
  ¼ pound salt pork, minced
  4 cups diced, peeled potatoes
  ½ cup chopped onion
  2 cups milk
  1 cup light cream
  3 tablespoons all-purpose flour
  1½ teaspoons salt

If using clams in shell, place in large kettle; add 1 cup water. Cover and bring to boiling. Reduce heat; steam just till shells open, 5 to 10 minutes. Remove clams from shell.

Dice clams; strain liquid, reserving ½ cup. Fry salt pork till crisp. Remove bits of pork; reserve. Add ½ cup clam liquid, 1½ cups water, potatoes, and onion to fat. Cook, covered, till potatoes are tender, 15 to 20 minutes.

Add clams 1¾ *cups* milk, and cream. Blend remaining milk and flour; stir in to chowder. Cook and stir till boiling. Add salt and dash pepper; top with salt pork. Makes 6 servings.

MANHATTAN CLAM CHOWDER

  2 dozen medium quahog clams or 2 7½-
        ounce cans clams or 1 pint shucked
        clams
  3 slices bacon, finely diced
  1 cup finely diced celery
  1 cup chopped onion
  1 16-ounce can tomatoes, cut up
  2 cups diced, peeled potatoes
  1 cup finely diced carrots
  1½ teaspoons salt
  ¼ teaspoon dried thyme leaves, crushed
  2 tablespoons all-purpose flour

If using clams in shell, place in large kettle; add 1 cup water. Cover and bring to boiling. Reduce heat; steam just till shells open, 5 to 10 minutes. Remove clams from shells.

Dice clams finely. Strain liquid, reserving ½ cup. Partially cook bacon. Add celery and onion; cook till tender. Add 3 cups water, clam liquid, tomatoes, potatoes, carrots, salt, thyme, and dash pepper. Cover; simmer 35 minutes. Blend flour with 2 tablespoons cold water. Stir into chowder; cook and stir till boiling. Add clams; heat. Makes 6 to 8 servings.

CURRIED CRAB SOUP

This cold soup makes a spectacular appearance at a party when served in glass icers —

  3 tablespoons butter or margarine
  2 tablespoons all-purpose flour
  ½ to 1 teaspoon curry powder
  1 teaspoon salt
  4 cups milk
        •   •   •
  1 7½-ounce can crab meat, drained,
        chopped, and cartilage removed
  ¼ cup dry white wine
  1 cup dairy sour cream
        Snipped chives

In saucepan melt butter. Blend in flour, curry, and salt. Add milk all at once; cook, stirring constantly, till thickened and bubbly. Add crab meat and wine; heat through. Cool. Blend about ½ cup of the soup with sour cream till smooth; stir sour cream mixture into soup. Chill thoroughly, several hours or overnight. Serve cold in bowls surrounded with crushed ice. Garnish with chives. Makes 10 to 12 servings.

CRAB GUMBO

Use either crab or shrimp —

  ½ cup chopped onion
  2 tablespoons butter or margarine
  1 16-ounce can tomatoes, cut up
  1 8-ounce can tomato sauce
  1 13¾-ounce can chicken broth
  ½ teaspoon sugar
  ⅛ teaspoon pepper
  1 bay leaf
        •   •   •
  1 15½-ounce can cut okra, drained
  1 7½-ounce can crab, drained, chopped,
        and cartilage removed or 2 4½-
        ounce cans shrimp, drained
  3 cups hot cooked rice

In 3-quart saucepan cook onion in butter or margarine till tender but not brown. Add tomatoes, tomato sauce, chicken broth, sugar, pepper, and bay leaf. Bring to boiling; reduce heat and simmer, uncovered, about 30 minutes. Remove bay leaf. Add okra, and crab or shrimp; heat through. Serve gumbo over hot cooked rice in soup plates. Makes 6 servings.

SEAFOOD CHOWDER

2 pounds fresh or frozen haddock fillets
    or other fish fillets
4 ounces salt pork, diced
1 cup chopped onion
4 cups peeled and cubed potatoes
    (6 medium)
2 cups water
2 teaspoons salt
¼ teaspoon pepper
2 cups milk
1 14½-ounce can evaporated milk
2 tablespoons all-purpose flour

Thaw frozen fillets. In large saucepan cook diced salt pork slowly till golden brown. Drain, reserving 1 tablespoon fat. Set aside cooked salt pork. Return the 1 tablespoon fat to saucepan. Add onion; cook till tender but not brown. Add cubed potatoes and water. Add fillets; sprinkle with salt and pepper. Bring to boiling; cook over low heat till potatoes are tender and the fish flakes easily when it is tested with a fork, about 15 to 20 minutes.

With slotted spatula, remove fish. Break fish into bite-sized pieces; return to saucepan. Combine milk and evaporated milk. Gradually stir milk into flour till smooth; add to fish mixture. Add reserved, cooked salt pork and cook over low heat till soup mixture is heated through but do not let boil. Makes 8 servings.

Lift haddock fillets *from the simmering broth after they have been cooked. Using a slotted spatula helps to balance the pieces and drains away the broth.*

Menu

MIDNIGHT SUPPER
Cheese Dip
Chips and Vegetable Dippers
Seafood Chowder
Crackers
Fruit Cup
Tea   Coffee

After the theater, a game, prom, or New Year's Eve party, the gang is not necessarily ready to end the evening. So, plan a midnight supper. Everyone will relive the highlights of the game or analyze the play over this warming menu.

Have the foods ready earlier in the day and refrigerated. Then, set out the dip and chips to pacify the group while you reheat the soup and put other items on the table.

This satisfying but not too filling supper makes a happy ending to a gala evening.

FISH CHOWDER

½ cup chopped onion
¼ cup chopped green pepper
2 tablespoons butter or margarine
1 10¾-ounce can condensed tomato soup
1 14½-ounce can evaporated milk
1 chicken bouillon cube, crushed
    Dash garlic powder
1 pound haddock fillets or other fish
    fillets, cooked and flaked (2 cups)

In 3-quart saucepan cook onion and green pepper in butter or margarine till tender but not brown. Add soup, evaporated milk, bouillon cube, and garlic powder. Stir in the cooked fish. Heat through. Makes 4 servings.

In the New England style

Ladle steaming Seafood Chowder into heated, shallow soup bowls and top servings with large, unsalted crackers. Pass additional crackers, slices of cheese, raw vegetable sticks, or relishes for accompaniments.

SOLE-SHRIMP KETTLE

1 pound fresh or frozen sole fillets or
    other fish fillets
1 large onion, thinly sliced
¼ cup butter or margarine
3 chicken bouillon cubes, crushed
4 cups hot water
2 tablespoons lemon juice
1 teaspoon salt
⅛ teaspoon white pepper
1 pound fresh or frozen shelled shrimp
2 medium tomatoes, peeled and chopped
1 tablespoon snipped chives

Thaw frozen fillets. Cut fillets into 1-inch chunks. In large saucepan cook onion in butter till tender. Add fish, bouillon cubes, water, lemon juice, salt, pepper, shrimp, and tomatoes. Bring to boiling. Reduce heat and simmer till fish flakes easily when tested with a fork and shrimp turns pink, 2 to 3 minutes. Sprinkle top with snipped chives. Makes 8 servings.

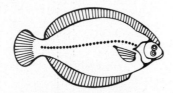

FISH AND CHEESE SOUP

1 pound fresh or frozen perch fillets
    or other fish fillets
¼ cup finely chopped onion
¼ cup diced carrot
¼ cup diced celery
2 tablespoons butter or margarine
        • • •
¼ cup all-purpose flour
¼ teaspoon salt
    Dash paprika
3 cups milk
1 13¾-ounce can chicken broth
2 ounces process American cheese,
    cubed (½ cup)

Thaw fish; cut into bite-sized pieces. Cook onion, carrot, and celery in butter till tender. Blend in flour, salt, and paprika. Add milk and chicken broth. Cook and stir till thickened and bubbly. Add fish; return to boiling. Reduce heat and cook, stirring gently, till fish flakes easily, 5 to 8 minutes. Stir in cheese till melted. Serves 6.

BOOKBINDER'S SNAPPER SOUP

Serve hearty bowlfuls of this sherry-laced turtle soup, a specialty from the Old Original Bookbinder's in Philadelphia—

1½ pounds veal knuckle, cut in 2-inch
        pieces
¼ cup butter
1 cup chopped onion
1 branch celery, chopped
1 small carrot, diced
1 teaspoon salt
1 whole clove
1 small bay leaf
¼ teaspoon pepper
¼ teaspoon dried thyme leaves, crushed
        • • •
¼ cup all-purpose flour
3 10½-ounce cans condensed beef broth
1 cup canned tomatoes
1 pound frozen snapper turtle meat, cut
    in small pieces
        • • •
½ cup dry sherry
    Dash bottled hot pepper sauce
1 slice lemon

In shallow roasting pan combine first 10 ingredients. Bake at 400° for 30 minutes. Push bones to one side; blend in flour. Bake at 350° for 30 minutes longer. Transfer to kettle. Add broth and tomatoes. Cover and simmer 1½ hours.

   Meanwhile, simmer turtle meat, covered, in ¾ cup water till tender, 1 to 1½ hours. Add sherry, hot pepper sauce, and lemon slice. Cover; simmer 10 minutes. Strain veal soup; skim off fat. Combine veal and turtle soups; heat. Season with salt and pepper. Serves 6.

SALMON CHOWDER

Drain one 16-ounce can salmon, reserving liquid. Add milk to salmon liquid to equal 2¾ cups. Remove skin and bones from salmon; break into chunks. In 3-quart saucepan cook ¼ cup chopped onion in ¼ cup butter or margarine till tender. Blend in 3 tablespoons all-purpose flour, ½ teaspoon salt, and dash pepper; add milk and 1 bay leaf. Cook and stir till thickened and bubbly. Add salmon chunks; 2 cups cubed, peeled, cooked potatoes (about 2 medium); and 1 tablespoon snipped parsley. Heat through. Serve in soup bowls. Serves 5.

OYSTER STEW

2 tablespoons all-purpose flour
1½ teaspoons salt
1 teaspoon Worcestershire sauce
Dash bottled hot pepper sauce
1 pint shucked oysters, undrained
¼ cup butter or margarine
1 quart milk, scalded

In saucepan blend flour, salt, Worcestershire sauce, hot pepper sauce, and 2 tablespoons water. Add oysters and butter. Simmer over very low heat and stir gently till edges of oysters curl, 3 to 4 minutes. Add hot milk; remove from heat and cover. Let stand 15 minutes. Reheat briefly. Top servings with pats of butter, if desired. Makes 4 or 5 servings.

HEARTY OYSTER STEW

½ cup finely diced carrots
½ cup finely diced celery
½ cup butter or margarine
2 tablespoons all-purpose flour
1½ teaspoons salt
1 teaspoon Worcestershire sauce
Dash bottled hot pepper sauce
• • •
2 10-ounce cans frozen oysters, thawed
4 cups milk, scalded, or 3 cups milk and
1 cup light cream, scalded

In large saucepan cook carrots and celery in ¼ cup butter till tender. Blend flour, salt, Worcestershire sauce, hot pepper sauce, and 2 tablespoons water till smooth. Add to vegetables. Add oysters and the liquid. Return to boiling; simmer over very low heat 3 to 4 minutes, stirring gently. Add hot milk. Remove from heat. Cover; let stand 15 minutes.

Place remaining butter in tureen. Reheat stew to serving temperature. Pour into tureen. Dash with paprika, if desired. Serves 4 to 6.

QUICK TOMATO-OYSTER BISQUE

Thaw one 10-ounce can frozen condensed oyster stew; remove oysters and chop. In 2-quart saucepan combine oyster stew and one 10¾-ounce can condensed tomato rice soup; gradually stir in 1¼ cups milk. Add oysters. Cook and stir till heated through. Serves 4.

Brighten up a cold day *with steaming bowls of soup. Macaroni-Oyster Chowder contains all the foods that are needed to make a complete, balanced lunch.*

MACARONI-OYSTER CHOWDER

Shell macaroni accents creamy chowder—

1 10-ounce can frozen oysters, thawed
2½ cups water
1 cup chopped carrot
1 cup chopped celery
⅓ cup chopped onion
2 teaspoons salt
3½ ounces small shell macaroni (1 cup)
• • •
4 cups milk
¼ cup snipped parsley
¼ teaspoon pepper
⅛ teaspoon ground sage
2 tablespoons all-purpose flour
¼ cup butter or margarine
Oyster crackers

Drain liquid from oysters into large saucepan; add water, carrot, celery, onion, and salt. Heat to boiling. Gradually add macaroni to boiling liquid. Cook, covered, till macaroni is tender, about 10 to 12 minutes.

Stir in *3 cups* milk, parsley, pepper, and sage. Thoroughly blend the remaining 1 cup of milk thickened and bubbly. Meanwhile, cook oysters in butter or margarine till edges of oysters curl; stir oysters into chowder. Serve with oyster crackers. Makes 6 servings.

Need a quick luncheon or supper idea? Bring out a trayful of seaworthy sandwiches or a bowl of well-seasoned seafood salad and watch the food disappear before your eyes.

Sandwiches can best be described by the word versatile. See how many different varieties of sandwiches you can assemble. Then, stack up hearty man-sized sandwiches for Dad's stag party and serve them hot or cold. Or create dainty, finger-sized sandwiches for Mom's bridge group. Make low-calorie open-facers by leaving off the top slice of bread, or make hefty triple-deckers by adding a third slice of bread.

Choose from the wide assortment of breads available—white, rye, whole wheat, potato, cheese, pumpernickel, French and Italian loaves, or buns, rolls, and English muffins. For sandwich fillings, cook and flake your own fish or buy seafood canned or frozen ready to use. With the sandwich ingredients on hand, make up a batch of sandwiches or let do-it-yourself sandwich makers concoct their own.

If seafood salads are more to your liking, and who doesn't enjoy a refreshingly cool or a mouth-watering hot salad accompanied with freshly baked bread or muffins, look over the wide array of hot, molded, and chilled salad mixtures. The hot salads can be presented in individual baking shells or casseroles, while the molded salads can be prepared in plain or fancy fish molds, then attractively garnished with salad greens, such as the Salmon Mousse pictured here.

Sandwiches and Salads

CREATE A HOT OR COLD SANDWICH

CREOLE SANDWICHES

2 tablespoons chopped onion
2 tablespoons chopped green pepper
1 tablespoon butter or margarine
1 8-ounce can whole tomatoes, cut up
3 tablespoons sliced pimiento-stuffed
    green olives
1 teaspoon sugar
    Dash garlic salt
4 frozen fish portions
4 hamburger buns, split and toasted

In small saucepan cook onion and green pepper in butter till tender but not brown. Stir in tomatoes, olives, sugar, ¼ teaspoon salt, garlic salt, and dash pepper. Simmer till thickened, about 15 to 20 minutes. Panfry fish according to package directions. Butter buns, if desired. Place fish portions on bottom halves of buns. Spoon some sauce over fish, then put tops of buns in place. Makes 4 sandwiches.

LUNCHEON STACK-UPS

1 pound fresh or frozen fish fillets
1 10-ounce package frozen asparagus
    spears
¼ cup chopped onion
2 tablespoons butter or margarine
2 tablespoons all-purpose flour
¼ teaspoon dried basil leaves, crushed
1¼ cups milk
2 tablespoons chopped canned pimiento
3 English muffins, split, toasted, and
    buttered

Thaw frozen fillets; cut into 6 pieces. Steam fish. Cook asparagus according to package directions; drain. Cook onion in butter till golden; blend in flour, ½ teaspoon salt, and basil. Add milk; cook and stir till thickened and bubbly. Add pimiento; heat through.

To serve, place 2 muffin halves on each plate, top with fillets, then asparagus. Pour cream sauce over stack-ups. Makes 3 servings.

Menu

TEEN-AGE GATHERING
Onion Dip
Corn Chips   Potato Chips
Creole Sandwiches
Celery, Carrots, Radishes
Ice Cream Sundaes
Milk

Anytime teen-agers get together, there's bound to be a party. Be prepared for such impromptu parties as well as any planned parties by stocking adequate supplies. By keeping hamburger buns, fish portions, chips, and ice cream in the freezer, you will have the basic ingredients needed to serve this menu on short notice.

Let the teen-agers join in and do the cooking themselves. When everything is ready, they will enjoy the rewards of their efforts.

SARDINE AND CHEESE SANDWICH

Spread 4 slices toasted rye bread with butter. Drain two 3¾-ounce cans sardines in oil; arrange on toast. Combine ⅓ cup chili sauce and 2 tablespoons chopped onion; spoon over sardines. Place on baking sheet and bake at 450° for 10 minutes. Top with ½ cup shredded process American cheese. Return to oven; heat just till cheese melts. Makes 4 sandwiches.

Hearty enough for a Viking sailor

Be prepared to serve a second round of hot Creole → Sandwiches and to replenish mugs with cold milk. This dressed-up version of the fish-wiches will appeal to robust appetites as well as hard-to-please appetites.

Sprinkle sesame seed *on sides of sandwiches before browning to add extra crunch. Complement the texture of French Salmon-Wiches with creamy soup.*

FRENCH SALMON-WICHES

Dill accents the flavor of salmon —

    1 7¾-ounce can salmon
    1 teaspoon instant minced onion
    2 teaspoons water
    ¼ cup mayonnaise or salad dressing
    2 tablespoons chopped green pepper
    ¼ teaspoon salt
    ¼ teaspoon dried dillweed
        • • •
    8 slices bread
    1 beaten egg
    2 tablespoons milk
      Sesame seed
    ¼ cup shortening, butter, or margarine

Drain salmon, reserving liquid. Remove bones and skin from salmon; flake. Soak onion in water 5 minutes. Blend together salmon, onion, mayonnaise or salad dressing, green pepper, salt, and dillweed. Spread mixture evenly on 4 slices of bread; top with remaining bread.

In shallow dish combine reserved salmon liquid, beaten egg, and milk; dip each sandwich in the egg mixture. Sprinkle both sides of sandwiches with sesame seed. Heat shortening, butter, or margarine in skillet; place sandwiches in skillet and brown on both sides. Continue cooking till sandwiches are heated through. Serve while hot. Makes 4 sandwiches.

GRILLED SANDWICHES

Use prepared salad dressing or make your own —

    1 pound pollock fillets or other fish
      fillets, cooked and flaked (2 cups)
    ¼ cup Thousand Island salad dressing
    12 slices bread
    6 slices process Swiss cheese
    6 tablespoons butter or margarine,
      softened
    2 teaspoons finely chopped onion

Combine flaked fish and dressing; spread on 6 slices bread. Place one slice cheese on each and top with remaining bread. Blend butter or margarine and onion together. Spread on both sides of sandwiches. Grill till golden brown and cheese melts, about 4 to 5 minutes on each side. Serve while hot. Makes 6 sandwiches.

HADDOCK ON CORNBREAD

Combine 1½ pounds haddock fillets or other fish fillets, cooked and flaked (3 cups); ⅔ cup mayonnaise or salad dressing; 3 tablespoons chopped canned pimiento; ¼ cup finely chopped green pepper; and ½ teaspoon salt. Split 4 toaster-style corn muffins in half; butter halves. Spread fish mixture over muffins; top each with a slice of process American cheese. Bake at 350° for 20 minutes. Serves 8.

SANDWICH TOWERS

    8 fish sticks
    4 thin slices fully cooked ham
    4 slices white bread, toasted
      and buttered
    1 8½-ounce can pineapple slices,
      well drained
    1 8-ounce jar process cheese spread
    2 tablespoons milk

Prepare fish sticks according to package directions. Place one slice ham atop each piece of toast. Top each with two cooked fish sticks and a pineapple slice. Place sandwiches on baking sheet. Heat in 400° oven about 3 to 4 minutes.

Meanwhile, in small saucepan melt cheese spread with milk over low heat. Transfer sandwiches to luncheon plates; drizzle with cheese sauce. Serve while hot. Makes 4 sandwiches.

TUNA-BERRY SANDWICHES

Cranberry sauce is hidden inside—

> 1 6½- or 7-ounce can tuna, drained
>   and flaked
> ¼ cup finely chopped celery
> 2 tablespoons chopped walnuts
> ¼ cup mayonnaise or salad dressing
> • • •
> 8 slices bread
> 1 8-ounce can jellied cranberry
>   sauce, sliced ¼ inch thick
> • • •
> 2 beaten eggs
> 3 tablespoons milk
>   Dash salt

Combine tuna, celery, nuts, and mayonnaise. Spread filling on 4 slices bread. Arrange cranberry slices atop filling; top with remaining bread. Combine eggs, milk, and salt. Dip sandwiches in egg mixture. Brown on medium-hot, lightly greased griddle, about 6 to 8 minutes, turning once. Makes 4 sandwiches.

CRAB AND CHEESE SANDWICH

Plan this sandwich for an elegant late supper—

> 3 tablespoons butter or margarine
> 3 tablespoons all-purpose flour
> 1 teaspoon chicken-flavored gravy base
> ¾ teaspoon dry mustard
> ¼ teaspoon salt
> 1¾ cups milk
> • • •
> 4 ounces sharp Cheddar cheese,
>   shredded (1 cup)
> 3 English muffins, split, toasted,
>   and buttered
> 12 ounces cooked crab meat or 2 6-ounce
>   packages frozen crab meat, thawed

Melt butter or margarine in saucepan over low heat. Blend in flour, chicken base, dry mustard, and salt. Add milk all at once. Cook and stir till mixture is thickened and bubbly; cook 2 minutes more. Remove from heat; add cheese, stirring to melt. Arrange muffin halves on ovenproof plates or platter; top each with crab meat. Cover with cheese sauce. Broil 4 to 5 inches from heat just till hot and bubbly, but not brown. Serve immediately. Makes 6 sandwiches.

SALMON-BLUE CHEESE BROILERS

Drain and flake one 16-ounce can salmon. Mix salmon with ⅓ cup mayonnaise; one 3-ounce can chopped mushrooms, drained; and 2 tablespoons crumbled blue cheese.

Toast and butter 8 slices of rye or white bread. Spread toast with salmon mixture. Sprinkle grated Parmesan cheese over sandwiches. Broil 5 inches from heat till mixture is hot, about 6 to 7 minutes. Makes 8 sandwiches.

TUNA BURGERS

> 1 6-ounce can evaporated milk
> 3 slices white bread with
>   crusts removed
> ½ envelope French salad dressing mix
> 2 6½- or 7-ounce cans tuna, drained
> 4 English muffins or hamburger buns,
>   split
>   Pimiento-stuffed olive slices

Pour milk over bread in mixing bowl; add salad dressing mix. Stir with fork till well blended. Stir in tuna. Spoon tuna mixture onto 8 English muffin halves or hamburger bun halves. Place sandwiches under broiler 6 inches from heat; broil till tuna is lightly browned and heated through, about 4 minutes. Garnish with olive slices. Makes 8 open-faced sandwiches.

Try a new way *of making tuna sandwich filling. Stir packaged French salad dressing mix into Tuna Burgers before broiling for a quick, easy, flavor addition.*

Broil the whole meal *at the same time. Shrimp Boat Supper teams up French bread halves filled with a shrimp mixture and herb-seasoned tomato halves.*

SHRIMP BOAT SUPPER

    1 10- to 12-inch loaf French bread
    2 tablespoons butter or margarine,
        melted
    1 pound shelled shrimp, cooked
    1 cup cooked peas
    1 cup diced celery
    ¼ cup chopped canned pimiento
    ½ cup mayonnaise or salad dressing
    ¼ teaspoon salt
        Dash pepper
    3 firm, ripe medium tomatoes
    2 tablespoons French salad dressing
        Dried basil leaves, crushed
    6 slices sharp process American
        cheese, halved diagonally

Halve bread lengthwise. With fork, remove ½ cup crumbs from each half. Reserve crumbs. Brush cut surfaces of bread with melted butter. Combine shrimp, peas, celery, pimiento, and reserved crumbs. Toss lightly with mayonnaise, salt, and pepper. Spoon evenly into each "boat." Place on rack of broiler pan.

Halve tomatoes; brush with French salad dressing; sprinkle with salt, pepper, and basil. Place on broiler rack with shrimp boats. Broil 6 inches from heat for about 3 minutes. Top boats with diagonal cheese slices. Return to broiler till cheese bubbles and melts, about 2 minutes. Serve immediately. Makes 6 servings.

PUFFED LOBSTER SANDWICH

    1 10-ounce package frozen asparagus
        spears
    6 slices bread
    1 5-ounce can lobster, drained and
        flaked
    ⅓ cup mayonnaise or salad dressing
    ¼ cup finely chopped celery
    2 tablespoons finely chopped canned
        pimiento
    4 ounces process Swiss cheese,
        shredded (1 cup)
    3 egg yolks
    ¼ cup mayonnaise or salad dressing
    3 stiffly beaten egg whites

Cook asparagus according to package directions; drain. Toast bread on one side. Mix together the lobster, ⅓ cup mayonnaise, celery, and pimiento. Spread mixture over untoasted side of bread. Sprinkle shredded cheese over each; arrange asparagus on each sandwich.

Beat egg yolks, ¼ teaspoon salt, and dash pepper till thick and lemon-colored; stir in the ¼ cup mayonnaise. Fold into egg whites. Pile mixture atop asparagus. Bake at 350° till topping mixture is golden brown, about 18 minutes. Serve immediately. Makes 6 sandwiches.

TUNA CHIPPERS

    1 6½- or 7-ounce can tuna, drained
        and flaked
    ¼ cup finely chopped celery
    ¼ cup mayonnaise or salad dressing
    1 teaspoon prepared horseradish
    1 teaspoon prepared mustard
    1 teaspoon lemon juice
    8 slices bread
    ½ cup milk
    2 beaten eggs
    1¼ cups crushed potato chips

Blend together tuna, celery, mayonnaise, horseradish, mustard, lemon juice and dash pepper. Spread tuna mixture on 4 slices bread. Top with remaining bread. Combine milk and beaten eggs in shallow dish. Dip each sandwich in egg mixture, then in crushed potato chips. Pat to secure chips to bread, turning to coat both sides of sandwiches. Brown on medium-hot, lightly greased griddle till crisp, about 4 to 5 minutes on each side. Makes 4 sandwiches.

CRAB IN FRENCH ROLLS

1 7½-ounce can crab meat, drained
     and cartilage removed
4 ounces Cheddar cheese, shredded
     (1 cup)
⅓ cup sliced pimiento-stuffed green
     olives
¼ cup butter or margarine, melted
1 small clove garlic, minced
6 French rolls

Chop crab meat coarsely; thoroughly combine all ingredients except French rolls. Split French rolls; spread crab mixture over bottom halves and replace tops. Wrap in foil; heat at 350° for 15 to 20 minutes. Serves 6.

TUNA-CHEDDAR SANDWICH

1 6½- or 7-ounce can tuna, drained
4 ounces natural Cheddar cheese, finely
     diced (1 cup)
⅓ cup diced green pepper
2 tablespoons chopped canned pimiento
½ cup mayonnaise or salad dressing
½ teaspoon onion salt
12 slices whole wheat bread, buttered
     Lettuce leaves

Mix together tuna, diced cheese, green pepper, pimiento, mayonnaise or salad dressing, and onion salt. Spread tuna filling on 6 slices bread. Top with lettuce leaves and the remaining slices of bread. Makes 6 servings.

SHRIMP SALAD SANDWICH

1 3-ounce package cream cheese,
     softened
2 teaspoons milk
1 teaspoon prepared mustard
          •   •   •
1 4½-ounce can shrimp, drained
¼ cup finely chopped celery
8 slices white bread, buttered
     Lettuce leaves

Blend cream cheese, milk, and mustard together till smooth. Chop shrimp. Add shrimp and celery to cream cheese mixture. Mix well. Spread filling on 4 slices bread. Top with lettuce and remaining 4 slices bread. Serves 4.

LOBSTER ROLLS

Serve this elegant lobster and egg mixture in French or potato rolls—

1 5-ounce can lobster, drained
     and broken into pieces
2 hard-cooked eggs, chopped
⅓ cup mayonnaise or salad dressing
2 tablespoons chopped green pepper
2 tablespoons chili sauce
1 tablespoon sliced green
     onion with tops
1 teaspoon lemon juice
6 potato rolls or French rolls,
     split and buttered
     Lettuce leaves

Combine lobster and eggs. Blend together mayonnaise, green pepper, chili sauce, onion, and lemon juice. Toss lightly with egg and lobster mixture. Chill. Spread filling on bottom halves of buns. Top with lettuce and then cover with tops of buns. Makes 6 sandwiches.

CRAB LUNCHEON SANDWICHES

Crab, dill, and sour cream make an outstanding combination for sandwich filling—

¼ cup dairy sour cream
2 tablespoons mayonnaise or salad
     dressing
1 teaspoon lemon juice
¼ teaspoon prepared mustard
⅛ teaspoon dried dillweed
1 7½-ounce can crab meat, drained,
     flaked, and cartilage removed
¼ cup diced celery
4 French rolls, split and buttered
     Lettuce leaves

Blend together the sour cream, mayonnaise, lemon juice, mustard, and dillweed. Stir in crab meat and celery. Chill. Spread filling on bottom halves of rolls. Top with lettuce leaves and replace top halves of rolls. Serve the sandwiches immediately. Makes 4 sandwiches.

EGG-TOMATO-SARDINE SANDWICH

Use this sandwich for parties or quick snacks—

For each sandwich, butter 1 slice rye bread generously. Mix chopped hard-cooked egg with mayonnaise or salad dressing to moisten; spread on the buttered bread. Arrange canned sardines and small tomato wedges atop the egg filling. Garnish with springs of parsley or dill.

CLAM PINWHEEL SANDWICHES

For appetizers, serve ham and clam pinwheels on slices of party rye bread—

  1 8-ounce package cream cheese, softened
  1 8-ounce can minced clams, well drained
  4 slices Danish-style boiled ham
  8 slices whole wheat bread
  1/3 cup mayonnaise or salad dressing
  1 1/3 cups shredded lettuce

In small mixer bowl blend cream cheese and clams; spread mixture evenly over ham slices, using about 1/3 cup for each slice. Starting from narrow end, roll up tightly. Chill. Slice each ham roll into 10 tiny pinwheels. Spread bread with mayonnaise; top with shredded lettuce. Arrange 5 ham pinwheels on each sandwich in diagonal line. Makes 8 sandwiches.

SHRIMP CAPERS

Pipe mayonnaise with tube or swirl with spoon—

For each sandwich, spread 1 thin slice French bread with butter. Cover with a ruffly leaf of lettuce. Arrange tiny canned shrimp, overlapping, in two rows atop lettuce. Pipe mayonnaise through a pastry tube down the center of sandwich. Garnish with drained capers.

Smorgasbord of fish

← *Choose a favorite fish. The selection includes a choice of Caviar-Stuffed Eggs (see page 31), Egg-Tomato-Sardine Sandwich, Clam Pinwheel Sandwiches, Shrimp Capers, and Beet-Herring Salad (see page 66).*

SARDINE SANDWICHES

  2 3¾-ounce cans sardines in oil
  2 hard-cooked eggs, chopped
  2 tablespoons snipped chives
  2 tablespoons mayonnaise
  1 tablespoon lemon juice
  12 slices whole wheat bread

Drain sardines and mash. Combine sardines, eggs, chives, mayonnaise, and lemon juice. Spread whole wheat bread with additional mayonnaise, if desired. Spread sardine filling on 6 slices of bread. Top with lettuce, if desired, and remaining 6 slices of bread. Serves 6.

HALIBUT ON PUMPERNICKEL

  1 pound halibut fillets or other fish fillets, cooked, flaked, and chilled (2 cups)
  ¼ cup dairy sour cream
  ¼ cup mayonnaise or salad dressing
  1 tablespoon chopped onion
  ¼ teaspoon salt
  ¼ teaspoon dried dillweed
     • • •
  16 slices pumpernickel or rye bread, buttered
  Lettuce

Blend together flaked fish, sour cream, mayonnaise, onion, salt, and dillweed. Spread filling on 8 slices bread; top with lettuce and the remaining 8 slices bread. Makes 8 servings.

FISH SALAD CLUB SANDWICH

  1 pound perch fillets or other fish fillets, cooked and flaked (2 cups)
  ½ cup chopped celery
  ½ cup bottled tartar sauce
  18 slices bread, toasted and buttered
  Lettuce
  Thin tomato slices

Combine flaked perch, celery, tartar sauce, and ¼ teaspoon salt. Chill. Spread about 1/3 cup perch mixture on 6 slices of toast. Top each with a second slice of toast; place lettuce and tomato slices atop. Cover with third slice of toast. Secure with wooden picks; cut diagonally into quarters. Makes 6 sandwiches.

ITALIAN SANDWICH

Make one long sandwich loaf or six individual loaves to take on a picnic —

¼ cup mayonnaise or salad dressing
1 teaspoon vinegar
1 clove garlic, crushed
¼ teaspoon dried basil leaves, crushed
¼ teaspoon dried oregano leaves, crushed

• • •

1 long loaf French bread or 6 hard rolls
¼ cup butter or margarine, softened

• • •

Romaine leaves
6 ounces sliced mozzarella cheese
½ medium onion, sliced and separated into rings
2 tomatoes, sliced
1 2-ounce can anchovy fillets, drained
½ cup sliced pitted ripe olives

Blend together the mayonnaise, vinegar, garlic, basil, and oregano. Cut bread in half, lengthwise; spread with butter, then with mayonnaise mixture. On bottom half of bread, arrange the romaine, slices of cheese, onion rings, tomatoes, anchovy fillets, and olive slices. Replace top half of bread or rolls. Secure with wooden picks. Slice French bread loaf into 6 sandwiches. Makes 6 servings.

Serve lunch in a hurry. *Remove marinated cucumber slices from the refrigerator and stack sliced salmon on dark bread for a colorful Smoked Salmon Platter.*

LOX AND BAGELS

4 bagels
1 3-ounce package cream cheese, softened
8 ounces sliced smoked red salmon (lox)

Split bagels lengthwise. Heat bagels, if desired. Spread cut surfaces generously with softened cream cheese. Arrange salmon slices (lox) on the 8 halves. Serve with lemon wedges or freshly ground pepper, if desired. Serve at breakfast or cut into small wedges for appetizers. Makes 8 open-faced sandwiches.

SMOKED SALMON SANDWICH

¼ cup mayonnaise or salad dressing
1 tablespoon finely chopped onion
1 tablespoon snipped parsley
1 teaspoon lemon juice
8 slices pumpernickel or dark bread
4 ounces sliced smoked red salmon (lox)

Blend together the mayonnaise or salad dressing, onion, parsley, and lemon juice. Spread on bread; place salmon on 4 slices bread. Top with remaining bread. Makes 4 sandwiches.

SMOKED SALMON PLATTER

⅓ cup salad oil
3 tablespoons vinegar
1½ teaspoons snipped dill or ½ teaspoon dried dillweed
¼ teaspoon sugar
¼ teaspoon salt
⅛ teaspoon pepper
1 large cucumber, sliced paper thin
4 ounces sliced smoked red salmon (lox)
4 slices dark bread, buttered

Beat together the salad oil and vinegar; stir in dill, sugar, salt, and pepper. Pour over cucumber slices. Refrigerate several hours or overnight. To serve, place slices of red salmon on buttered bread. Arrange the sandwiches and cucumber salad on a serving platter. Garnish with sprigs of parsley, lemon wedges, olives, and radishes, if desired. Makes 4 servings.

HAM AND TUNA SANDWICHES

1 6½- or 7-ounce can tuna,
    drained and flaked.
1 4½-ounce can deviled ham
3 hard-cooked eggs, chopped
¼ cup finely chopped celery
2 tablespoons chopped dill pickle
½ teaspoon grated onion
⅓ cup mayonnaise or salad dressing
16 slices white bread, buttered
    Lettuce leaves

Thoroughly combine tuna, deviled ham, chopped egg, celery, pickle, and onion; blend in mayonnaise and chill. Spread 8 slices bread with tuna mixture. Top each with a lettuce leaf, then remaining bread. Makes 8 sandwiches.

PERCH-PINEAPPLE FINGERS

1 pound perch fillets or other fish
    fillets, cooked and flaked (2 cups)
1 8¾-ounce can crushed pineapple,
    drained
½ cup mayonnaise or salad dressing
¼ cup finely chopped walnuts
10 slices bread, crusts removed and
    buttered

Combine flaked fish, pineapple, mayonnaise, walnuts, and ¼ teaspoon salt. Chill. Spread mixture on bread; cut each slice into 3 "fingers." Garnish with watercress or parsley, if desired. Makes 30 open-faced tea sandwiches.

BASIC TUNA SALAD SANDWICH

Add additional ingredients to vary this recipe—

1 6½- or 7-ounce can tuna, drained
    and flaked
½ cup mayonnaise or salad dressing
¼ cup chopped celery
2 teaspoons finely chopped onion
1 teaspoon lemon juice
12 slices bread, buttered
    Lettuce leaves

Combine tuna, mayonnaise or salad dressing, celery, onion, and lemon juice. Spread filling on 6 slices bread. Top with lettuce leaves and remaining bread slices. Makes 6 sandwiches.

Alternating as hearty and dainty, *Ham and Tuna Sandwiches will satisfy robust appetites and also delight the ladies when served as small tea sandwiches.*

HERRING SUBMARINES

4 French rolls (about 8 inches long)
¼ cup butter or margarine, softened
2 teaspoons prepared mustard
2 cups shredded lettuce
1 12-ounce jar pickled herring fillets,
    drained
4 slices process Swiss cheese
2 tomatoes, sliced

Split rolls lengthwise, *but do not cut all the way through.* Scoop out some of the centers. Combine softened butter and mustard; spread on cut sides of rolls. Line bottoms of rolls with lettuce; pile on herring. Cut cheese slices into 4 triangles; arrange over herring. Top with tomato slices. Close sandwiches and anchor with wooden picks; garnish with pickles and olives, if desired. Makes 4 generous servings.

HADDOCK OPEN-FACED SANDWICH

Cook and flake ½ pound haddock fillets or other fish fillets. Combine with ½ cup mayonnaise or salad dressing; ½ cup finely chopped watercress *or* lettuce; ⅓ cup small-curd cottage cheese; ¼ cup chopped walnuts; 2 teaspoons lemon juice; ¼ teaspoon salt; and dash pepper. Spread mixture on 6 slices buttered toast. Serve open-faced with cherry tomatoes. Serves 6.

VARY THE MENU WITH A HEARTY SALAD

TUNA WALDORF SALAD

2 3-ounce packages lime-flavored gelatin
1 unpeeled apple, thinly sliced
1 cup chopped unpeeled apple
½ cup diced celery
½ cup broken pecans
Lettuce
2 6½- or 7-ounce cans tuna, chilled, drained, and broken in large pieces
1 cup mayonnaise or salad dressing
2 tablespoons lemon juice
2 tablespoons milk

Dissolve lime-flavored gelatin in 1¾ cups boiling water. Stir in 2 cups cold water; chill till partially set. Spoon part of the mixture into a 5½-cup ring mold. Arrange unpeeled apple slices in gelatin around bottom; chill. Fold chopped apple, celery, and pecans into remaining gelatin. Hold at room temperature till gelatin in mold is almost set, then carefully spoon over top of first layer. Chill till firm. Unmold gelatin onto lettuce-lined plate. Fill center of ring with chilled tuna pieces. Blend together mayonnaise or salad dressing, lemon juice, and milk. Drizzle some dressing over tuna. Pass remaining dressing. Makes 6 servings.

MOLDED TUNA RING

In saucepan soften 1 envelope unflavored gelatin (1 tablespoon) in ¼ cup cold water. Stir over low heat till gelatin is dissolved. Stir in one 10¾-ounce can condensed tomato soup; heat through. Gradually blend into one 3-ounce package softened cream cheese. Add ½ cup mayonnaise, 1½ teaspoons prepared horseradish, and dash bottled hot pepper sauce; beat smooth with rotary beater. Chill till partially set.

Fold in one 6½- or 7-ounce can tuna, drained and flaked; ½ cup chopped celery; and 1 tablespoon finely chopped onion. Turn into a 3½-cup ring mold. Chill several hours or overnight. Unmold onto lettuce. Makes 4 or 5 servings.

Menu

CLUB LUNCHEON
Pineapple Juice Cocktail
Tuna Waldorf Salad
Relish Tray
Cloverleaf Rolls   Butter Roses
Strawberries in Meringue Shells
Iced Tea

It's your turn to have the club luncheon and you want something special to serve. Try a menu like this one. The recipes are easy to prepare the day before, so those few morning hours can be spent leisurely putting everything in order.

These light, refreshing foods will appeal to guests who are calorie watchers. Yet, there is a gourmet flair to display your culinary skills.

TUNA CALICO MOLD

Dissolve two 3-ounce packages lime-flavored gelatin in 2 cups boiling water. Stir in 1½ cups cold water, 3 tablespoons lemon juice, and dash salt. Chill till partially set.

Fold in one 9¼-ounce can tuna, drained and flaked; one 10-ounce package frozen mixed vegetables, cooked and drained; ½ cup chopped celery; and 2 tablespoons finely chopped onion. Turn into 6½-cup mold; chill till firm. Unmold; pass mayonnaise. Serves 6.

A new way with classic Waldorf Salad

Arrange Tuna Waldorf Salad with an artistic touch. Thin apple slices are layered in the gelatin mold to make an interesting design. At serving time, mound chunks of tuna in center and drizzle with dressing. →

BEET-JELLIED GEFILTE FISH

Small gefilte fish balls made in your kitchen can replace the commercial product—

Drain one 16-ounce can sliced or shoestring beets, reserving liquid. Add water to liquid to make 2½ cups. Chop beets very fine; chill.

Soften 1 envelope unflavored gelatin (1 tablespoon) in ¼ cup cold water. In small saucepan heat *1 cup* of the beet liquid to boiling. Remove from heat and add the softened gelatin, one 3-ounce package lemon-flavored gelatin, and 3 tablespoons sugar; stir till dissolved. Add the remaining beet liquid, ¼ cup lemon juice, ½ teaspoon seasoned salt, and 3 tablespoons prepared horseradish. Chill the mixture till partially set. Fold in chopped beets.

Turn mixture into a 6½-cup ring mold. Drain and slice one 16-ounce jar gefilte fish. Arrange evenly thoughout the jellied mixture. Chill the mold 4 to 5 hours or overnight. Unmold onto a serving plate. If desired, garnish with curly endive, deviled eggs, cucumber slices, and celery curls dusted with paprika. Serve with a bowl of Cucumber Dressing. Serves 8.

Cucumber Dressing: In a bowl combine 1 cup dairy sour cream; ½ cup chopped, peeled, and seeded cucumber; 1 tablespoon prepared horseradish; 1 teaspoon grated onion; ½ teaspoon salt; and dash freshly ground pepper. Chill thoroughly. Pass with gefilte fish mold.

Molding gefilte fish *and beets in a full-flavored gelatin mixture makes a versatile salad. Beet-Jellied Gefilte Fish serves as a main course or appetizer.*

BEET-HERRING SALAD

This salad is pictured on page 60—

    1½ cups diced, peeled, cooked potatoes
    1 16-ounce can diced beets,
        well drained (1½ cups)
    1 8-ounce jar pickled herring in wine
        sauce, drained and diced
    ½ cup diced unpeeled apple
    ¼ cup chopped sweet pickle
    ¼ cup chopped onion
    ¼ cup vinegar
    2 tablespoons sugar
    2 tablespoons water
    ¼ teaspoon salt
    1 hard-cooked egg

Combine potatoes, beets, herring, apple, pickle, and onion. Blend together vinegar, sugar, water, salt, and dash pepper. Toss with beet mixture. Pack salad into 4-cup mold or bowl; chill. Drain and unmold on serving plate. Cut egg in wedges; remove yolk. Arrange egg white wedges spoke fashion atop salad. Sieve yolk over center. If desired, garnish plate with sprigs of watercress. Makes 6 to 8 servings.

CLAM-TOMATO MOLD

    1 7½-ounce can minced clams
    1 envelope unflavored gelatin
    1½ cups tomato juice
    1 tablespoon lime juice
    2 tablespoons chopped onion
    2 sprigs parsley
        Few celery leaves
    1 tablespoon sugar
    ½ teaspoon salt
    2 whole cloves
    ½ cup sliced celery
    ¼ cup sliced pitted ripe olives
        Lettuce

Drain clams, reserving liquid. Soften gelatin in reserved liquid. In saucepan combine tomato juice, lime juice, onion, parsley, celery leaves, sugar, salt, and whole cloves. Simmer, covered, 5 minutes. Strain, discarding cooked vegetables and spices. Dissolve softened gelatin in hot tomato juice. Chill aspic till partially set. Fold in clams, celery, and olives. Turn into 3½-cup ring mold. Chill firm. Unmold onto lettuce-lined plate. Makes 4 or 5 servings.

CRAB-FILLED TOMATO ASPIC

2 envelopes unflavored gelatin
2 cups tomato juice
1 8-ounce can tomato sauce
2 tablespoons lemon juice
1 teaspoon Worcestershire sauce
½ teaspoon onion salt
Few drops bottled hot pepper sauce

• • •

1 7½-ounce can crab, drained,
    flaked, and cartilage removed
¾ cup diced celery
½ cup dairy sour cream
¼ cup mayonnaise or salad dressing
2 tablespoons lemon juice
Lettuce

In saucepan soften gelatin in tomato juice. Stir over low heat till gelatin is dissolved. Stir in tomato sauce, 2 tablespoons lemon juice, Worcestershire sauce, onion salt, and hot pepper sauce. Pour into 3½-cup ring mold; chill till firm. Meanwhile, toss together crab and celery. Blend in sour cream, mayonnaise, and 2 tablespoons lemon juice; chill thoroughly. To serve, unmold salad onto lettuce-lined plate. Spoon crab salad into center of ring. If desired, sprinkle crab mixture with paprika. Serves 6.

PARTY CRAB RING

1 envelope unflavored gelatin
    (1 tablespoon)
½ cup dairy sour cream
½ cup mayonnaise or salad dressing
1 tablespoon lemon juice
1 7½-ounce can crab meat, drained,
    flaked, and cartilage removed
1 hard-cooked egg, chopped
¼ cup sliced pimiento-stuffed green
    olives
2 tablespoons finely chopped green
    onion

In saucepan soften gelatin in 1 cup cold water; stir over low heat till gelatin is dissolved. Cool slightly. Combine sour cream, mayonnaise, lemon juice, and ¼ teaspoon salt; beat smooth. Gradually stir in gelatin. Chill till partially set. Whip till fluffy. Fold in crab, hard-cooked egg, olives, and green onion. Turn into 4½-cup ring mold. Chill till firm. Loosen carefully; unmold and trim with lettuce, if desired. Serves 4 to 6.

LOBSTER MOUSSE

Another time, prepare this salad in small molds for individual servings —

1 3-ounce package lemon-flavored
    gelatin
1 cup boiling water
1 3-ounce package cream cheese,
    softened
1 cup cold milk
½ cup mayonnaise or salad dressing
1 5-ounce can lobster, drained and
    flaked
½ cup chopped celery
1 tablespoon finely chopped onion

Dissolve gelatin and ¼ teaspoon salt in boiling water. With rotary beater gradually beat hot gelatin mixture into softened cream cheese. Beat in milk and mayonnaise till smooth. Chill till partially set. Fold in remaining ingredients. Turn into a 3½-cup mold. Chill till firm. Unmold. Makes 4 to 6 servings.

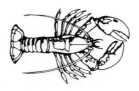

LOBSTER-PINEAPPLE MOLD

2 envelopes unflavored gelatin
    (2 tablespoons)
1 cup cold water
1 cup mayonnaise or salad dressing
1 cup dairy sour cream
2 tablespoons lemon juice
    Dash salt
2 5-ounce cans lobster, drained
    and flaked
1 8¾-ounce can crushed pineapple
¾ cup chopped celery
    Lettuce

In small saucepan soften gelatin in cold water. Stir over low heat till gelatin is dissolved. Cool slightly. With rotary beater beat in mayonnaise or salad dressing, sour cream, lemon juice, and salt till smooth. Chill till partially set. Fold in lobster, undrained pineapple, and celery. Turn into 6½-cup mold. Chill till firm. Unmold; trim with lettuce. Serves 8.

SHRIMP-IN-CUCUMBER RING

Pile marinated shrimp in center of mold —

1 3-ounce package lime-flavored
   gelatin
2 tablespoons lime juice
1 13½-ounce can crushed pineapple
¾ cup shredded unpeeled cucumber
2 tablespoons sliced green onion

• • •

1 cup salad oil
½ cup vinegar
1 teaspoon salt
½ teaspoon dried dillweed
   Dash freshly ground black pepper
1 pound shelled shrimp, cooked
   Lettuce

Dissolve gelatin in 1 cup boiling water. Stir in lime juice. Chill till partially set. Combine undrained pineapple, cucumber, and green onion. Fold into gelatin. Turn into 4½-cup ring mold. Chill till firm. Combine oil, vinegar, salt, dillweed, and pepper. Pour over cooked shrimp in shallow dish. Cover; chill at least 24 hours, spooning marinade over shrimp occasionally. Drain shrimp. Unmold salad on lettuce-lined plate and fill center with the drained, chilled shrimp. Makes 4 to 6 servings.

FISH-POTATO SALAD

1 3-ounce package lemon-flavored
   gelatin
1¼ cups boiling water
2 tablespoons vinegar
½ cup mayonnaise or salad dressing
2 teaspoons lemon juice
½ teaspoon salt
¼ teaspoon dried dillweed
1 pound fish fillets, cooked and flaked
   (about 2 cups)
1 cup diced, peeled, cooked potatoes
½ cup diced cucumber

Dissolve gelatin in boiling water; stir in vinegar. Chill till partially set; beat till soft peaks form, 8 to 10 minutes. In bowl blend mayonnaise, lemon juice, salt, and dillweed. Add fish and potatoes; toss. Fold with cucumber into gelatin. Chill till mixture mounds. Spoon into 8x8x2-inch pan. Chill till mixture is firm. Cut into serving portions. Makes 6 servings.

SHRIMP FIESTA MOLD

2 3-ounce packages lime-flavored
   gelatin
2 tablespoons lemon juice
2 teaspoons prepared horseradish
   Few drops bottled hot pepper sauce
2 4½-ounce cans shrimp, drained and
   cut up
2 medium oranges, peeled and chopped
   (about 1 cup)
   Lettuce
   Mayonnaise or salad dressing

Dissolve gelatin in 2 cups boiling water. Stir in 1 cup cold water, lemon juice, horseradish, and hot pepper sauce. Chill till partially set. Fold in the shrimp and chopped oranges. Turn into 5-cup mold. Chill till firm. Unmold on lettuce-lined plate and pass mayonnaise or salad dressing. Makes 6 servings.

SALMON MOLD

¼ cup sugar
1 envelope unflavored gelatin
   (1 tablespoon)
¼ cup vinegar
1 tablespoon lemon juice
1 cup diced peeled cucumber
½ cup diced celery
1 16-ounce can salmon
1 envelope unflavored gelatin
   (1 tablespoon)
½ cup mayonnaise or salad dressing
1 teaspoon lemon juice
   Lettuce

In saucepan combine sugar, 1 envelope gelatin, and ¼ teaspoon salt; stir in 1¼ cups water, vinegar, and 1 tablespoon lemon juice. Cook and stir just till mixture boils and gelatin is dissolved. Remove from heat; chill till partially set. Fold in cucumber and celery; turn into 5-cup mold. Chill till almost set.

   Drain salmon, reserving liquid; add enough water to liquid to make ½ cup. Remove bones and skin from salmon; flake. Soften 1 envelope gelatin in ¼ cup water; dissolve over hot water. Combine mayonnaise, the reserved salmon liquid, and 1 teaspoon lemon juice. Stir in salmon; blend in dissolved gelatin and spoon over cucumber layer. Chill till firm, 3 to 4 hours. Unmold; trim with lettuce. Serves 6.

SEAFOOD SOUFFLÉ SALAD

1 3-ounce package lemon-flavored
    gelatin
1 tablespoon lemon juice
½ cup mayonnaise or salad dressing
1 cup diced, peeled avocado
¾ cup diced, shelled, cooked shrimp
¼ cup diced celery
1 tablespoon finely chopped onion

Dissolve gelatin and ¼ teaspoon salt in 1 cup boiling water. Stir in ½ cup cold water and the lemon juice. Gradually beat gelatin mixture into mayonnaise till smooth. Chill till partially set. Beat till fluffy. Fold in avocado, shrimp, celery, and onion. Chill again till mixture mounds when spooned. Turn into 4-cup mold; chill till firm. Makes 4 to 6 servings.

SALMON MOUSSE

This salad is pictured on page 52 —

1 16-ounce can salmon
2 envelopes unflavored gelatin
1 cup mayonnaise or salad dressing
2 tablespoons lemon juice
2 teaspoons prepared horseradish
½ teaspoon paprika
½ cup diced celery
¼ cup chopped pimiento-stuffed
    green olives
1 tablespoon finely chopped onion
½ cup whipping cream

Drain salmon, reserving liquid. Remove skin and large bones; flake salmon. Add cold water to reserved liquid to equal 1¾ cups. In saucepan soften gelatin in salmon liquid. Stir over low heat till gelatin is dissolved; cool slightly. Blend together mayonnaise and next 3 ingredients; gradually stir in cooled gelatin mixture. Chill till partially set. Fold in salmon, celery, olives, and onion. Whip cream just till soft peaks begin to form; fold into salad. Turn into a 5½-cup fish mold. Chill till firm. Trim with lettuce, if desired. Makes 5 servings.

RED AND WHITE SALAD

1 envelope unflavored gelatin
    (1 tablespoon)
1 cup orange juice
1 teaspoon lemon juice
1 8-ounce can jellied cranberry sauce
    Few drops red food coloring
1 envelope unflavored gelatin
    (1 tablespoon)
1 cup chicken broth
1 tablespoon lemon juice
½ cup mayonnaise or salad dressing
½ pound fish fillets, cooked and
    flaked (about 1 cup)
½ cup chopped celery
2 tablespoons chopped pimiento-
    stuffed green olives

In saucepan soften 1 envelope gelatin in orange juice. Stir over low heat till gelatin is completely dissolved. Add the 1 teaspoon lemon juice, cranberry sauce, and red food coloring; beat till smooth. Pour mixture into 5-cup straight-sided mold. Chill till almost firm.

Meanwhile, soften 1 envelope gelatin in ½ cup cold water; stir over low heat till gelatin dissolves. Add chicken broth and 1 tablespoon lemon juice; beat in mayonnaise with rotary beater till smooth. Chill till partially set. Fold in fish, celery, and olives. Spoon over cranberry layer. Chill till firm. Unmold and trim with lettuce, if desired. Makes 6 servings.

SALMON-SOUR CREAM MOLD

1 envelope unflavored gelatin
    (1 tablespoon)
1 envelope sour cream sauce mix
½ cup mayonnaise or salad dressing
2 teaspoons lemon juice
¼ teaspoon dried dillweed
1 16-ounce can salmon
½ cup diced celery

Soften gelatin in ½ cup cold water; stir over low heat till gelatin dissolves. Cool. Prepare sour cream sauce mix according to package directions. Blend in mayonnaise, lemon juice, and dillweed. Gradually stir in gelatin.

Drain salmon, discarding skin and large bones. Flake. Fold salmon and celery into sour cream mixture. Turn into 3½-cup mold. Chill till firm, 4 to 5 hours. Unmold. Makes 4 servings.

CRAB-ARTICHOKE SALAD

    ½ cup whipping cream
    1 cup mayonnaise or salad dressing
    ¼ cup catsup or chili sauce
    2 teaspoons lemon juice
      Salt
          • • •
      Salad greens, torn in bite-sized
        pieces (6 cups)
   12 ounces frozen king crab legs, thawed
        and shelled, or one 6-ounce package
        frozen crab meat, thawed, or one
        7½-ounce can crab meat, drained
    1 9-ounce package frozen artichoke
        hearts, cooked, drained, and chilled
    2 hard-cooked eggs, chopped

Prepare salad dressing by whipping cream. Combine whipped cream, mayonnaise or salad dressing, catsup or chili sauce, and lemon juice. Add salt to taste. Chill thoroughly. Combine greens in salad bowl. Top with crab meat chunks, artichoke hearts, and chopped egg. Toss salad with chilled dressing. Serves 4 to 6.

CRAB-TOMATO FANS

    1 7½-ounce can crab meat, drained,
        flaked, and cartilage removed
    ¼ cup chopped celery
    ¼ cup chopped, unpeeled cucumber
    ¼ teaspoon salt
    ¼ cup mayonnaise or salad dressing
    4 medium tomatoes
      Lettuce
      Lemon wedges

Combine crab meat, celery, cucumber, and salt. Stir in mayonnaise. Chill. Turn tomatoes stem end down. Make 5 downward slices (parallel to one another), cutting to *but not through* bottom. Sprinkle cut surfaces lightly with salt. Fill between slices with crab meat salad. Serve on lettuce leaves with lemon wedges. Serves 4.

Gourmet meal in a bowl

← *Pour creamy dressing over Crab-Artichoke Salad to add the final touch to this main dish salad. Then complete the menu with hot miniature corn muffins, butter, iced tea, and chocolate soufflé for dessert.*

GENE'S DUNGENESS CRAB SALAD

Toss chunks of crab meat in a sharp dressing for an elegant salad like those served at Gene's Lobster House in Madeira Beach, Florida—

    ½ cup mayonnaise or salad dressing
    ¼ cup chili sauce
    2 tablespoons catsup
    2 teaspoons prepared horseradish
    ½ teaspoon lemon juice
      Dash bottled hot pepper sauce
      Dash Worcestershire sauce
    1 pound fresh or frozen cooked
        Dungeness crab meat or 2 7½-ounce
        cans crab meat, drained and
        cartilage removed
      Lettuce

Combine first 7 ingredients and mix well; chill. Chill crab meat; cut into large pieces. Toss dressing with crab meat. Season with salt and pepper to taste. Arrange lettuce cups on 4 to 6 chilled plates. Fill bottoms of cups with shredded lettuce. Top with crab salad.

   Garnish each plate with 2 lemon wedges, 1 wedge of dill pickle, 2 wedges of hard-cooked egg, 2 wedges of tomato, and a sprig of parsley, if desired. Makes 4 to 6 servings.

LOW-CALORIE CRAB SALAD

    2 6-ounce packages frozen crab meat,
        thawed
    1 10-ounce package frozen asparagus
        spears, cooked, drained, and
        chilled
      Lettuce
    ½ cup low-calorie mayonnaise-type
        dressing
    1 tablespoon lemon juice
    1 teaspoon drained capers
    ½ teaspoon prepared mustard
    ½ teaspoon Worcestershire sauce
    3 hard-cooked eggs, sliced

Break crab into chunks, removing cartilage. Place 3 asparagus spears on each of 6 lettuce-lined plates and ⅓ cup crab meat over the asparagus. Blend together the dressing, lemon juice, capers, mustard, and Worcestershire sauce. Spoon 1 tablespoon of the mayonnaise mixture atop each salad. Trim with slices of hard-cooked egg. Makes 6 servings.

SHRIMP-EGG SALAD

Marinate the shrimp at least 24 hours —

12 ounces fresh or frozen shelled shrimp
1 stalk celery, cut up
1 tablespoon mixed pickling spices
½ cup sliced celery
¼ cup chopped onion
¼ cup diced green pepper
2 bay leaves
⅔ cup salad oil
⅓ cup vinegar
1 tablespoon capers and juice
¾ teaspoon salt
3 drops bottled hot pepper sauce
2 hard-cooked eggs, sliced
Lettuce

In saucepan combine shrimp, cut up celery stalk, pickling spices, and 1 tablespoon salt with enough boiling water to cover shrimp. Return to boiling. Remove from heat and let stand 3 minutes. Drain. Layer drained shrimp, ½ cup celery, onion, and green pepper in shallow bowl. Add the bay leaves. Combine remaining ingredients except eggs and lettuce; pour over shrimp mixture in bowl. Chill at least 24 hours. Drain; remove bay leaves. Reserve marinade. Add hard-cooked eggs to shrimp mixture and toss lightly. Serve mixture on lettuce. Pass marinade or mayonnaise. Makes 4 or 5 servings.

Menu

PATIO DINNER
Melon Ball Compote
Curry-Lobster-Potato Salad
Green Beans
Bread Sticks   Butter
Cream Puffs
Tea or Coffee

Move the evening or noon meal outside for a relaxing treat. The menu features cool foods that make a refreshing dinner on warm days.

Serve the meal from individual trays. Arrange the food on each tray in the kitchen, and then let everyone carry his own tray outdoors. This saves time and the work of transporting all the food and serving dishes back and forth. To add that extra touch, decorate each tray with a flower, paper decoration, or game card that will be used for a group game after the meal.

SPINACH-SHRIMP SALAD

⅔ cup salad oil
⅓ cup orange juice
2 tablespoons sugar
1 tablespoon vinegar
½ teaspoon grated orange peel
¼ teaspoon salt
¼ teaspoon dry mustard
Dash bottled hot pepper sauce
• • •
1 large avocado, peeled and sliced into rings
1 tablespoon orange juice
1 pound fresh spinach, torn in pieces (12 cups)
1 pound shelled shrimp, cooked
3 oranges, sectioned

In screw-top jar combine salad oil, ⅓ cup orange juice, sugar, vinegar, orange peel, salt, mustard, and hot pepper sauce. Shake well and chill. Sprinkle avocado rings with 1 tablespoon orange juice. Combine avocado, spinach, shrimp, and orange sections in salad bowl. Toss with chilled dressing. Makes 6 to 8 servings.

Slice avocado into rings *for an attractive addition to Spinach-Shrimp Salad. Toss salad and the orange-flavored dressing gently so the rings do not break.*

CURRY-LOBSTER-POTATO SALAD

4 cups diced, peeled, cooked potatoes
1 5-ounce can lobster, drained and
     flaked
¼ cup sliced celery
3 tablespoons snipped parsley
2 tablespoons chopped green pepper
2 tablespoons sliced green onion
¾ cup mayonnaise or salad dressing
2 tablespoons lemon juice
¼ teaspoon curry powder
     Lettuce
1 hard-cooked egg, cut in wedges

Combine potatoes, lobster, celery, parsley, green pepper, and green onion; toss lightly. Blend together mayonnaise, lemon juice, ½ teaspoon salt, and curry; fold into potato-lobster mixture. Pack into an 8½x4½x2½-inch loaf dish; chill. Unmold on lettuce-lined plate; garnish with hard-cooked egg wedges. Serves 4 or 5.

CRAB-STUFFED AVOCADO

Spoon an elegant crab mixture over avocado halves like the salad featured at The Boston Half Shell in Denver, Colorado—

12 ounces cooked crab meat, broken
     into chunks
2 hard-cooked eggs, chopped
¼ cup chopped ripe olives
3 tablespoons capers, drained
⅔ cup mayonnaise or salad dressing
¼ cup chili sauce
2 tablespoons dairy sour cream
2 teaspoons prepared horseradish
2 teaspoons lemon juice
¼ teaspoon salt
     Dash freshly ground pepper
¼ cup whipping cream
4 large avocados, halved, seeded and
     peeled

Combine crab, eggs, olives, and capers; chill. Blend together mayonnaise, chili sauce, sour cream, horseradish, lemon juice, salt, and pepper; chill. Just before serving, whip cream; fold into dressing. Combine enough dressing with crab mixture to moisten. Place avocado halves on lettuce cups. Spoon filling atop. Garnish with sliced olives, lemon wheels, pickles, and parsley, if desired. Serves 8.

LOBSTER AND ORANGE COMBO

1 5-ounce can lobster, drained and
     broken into ½-inch pieces
½ cup thinly sliced celery
¼ cup mayonnaise or salad dressing
1 tablespoon lemon juice
1 11-ounce can mandarin oranges,
     chilled and drained
     Lettuce
2 teaspoons thinly sliced green onion

Combine lobster and celery. Chill. Combine mayonnaise, lemon juice, and ¼ teaspoon salt. Just before serving, arrange mandarin oranges in circles on two lettuce-lined plates. Toss lobster with dressing and pile atop oranges. Garnish with sliced green onion. Serves 2.

ORIENTAL LOBSTER SALAD

Drain two 5-ounce cans lobster and break into large pieces. Cook one 7-ounce package Chinese pea pods according to package directions; drain. Toss together cooked pea pods, 1 cup diced celery, and lobster; chill thoroughly.

Combine ¾ cup mayonnaise or salad dressing, 2 teaspoons lemon juice, and 2 teaspoons soy sauce; chill. Add mayonnaise mixture to lobster mixture and toss lightly. Spoon into 6 lettuce cups. Sprinkle ¼ cup toasted slivered almonds over tops of salads. Makes 6 servings.

MACARONI-SHRIMP SALAD

8 ounces shelled shrimp, cooked and
     cut in halves lengthwise
¾ cup small macaroni shells, cooked
⅓ cup chopped celery
2 tablespoons sliced pimiento-
     stuffed green olives
1 tablespoon snipped parsley
½ cup mayonnaise or salad dressing
2 tablespoons red wine vinegar
2 teaspoons lemon juice
¼ teaspoon garlic salt
¼ teaspoon dry mustard
¼ teaspoon paprika

Combine shrimp, macaroni, celery, olives, and parsley. Blend together mayonnaise, vinegar, lemon juice, garlic salt, mustard, and paprika; toss with shrimp mixture. Chill. Serves 4.

Add an extra touch to *Salmon Buffet Bowl by garnishing the lettuce. Dip the tips of romaine into water and then into paprika for a bright trim around edges.*

SALMON BUFFET BOWL

Prepare the dressing ahead of time —

  1 cup mayonnaise or salad dressing
¼ cup chili sauce
¼ cup finely chopped green pepper
¼ cup finely chopped green onion
  1 teaspoon lemon juice
½ cup whipping cream
  1 large head romaine
  1 16-ounce can salmon, chilled, drained,
     and broken into chunks
  2 tomatoes, cut in wedges
  2 hard-cooked eggs, sliced lengthwise
    Snipped parsley

Blend together mayonnaise, chili sauce, green pepper, green onion, and lemon juice; chill. At serving time, whip cream just till soft peaks form; fold into mayonnaise mixture.

    Line salad bowl with outer leaves of romaine. Tear up remaining romaine and place in bowl. Place salmon chunks across center of lettuce. Surround salmon with tomato wedges and egg slices. Garnish with snipped parsley. Spoon some of the dressing in center of salad. Pass the remaining dressing. Makes 4 servings.

SALMON-EGG STUFFED TOMATOES

  1 7¾-ounce can salmon,
    drained and flaked
  1 tablespoon lemon juice
  6 hard-cooked eggs, chopped
⅓ cup chopped celery
⅓ cup mayonnaise or salad dressing
  2 tablespoons sweet pickle relish
½ teaspoon dried dillweed
½ teaspoon salt
    Dash pepper
  6 medium tomatoes

Sprinkle salmon with lemon juice; mix with eggs, celery, mayonnaise, relish, dillweed, ½ teaspoon salt, and pepper. Chill. Turn tomatoes stem end down. Cut each tomato into 6 wedges, *cutting to, but not through,* base of tomato. Spread wedges apart slightly. Sprinkle cut surfaces with salt. Fill tomatoes with salmon mixture. Serve on lettuce, if desired. Serves 6.

TUNA-DRESSED SALAD

  1 6½- or 7-ounce can tuna, drained
  1 cup dairy sour cream
¼ cup mayonnaise or salad dressing
¼ cup chili sauce
  2 tablespoons lemon juice
½ teaspoon Worcestershire sauce
¼ teaspoon dry mustard
¼ teaspoon dried oregano leaves,
    crushed

     • • •

  2 cups torn lettuce
  4 cups cubed, peeled, cooked potatoes,
    chilled
  1 9-ounce package frozen cut green
    beans, cooked and chilled
  4 ounces natural Swiss cheese, cut in
    2-inch sticks (1 cup)
½ cup plain croutons
  1 tomato, cut in wedges
    Salt and pepper

Combine first 8 ingredients in blender container or mixing bowl; blend or beat with electric mixer till smooth. Chill thoroughly.

    At serving time, line large salad bowl with torn lettuce. Arrange chilled potatoes, green beans, Swiss cheese, croutons, and tomato wedges atop. Season with salt and pepper. Spoon dressing over salad; toss. Serves 4 to 6.

TANGY SEAFOOD TOSS

Please dieters and non-dieters alike with this flavorful, low-calorie salad—

1 tablespoon cornstarch
1 tablespoon sugar
½ teaspoon paprika
½ teaspoon dry mustard
¼ teaspoon salt
⅛ teaspoon pepper
1 16-ounce can grapefruit sections (2 cups)*
¼ cup catsup
2 tablespoons salad oil
4 cups torn lettuce
1 7-ounce can water-pack tuna, drained and broken into chunks
½ medium cucumber, sliced
⅓ cup sliced radishes

In saucepan combine cornstarch, sugar, paprika, dry mustard, salt, and pepper. Drain grapefruit, reserving liquid; gradually blend grapefruit liquid into cornstarch mixture. Cook and stir till thickened and bubbly. Remove from heat; stir in catsup and salad oil. Chill. Arrange lettuce, tuna, cucumber, radishes, and grapefruit in bowl. Chill. Serve with dressing. Serves 4.

*If desired, substitute 2 cups fresh grapefruit sections and use 1 cup grapefruit juice. Increase sugar to 3 tablespoons.

Include Tuna-Tomato Stars in summertime menus. This brightly colored combination makes a refreshing meal for family or company on summer days.

HEARTY TUNA SALAD

Cook one 10-ounce package frozen Italian green beans according to package directions; drain and cool. Combine beans; one 6½- or 7-ounce can tuna, drained and flaked; 1 cup thinly sliced celery; ½ cup mayonnaise or salad dressing; 1 tablespoon lemon juice; 1½ teaspoons soy sauce; and dash garlic powder. Chill. Before serving, add 1 cup chow mein noodles to tuna mixture; toss together lightly. Serve tuna salad in lettuce cups. Makes 4 servings.

TOMATO-TUNA CUPS

1 6½- or 7-ounce can tuna, drained and flaked
½ cup mayonnaise or salad dressing
½ cup chopped celery
⅓ cup chopped green pepper
2 tablespoons chopped onion
½ to 1 teaspoon curry powder
6 medium tomatoes

Lightly toss together the tuna, mayonnaise, celery, green pepper, onion, curry, ¼ teaspoon salt, and dash pepper. With stem end down, cut each tomato into 6 wedges, *cutting to, but not through,* base of tomato. Spread wedges apart slightly. Sprinkle cut surfaces lightly with salt. Fill tomatoes with tuna mixture. Serve in lettuce cups, if desired. Makes 6 servings.

TUNA-TOMATO STARS

1 6½- or 7-ounce can tuna, drained
1 tablespoon lemon juice
⅓ cup mayonnaise or salad dressing
2 hard-cooked eggs, chopped
¼ cup thinly sliced small sweet pickle
2 tablespoons finely chopped onion
2 tablespoons diced canned pimiento
4 medium tomatoes
Lettuce

Break tuna in chunks; sprinkle with lemon juice. Add mayonnaise, eggs, sweet pickle, onion, pimiento, and ¼ teaspoon salt; mix gently. Chill. With stem end down, cut each tomato into 6 wedges, *cutting to, but not through,* base of tomato. Spread wedges apart slightly; sprinkle cut surfaces lightly with salt. Fill with tuna salad; serve on lettuce. Serves 4.

Be prepared for the unexpected *by having the ingredients for Speedy Nicoise Salad on hand. In moments, canned foods are transformed into a meal.*

SPEEDY NICOISE SALAD

    1 16-ounce can whole green
        beans, drained
    1 15-ounce can artichoke hearts, drained
        and quartered
    1 6½- or 7-ounce can tuna, drained
        and flaked
    ½ cup sliced pitted ripe olives
    2 tablespoons sliced canned pimiento
    2 tablespoons anchovy fillets
    ¼ cup Italian salad dressing

           • • •

    Lettuce
    1 16-ounce can sliced tomatoes

Combine drained beans, artichoke hearts, tuna, sliced olives, pimiento, anchovy fillets, and salad dressing. Toss lightly. Serve salad in lettuce cups. To each serving, add 3 or 4 drained canned tomato slices. Makes 6 to 8 servings.

MARINATED SCALLOP SALAD

    4 medium potatoes
    1 pound fresh or frozen scallops
    2 cups water
    2 tablespoons lemon juice
    1 teaspoon salt
    1 bay leaf
    1 16-ounce can cut green beans, drained
    ¼ cup Italian salad dressing
    1 cup sliced celery
    2 tablespoons chopped green onion

           • • •

    ½ cup mayonnaise or salad dressing
    ¼ cup dairy sour cream
    1 teaspoon prepared horseradish
    ¼ teaspoon dried dillweed
    Lettuce

Boil potatoes in salted water till tender. Thaw frozen scallops; cut large scallops in half. In saucepan bring water, lemon juice, salt, and bay leaf to a boil; add scallops and return to boiling. Simmer 1 minute. Drain scallops; remove and discard the bay leaf.

Remove jackets from warm potatoes and slice about ¼ inch thick (about 4 cups). While potatoes are still warm, combine them with scallops and green beans; toss with Italian salad dressing to coat. Chill in refrigerator at least 2 hours. Add celery and onion to scallop mixture. Blend together the mayonnaise or salad dressing, sour cream, horseradish, and dillweed. Toss the dressing mixture with scallop mixture. Serve salad in lettuce-lined bowl. Garnish with tomato, hard-cooked egg, or lemon wedges, if desired. Makes 8 servings.

CHEESE-ANCHOVY BOWL

Try this chef's salad variation—

    6 cups torn lettuce (1 medium head)
    1 cup torn curly endive
    1 cup torn watercress
    4 ounces natural Swiss cheese, cut in
        2-inch thin strips (1 cup)
    1 2-ounce can anchovy fillets, drained
        Italian salad dressing

Chill greens. In large salad bowl combine lettuce, endive, and watercress. Add Swiss cheese and anchovy fillets. Toss with about 3 tablespoons salad dressing. Makes 6 to 8 servings.

RICE AND TUNA SALAD

⅔ cup uncooked long-grain rice
1 6½- or 7-ounce can tuna, drained and
    broken into chunks
1 cup shredded carrot
1 cup diced celery
2 tablespoons chopped onion
• • •
½ cup mayonnaise or salad dressing
2 teaspoons lemon juice
¼ teaspoon Worcestershire sauce
¼ teaspoon salt
¼ teaspoon dried mixed salad
    herbs, crushed

Cook rice according to package directions. Add tuna, carrot, celery, and onion; chill. Blend together the mayonnaise or salad dressing, lemon juice, Worcestershire sauce, salt, and mixed salad herbs. Just before serving toss dressing with salad. Garnish with carrot curls and parsley, if desired. Serves 4.

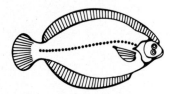

FLOUNDER SALAD BOWL

Transform leftover, cooked fish into a salad—

1 pound flounder fillets or other fish
    fillets, cooked and flaked (2 cups)
2 cups cubed, peeled, cooked potatoes
½ cup diced celery
½ cup shredded cucumber
½ cup chopped green pepper
6 slices bacon, crisp-cooked and
    crumbled
¼ cup sliced radishes
    Lettuce
½ cup mayonnaise or salad dressing
¼ cup catsup
½ teaspoon salt
    Dash pepper

Combine flaked fish, potatoes, celery, cucumber, green pepper, bacon, and radishes. Chill thoroughly. Turn into lettuce-lined bowl. Blend together mayonnaise, catsup, salt, and pepper. Pass dressing with salad. Serves 6.

APPLE-TUNA TOSS

In large salad bowl combine 4 cups torn lettuce; 2 cups diced, unpeeled apple; one 11-ounce can mandarin oranges, drained; one 6½- or 7-ounce can tuna, drained and broken in large chunks; and ⅓ cup coarsely chopped walnuts. Toss all ingredients together.

Combine ½ cup mayonnaise or salad dressing, 2 teaspoons soy sauce, and 1 teaspoon lemon juice; mix well. To serve, add dressing to salad; toss gently. Makes 4 to 6 servings.

SALMON BOWL

1 head Boston Lettuce, torn in pieces
½ to ¾ cup French salad dressing
1 16-ounce can whole green beans,
    drained
2 cups diced, peeled, cooked potatoes
1 7¾-ounce can salmon, drained and
    broken into chunks
2 tomatoes, peeled and cut in wedges
2 hard-cooked eggs, cut in wedges

In salad bowl sprinkle lettuce with a few tablespoons dressing. Arrange beans, potatoes, and salmon atop greens. Trim with tomato and egg. Pour remaining dressing over salad; sprinkle with snipped parsley, if desired. Serves 6.

HOT HALIBUT SLAW

Cabbage stays crisp in this hot salad—

4 slices bacon
¼ cup chopped onion
⅓ cup vinegar
1 teaspoon sugar
½ teaspoon salt
    Dash pepper
2 cups shredded cabbage
1 pound halibut fillets or other fish
    fillets, cooked and flaked (2 cups)

In skillet fry bacon till crisp. Drain bacon, reserving drippings. Crumble bacon; set aside. In same skillet cook onion in drippings till tender. Add vinegar, sugar, salt, and pepper; bring to boiling. Stir in cabbage and flaked fish. Cook, tossing lightly, just till heated through. Turn into serving bowl; sprinkle top with reserved crumbled bacon. Makes 4 servings.

Sprinkle a crunchy mixture *of corn flakes and American cheese over servings of Hot Tuna Salad for a quick topping. This recipe proves that you don't have to spend hours in the kitchen to serve an elegant entrée.*

HOT TUNA SALAD

Bake this salad in attractive seafood shells—

  1 6½- or 7-ounce can tuna,
      drained and flaked
  1 cup diced celery
  ½ cup mayonnaise or salad dressing
  ¼ cup slivered almonds, toasted
  2 tablespoons chopped ripe olives
  2 teaspoons lemon juice
  1 teaspoon minced onion
  ¼ cup crushed corn flakes
  1 tablespoon packaged (shaker
      container) grated American cheese
  1 tablespoon butter, melted

Combine tuna, celery, mayonnaise or salad dressing, toasted almonds, ripe olives, lemon juice, and onion; toss lightly. Pile into four individual baking shells or baking dishes. Bake at 350° for 10 minutes. Combine crushed corn flakes, cheese, and melted butter; sprinkle over the hot salads. Bake till browned, about 10 minutes more. Makes 4 servings.

LUNCHEON LOBSTER BAKE

  1 5-ounce can lobster, drained
  1½ cups soft bread crumbs (2 slices)
  ¾ cup mayonnaise or salad dressing
  ¾ cup milk
  6 hard-cooked eggs, finely chopped
  ⅓ cup chopped onion
  ¼ cup sliced pimiento-stuffed green
      olives
  ¾ teaspoon salt
  ½ cup soft bread crumbs
  2 tablespoons butter, melted
      Pimiento-stuffed olive slices

Cut lobster into chunks. Combine with 1½ cups crumbs, mayonnaise, milk, eggs, onion, ¼ cup sliced olives, salt, and dash pepper. Toss lightly. Pile into 6 individual greased baking dishes or 1-quart casserole. Combine ½ cup crumbs and the melted butter. Sprinkle over top of mixture. Bake at 350° till heated through, 20 to 25 minutes for individual baking dishes and 35 to 40 minutes for casserole. Garnish with olive slices. Makes 6 servings.

SALMON SKILLET SALAD

2 tablespoons salad oil
1 tablespoon all-purpose flour
1 tablespoon sugar
1 teaspoon instant minced onion
1 teaspoon garlic salt
½ teaspoon dry mustard
Dash pepper
½ cup water
¼ cup vinegar
1 16-ounce can salmon, drained
and broken into chunks
3 hard-cooked eggs, sliced
½ cup sliced celery
3 cups torn lettuce
½ cup thinly sliced unpeeled cucumber
1 large tomato, cut in wedges

In medium skillet blend salad oil, flour, sugar, instant onion, garlic salt, dry mustard, and pepper. Add water and vinegar; cook over medium heat till mixture boils, stirring constantly. In the hot sauce layer in order: salmon, sliced eggs, celery, lettuce, cucumber, and tomato wedges. Cook, covered, over medium heat till heated through, about 4 to 5 minutes. Remove from heat; toss mixture together lightly. Serve immediately. Makes 4 servings.

CRAB SALAD CUPS

6 frozen patty shells
2 cups bias-cut celery slices
1 7½-ounce can crab meat, drained,
flaked, and cartilage removed
1 5-ounce can water chestnuts,
drained and sliced
¼ cup sliced pitted ripe olives
2 tablespoons sliced green onion
½ cup mayonnaise or salad dressing
½ cup dairy sour cream
¼ cup dry white wine
¼ teaspoon garlic salt
¼ cup slivered almonds, toasted

Bake patty shells according to package directions. In 1½-quart casserole combine celery, crab meat, water chestnuts, olives, and green onion. Combine mayonnaise, sour cream, wine, and garlic salt; fold into crab mixture. Bake at 350° till bubbly, about 25 minutes. Spoon mixture into patty shells; sprinkle each serving with almonds. Makes 6 servings.

HOT SALMON SALAD

For casual entertaining, cook this salad at the table in an electric skillet—

4 ounces tiny shell macaroni (1 cup)
2 tablespoons Italian salad dressing
½ teaspoon dry mustard
½ teaspoon salt
Dash pepper
• • •
1 7¾-ounce can salmon, drained
and broken into chunks
½ cup sliced celery
½ cup chopped green pepper
½ cup mayonnaise or salad dressing
Green pepper rings

Cook macaroni according to package directions; drain. In skillet combine Italian dressing, mustard, salt, and pepper; heat just to boiling. Add drained macaroni, salmon, celery, chopped green pepper, and mayonnaise. Cook, tossing lightly, just till heated through. Garnish with green pepper rings. Serves 4.

SMOKED FISH POTATO SALAD

½ cup chopped onion
2 tablespoons butter or margarine
1 10½-ounce can condensed cream of
celery soup
⅓ cup milk
2 tablespoons sweet pickle relish
2 tablespoons vinegar
6 medium potatoes, peeled, cooked,
and cubed
1 pound smoked whiting or other
smoked fish, skinned, boned, and
flaked (1½ cups)
1 hard-cooked egg, cut in wedges

In saucepan cook onion in butter till just tender. Blend in condensed soup, milk, pickle relish, and vinegar. Gently stir in potatoes and whiting. Heat through. Trim with egg wedges. Sprinkle with paprika and garnish with parsley, if desired. Makes 6 servings.

The main part of a meal demands something extra special and what could be better than a shellfish or fish entrée? Keeping in mind that seafood is very nutritious, yet easy on the waistline, include fish and shellfish often when you are planning the week's menus.

For that special dinner party when the boss is invited, impress your guests with an elegant lobster or crab entrée. Or how about serving Spanish Paella, a tasty combination of shrimp, clams, and chicken? You will find many other shellfish recipes for everyday fare, too, including shrimp, scallops, abalone, clams, and oysters.

Main dishes prepared with fish are also family and guest pleasers. When you bring out a platter of fried fish or fish sticks, just watch the approving nods when the first bite is sampled. For casual entertaining, serve Fish and Chips as shown here, while elegant dining may call for a planked fish with all the trimmings. Host or hostess can carve this beauty at the table. Better rehearse the carving procedure first. Then, when company comes, the whole process can be done with little effort when you are "on deck."
Before you begin, however, check the carving directions to make this challenging task a bit easier.

How about transforming seafood and fish into one-dish meals by adding vegetables or other ingredients? These recipes are easy to serve and popular too! All that's needed to complete the meal is a salad, dessert, and beverage of your choice.

Entrées

ACCENT THE MEAL WITH SHELLFISH

CREOLE JAMBALAYA

2 cups cubed fully cooked ham
¾ cup chopped onion
1 clove garlic, minced
2 tablespoons butter or margarine
1 28-ounce can tomatoes, cut up
1 10½-ounce can beef broth
1 cup uncooked long-grain rice
1 bay leaf, crushed
1 teaspoon sugar
½ teaspoon dried thyme leaves, crushed
¼ teaspoon chili powder
    Dash freshly ground pepper
1 4½-ounce can shrimp, drained and
    cut in halves lengthwise
¼ cup sliced pitted ripe olives
1 medium green pepper, cut in
    1-inch squares

In a large saucepan cook ham, onion, and garlic in butter till onion is tender. Add tomatoes, beef broth, 1 cup water, rice, bay leaf, sugar, thyme, chili powder, and pepper. Cover and simmer till rice is tender, about 15 minutes.

Add shrimp, olives, and green pepper squares. Simmer, uncovered, to desired consistency, about 5 to 10 minutes. Makes 6 to 8 servings.

BARBECUED SHRIMP

8 ounces fresh or frozen shelled shrimp
⅓ cup salad oil
¼ cup sauterne
¼ cup soy sauce
½ clove garlic, crushed
¼ teaspoon ground ginger
¼ teaspoon paprika
    Dash pepper

Thaw frozen shrimp. Combine with remaining ingredients; let stand 30 minutes. Drain shrimp; thread on skewers. Broil about 4 to 5 inches from heat for 4 minutes; baste occasionally with marinade. Turn and broil till shrimp are cooked, 2 to 4 minutes. Makes 2 servings.

SHRIMP ÉTOUFFÉ

1½ pounds fresh or frozen shelled shrimp
2 tablespoons all-purpose flour
¼ cup butter or margarine
¼ cup finely chopped celery
2 tablespoons finely chopped green
    onion
1 clove garlic, minced
2 tablespoons snipped parsley
    Dash cayenne pepper
3 cups hot cooked rice

Thaw frozen shrimp. In 3-quart saucepan cook flour in butter till golden brown, about 5 minutes, stirring frequently. Stir in celery, onion, and garlic; cook and stir 3 to 4 minutes. Add parsley, 1 teaspoon salt, cayenne, 1 cup water, and uncooked shrimp. Simmer, covered, 15 minutes. Serve over rice. Makes 6 servings.

SHRIMP CREOLE

Use 12 ounces fresh or frozen shelled shrimp. Thaw frozen shrimp. Cook ½ cup chopped onion, ½ cup chopped celery, and 1 clove garlic, minced, in 3 tablespoons salad oil till tender but not brown. Add one 16-ounce can tomatoes, one 8-ounce can tomato sauce, 1 tablespoon Worcestershire sauce, 1½ teaspoons salt, 1 teaspoon sugar, ½ to 1 teaspoon chili powder, and dash bottled hot pepper sauce. Simmer, uncovered, 45 minutes. Mix 2 teaspoons cornstarch with 1 tablespoon cold water; stir into sauce. Cook; stir till bubbly. Add shrimp and ½ cup chopped green pepper. Cover; simmer 5 minutes. Serve over cooked rice. Serves 6.

Creole favorite

Discover why Creole Jambalaya is praised in many songs and legends. The delicate blend of seafood, vegetables, and piquant seasonings makes a dish that looks appealing and boasts a superb flavor.

Open a can of frozen soup *for the basis of Shrimp-Sauced Egg Patties. The shrimp soup adds flavor to the patties and the sauce with a minimum of effort.*

SHRIMP AND NOODLES

In saucepan mix one 10-ounce can frozen condensed cream of shrimp soup, thawed; ⅓ cup milk; and dash bottled hot pepper sauce. Bring to boiling. Stir small amount hot mixture into ½ cup dairy sour cream; return to hot mixture. Add 12 ounces shelled shrimp, cooked; heat. Serve over 4 ounces noodles, cooked. Serves 4.

Use a cook-and-serve skillet *when making Oriental Skillet Supper so that the arrangement of shrimp over the macaroni and cheese mixture will remain on top.*

SHRIMP-SAUCED EGG PATTIES

Sauce has a hint of curry—

    1 10-ounce can frozen condensed
       cream of shrimp soup
    8 hard-cooked eggs, chopped
    ¼ cup fine dry bread crumbs
    2 tablespoons milk
    2 teaspoons snipped parsley
    2 teaspoons chopped onion
    ¼ teaspoon salt
      Dash pepper
    ½ cup fine dry bread crumbs
    2 tablespoons salad oil
    ⅓ cup milk
    ¼ teaspoon curry powder

Thaw frozen soup; combine ¼ *cup* soup, chopped egg, the ¼ cup bread crumbs, 2 tablespoons milk, parsley, onion, salt, and pepper. Form mixture into 8 patties. Coat with the ½ cup bread crumbs. Heat salad oil in skillet; cook patties till golden, browning both sides.

For sauce, combine remaining soup, ⅓ cup milk, and curry powder; heat through. Pass sauce with the fried patties. Makes 4 servings.

ORIENTAL SKILLET SUPPER

    2 tablespoons butter or margarine
    1 medium apple, peeled, cored,
       and chopped (1 cup)
    ½ cup sliced celery
    ¾ teaspoon curry powder
              • • •
    1 chicken bouillon cube, crumbled
    2 cups water
    1 7¼-ounce package macaroni and
       cheese dinner mix
    ½ teaspoon salt
    ¾ cup milk
    1 4½-ounce can shrimp, drained

In skillet melt butter or margarine. Add chopped apple, sliced celery, and curry powder. Cook till apple and celery are crisp-tender. Remove from heat; add bouillon cube, water, macaroni part of the macaroni and cheese dinner mix, and salt. Return to heat; cover. Cook till macaroni is tender, 6 to 7 minutes, stirring occasionally. Stir in the package of cheese from dinner mix and the milk. Top with drained shrimp. Heat through. Makes 4 servings.

JOE'S STONE CRAB RESTAURANT SHRIMP CREOLE

Try this Southern favorite from Joe's Stone Crab Restaurant located in Miami Beach, Florida—

¼ cup chopped salt pork
½ cup chopped celery
½ cup chopped onion
1 28-ounce can tomatoes, cut up
¾ cup chili sauce
⅓ cup tomato paste
1 clove garlic, minced
1 teaspoon beef-flavored gravy base
½ teaspoon dried thyme leaves, crushed
¾ teaspoon salt
¼ teaspoon pepper
1½ pounds fresh or frozen shelled shrimp, cooked
Hot cooked rice

In large saucepan fry pork till crisp; remove bits of pork. Cook celery and onion in drippings till tender. Add tomatoes, chili sauce, tomato paste, garlic, gravy base, thyme, salt, and pepper. Simmer, covered, for 30 minutes. Stir in shrimp. Serve over hot cooked rice. Makes 8 servings.

SHRIMP Á LA KING

Save time by doubling the recipe. Serve one immediately and freeze one for a busy day—

1 7-ounce package frozen shelled shrimp
1 3-ounce can sliced mushrooms, drained
¼ cup chopped green pepper
¼ cup butter or margarine
2 tablespoons all-purpose flour
½ teaspoon salt
Several dashes white pepper
2 cups milk
1 tablespoon lemon juice
6 to 8 toast cups

Cook frozen shrimp according to package directions; drain. In medium saucepan cook mushrooms and green pepper in butter or margarine till tender. Blend in flour, salt, and white pepper. Add milk all at once. Cook quickly, stirring constantly till thickened and bubbly. Stir in cooked shrimp and lemon juice. Heat through. Serve in toast cups. Makes 6 to 8 servings.

Want a different way *of cooking shrimp? Curried-Coconut Shrimp solves the problem by combining a curry-flavored coconut coating with fried shrimp.*

CURRIED-COCONUT SHRIMP

2 pounds fresh or frozen shrimp in shells
1 cup sifted all-purpose flour
½ teaspoon sugar
½ teaspoon salt
1 slightly beaten egg
2 tablespoons salad oil
⅔ cup grated coconut
1½ to 2 teaspoons curry powder

Thaw frozen shrimp. Shell and devein shrimp, leaving last section and tail intact. Dry shrimp well. Combine flour, sugar, salt, egg, 1 cup ice water, and salad oil; beat smooth. Mix coconut and curry together. Dip dried shrimp into batter, then into coconut mixture. Fry in deep, hot fat (375°) till golden. Drain. Serves 6.

MUSTARD-GRILLED SHRIMP

Combine ½ cup prepared mustard, ½ cup water, 2 tablespoons sugar, 2 tablespoons vinegar, and 2 teaspoons prepared horseradish. Use 2 pounds fresh or frozen shelled jumbo shrimp. Thaw frozen shrimp. Add shrimp to mixture; chill several hours, stirring often. Drain, reserving marinade. Grill over *medium* coals, 6 to 8 minutes. Turn and baste twice with marinade. Makes 8 servings.

Menu

ORIENTAL DINNER
Chicken-Rice Soup
Chinese Peas and Shrimp
Chow Mein Noodles
Mandarin Orange Gelatin Salad
Sherbet   Fortune Cookies
Tea

Travel to a foreign land for dinner—at least in atmosphere. An oriental menu featuring many of the typical foods will transform mealtime into an adventure for the family.

Carry out the theme established in the menu by serving the dinner on a low table with cushions for seating. Use matchstick place mats and stainless steel flatware with bamboo handles for the table service. And to add that extraspecial oriental touch, don a long, silk kimono, or a dress that resembles one.

CHINESE PEAS AND SHRIMP

    12 ounces fresh or frozen shelled shrimp
    2 tablespoons salad oil
    1 7-ounce package frozen Chinese pea
        pods, thawed, or 2 cups fresh
        Chinese pea pods
    2 tablespoons thinly sliced green
        onion and tops
    2 teaspoons shredded peeled gingerroot
        or ½ teaspoon ground ginger
    1 clove garlic, minced
    1 teaspoon cornstarch
    ½ teaspoon sugar
    1 teaspoon soy sauce

Thaw frozen shrimp. Heat oil in heavy skillet till bubbly; add shrimp and cook quickly till pink, 3 to 5 minutes. Add pea pods, onion, ginger, and garlic; toss and cook over high heat for 1 minute. Combine cornstarch, sugar, and ½ teaspoon salt. Add soy sauce and 2 teaspoons cold water, mixing till smooth. Pour over shrimp mixture; toss and cook till thickened and clear, about 1 minute. Pass additional soy sauce, if desired. Makes 3 or 4 servings.

STUFFED SHRIMP

    24 fresh or frozen jumbo shrimp in
        shells
    2 tablespoons finely chopped celery
    2 tablespoons finely chopped green
        pepper
    1 clove garlic, minced
    2 tablespoons butter or margarine
    1 tablespoon all-purpose flour
    ¼ cup milk
    ½ cup soft bread crumbs (¾ slice)
    1 7½-ounce can crab meat, drained,
        cartilage removed, and chopped
    ½ teaspoon Worcestershire sauce
    ½ teaspoon lemon juice
    1 cup sifted all-purpose flour
    1 slightly beaten egg
    2 tablespoons salad oil
    ½ teaspoon sugar
        Shortening

Thaw frozen shrimp. Shell shrimp, leaving tails on. Butterfly shrimp by splitting down the back *almost but not all the way through*; devein. Cook celery, green pepper, and garlic in butter till tender; blend in 1 tablespoon flour. Stir in milk and cook till thickened. Add bread crumbs, crab, Worcestershire sauce, lemon juice, ½ teaspoon salt, and ⅛ teaspoon pepper. Stuff crab into slit shrimp, packing firmly. Chill 1 hour.

Beat together 1 cup flour, 1 cup ice water, egg, salad oil, sugar, and ½ teaspoon salt just till moistened (a few lumps should remain). Keep batter cool with a few ice cubes; use immediately. Pat shrimp dry; dip shrimp in batter. Fry in deep, hot fat (360°) till golden, 4 to 5 minutes. Makes 4 servings.

SHRIMP AND FRUIT SKEWERS

Combine ½ cup orange juice, ¼ cup vinegar, ¼ cup salad oil, ¼ cup soy sauce, and ½ teaspoon salt. Use 8 ounces fresh or frozen shelled shrimp. Thaw frozen shrimp. Pour mixture over shrimp in shallow dish; chill 1 hour. Remove shrimp from marinade. Thread shrimp and lemon wedges on skewers. On separate skewers, alternate preserved kumquats, crab apples, and banana chunks. Grill shrimp skewers over *medium* coals 6 to 8 minutes, turning often. Brush fruit with marinade; grill 3 to 4 minutes. Heat remaining marinade; serve with kabobs. Makes 3 or 4 servings.

SHRIMP-MANDARIN CREPES

    1 slightly beaten egg
1¼ cups milk
    1 tablespoon butter or margarine,
        melted
    1 cup sifted all-purpose flour
    1 3-ounce package cream cheese,
        softened
    1 pound shelled shrimp, cooked
    1 11-ounce can mandarin oranges
        Orange juice
 ⅓ cup sugar
    4 teaspoons cornstarch
    2 tablespoons butter or margarine

Combine egg, milk, 1 tablespoon melted butter, and flour; beat smooth. Lightly grease a 6-inch skillet; heat. Remove from heat and pour 2 tablespoons of batter into skillet; quickly tilt pan from side to side till batter covers bottom. Return to heat; brown crepe on one side only. To remove crepe, invert skillet over paper toweling. Repeat with remaining batter to make a total of 10 crepes. Spread unbrowned side of crepes with cream cheese.

Chop *half* the shrimp. Sprinkle over crepes and roll up each crepe. Arrange in chafing dish or skillet. Drain mandarin oranges, reserving syrup. Top crepes with the drained mandarin oranges and the whole cooked shrimp.

And enough orange juice to mandarin syrup to make 1½ cups. Mix sugar, cornstarch, and dash salt in saucepan. Blend in juice. Cook and stir till slightly thickened and clear. Remove from heat; stir in the 2 tablespoons butter. Spoon hot sauce over crepes; cover and heat through. Keep warm till served. If desired, pour brandy into long-handled ladle, ignite, and pour over crepes before serving. Serves 4 or 5.

SHRIMP KABOBS

Drain one 13½-ounce can pineapple chunks, reserving ¼ cup syrup. Use 12 ounces fresh or frozen shelled jumbo shrimp. Thaw frozen shrimp. Alternate pineapple, shrimp, and one 6-ounce can whole mushrooms, drained, on 4 skewers. Combine ¼ cup soy sauce, ¼ cup salad oil, reserved syrup, 2 tablespoons snipped parsley, ½ teaspoon salt, and dash pepper. Brush on kabobs. Grill over *medium-hot* coals 5 to 8 minutes; turn and brush with sauce occasionally. Makes 4 servings.

Use convenience foods *for a quick meal featuring Sweet-Sour Shrimp and refrigerated biscuits dipped in butter and grated Parmesan cheese before baking.*

SWEET-SOUR SHRIMP

    2 tablespoons cornstarch
    3 tablespoons sugar
    1 cup chicken broth
 ⅔ cup pineapple juice
 ¼ cup vinegar
    2 tablespoons soy sauce
    1 tablespoon butter or margarine
              • • •
    1 7-ounce package frozen Chinese
        pea pods, thawed
    2 4½-ounce cans shrimp, drained
    2 to 2½ cups hot cooked rice

In saucepan blend cornstarch and sugar; stir in chicken broth. Add pineapple juice, vinegar, soy sauce, and butter. Cook and stir till mixture comes to boiling; cover and simmer 5 minutes longer. Add pea pods and shrimp; heat through. Serve on hot rice. Makes 4 or 5 servings.

SHRIMP AU VIN

1½ pounds fresh or frozen shelled shrimp
3 tablespoons butter or margarine
3 tablespoons all-purpose flour
   Dash cayenne pepper
1 cup milk
⅔ cup dry white wine
¼ cup chopped green onion
6 tablespoons butter or margarine
6 to 8 patty shells
2 ounces sharp process American
   cheese, shredded (½ cup)

Thaw frozen shrimp. Chop coarsely. In saucepan melt 3 tablespoons butter; stir in flour, ½ teaspoon salt, and cayenne. Add milk; cook and stir till thickened and bubbly. Slowly stir in wine. In skillet cook shrimp and onion in 6 tablespoons butter till shrimp are pink, 2 to 3 minutes. Stir in sauce; heat through. Spoon into patty shells; top with cheese. Serves 6 to 8.

SHRIMP DE JONGHE

Cook 2 pounds fresh or frozen shelled shrimp. Arrange in 11¾x7½x1¾-inch baking dish. Combine ½ cup butter or margarine, melted; ½ cup dry white wine; ⅓ cup snipped parsley; 2 cloves garlic, minced; ½ teaspoon paprika; and dash cayenne pepper. Mix in 2 cups soft bread crumbs. Spread crumb mixture over shrimp. Bake at 350° till crumbs are brown, 25 minutes. Sprinkle with parsley. Serves 6 to 8.

SPAGHETTI MARINA

1 8-ounce package spaghetti
3 tablespoons butter or margarine
3 tablespoons all-purpose flour
½ teaspoon dried dillweed
1¾ cups milk
2 4½-ounce cans shrimp, drained
¼ cup sliced pitted ripe olives
1 tablespoon snipped parsley
1 tablespoon lemon juice

Cook spaghetti according to package directions; drain. In saucepan melt butter; stir in flour, dill, and dash salt. Add milk; cook and stir till slightly thickened and bubbly. Add shrimp, olives, parsley, and lemon juice. Heat through. Serve over hot spaghetti. Serves 4 or 5.

PEPPERED SHRIMP DIABLE

Spoon this zesty seafood mixture over rice as it is served at Charlie's Cafe Exceptionale in Minneapolis, Minnesota—

2 pounds fresh or frozen shelled
   shrimp
⅓ cup finely chopped green pepper
⅓ cup finely chopped onion
1 clove garlic, minced
2 tablespoons butter
⅓ cup tomato paste
½ cup vinegar
⅓ cup soy sauce
1 tablespoon prepared mustard
1 teaspoon coarsely cracked pepper
1 teaspoon paprika
1 teaspoon ground cumin
¼ cup all-purpose flour
   Rice pilaf or hot cooked rice

Thaw shrimp, if frozen. Cook green pepper, onion, and garlic in butter till tender, but not brown. Add tomato paste, vinegar, soy, mustard, pepper, paprika, and cumin. Simmer, covered, over low heat about 8 to 10 minutes. Season shrimp with salt and pepper; coat lightly with flour. Cook in about ½ inch of salad oil in skillet till golden on both sides, about 3 to 4 minutes. Add shrimp to sauce and heat through. Serve with rice pilaf. Makes 4 to 6 servings.

Serve Spaghetti Marina for the main course at a dinner party. Include an antipasto appetizer, a tossed salad, bread sticks, wine or coffee, and spumoni.

OYSTER LOAF

Oyster loaves are such a favorite in New Orleans that they are traditionally brought home by husbands as a peace offering—

>1 large loaf French or Italian bread
>¼ cup butter or margarine, softened
>1 quart shucked oysters
>⅓ cup all-purpose flour
>½ teaspoon salt
>¼ cup milk
>1 beaten egg
>1 cup cornmeal
>Shortening
>Lemon wedges or pickle slices
>Tartar sauce or chili sauce

Cut a ¾-inch slice off top of bread; remove center of loaf, leaving a ½-inch wall. Butter inside of loaf, and top slice. Toast in a 425° oven till lightly browned, 10 to 15 minutes. Meanwhile, drain oysters and pat dry between paper toweling. Combine flour, salt, and ⅛ teaspoon pepper. Mix milk and beaten egg. Roll oysters in seasoned flour, dip into milk mixture, then coat with the cornmeal.

Heat small amount of shortening in skillet. Panfry oysters till golden, about 2 to 3 minutes on each side. Drain on paper toweling. Pile oysters into loaf; replace top. Garnish with lemon wedges or pickle slices. To serve, slice the loaf and pass tartar sauce or chili sauce. Makes 6 servings.

PAN-ROASTED OYSTERS

Present this elegant dish as the main course the next time company comes for dinner—

>1 pint shucked small oysters
>¼ cup butter or margarine, melted
>1 3-ounce can sliced mushrooms, drained
>¼ cup dry red wine
>¼ cup snipped parsley
>½ teaspoon salt
>Toast points

Drain oysters. Arrange oysters in 11x7x1½-inch baking pan. Combine melted butter, mushrooms, wine, parsley, salt, and dash pepper. Pour over oysters. Bake at 400° till edges of oysters begin to curl, about 10 minutes. Serve over toast points. Makes 4 servings.

OYSTER BAKE

>1½ pints shucked oysters or 2 12-ounce
>   cans frozen oysters, thawed
>½ of 3½-ounce can French-fried onions
>2 tablespoons snipped parsley
>2 tablespoons grated Parmesan cheese
>2 tablespoons butter or margarine

Drain oysters. Sprinkle with salt and pepper. Arrange in buttered 8x1½-inch round baking pan or in 4 individual baking shells. Cover oysters with onions, parsley, and cheese. Dot with butter. Bake at 450° till browned, about 8 to 10 minutes in baking pan and 6 to 8 minutes in individual shells. Makes 4 servings.

DEVILED OYSTERS

>36 oysters in shells or 1 pint
>   shucked oysters
>2 tablespoons finely chopped onion
>3 tablespoons butter or margarine
>¼ cup all-purpose flour
>1 tablespoon prepared mustard
>1 teaspoon Worcestershire sauce
>½ teaspoon salt
>⅛ teaspoon ground nutmeg
>⅟₁₆ teaspoon cayenne pepper
>1 cup milk
>1 beaten egg
>1½ cups soft bread crumbs
>2 tablespoons butter or margarine,
>   melted

Shuck oysters in shells. Drain oysters well; chop and set aside. Cook onion in butter till tender but not brown. Blend in flour, mustard, Worcestershire sauce, salt, nutmeg, and cayenne pepper. Add milk; cook and stir till thickened and bubbly. Reduce heat. Stir a small amount of hot mixture into egg; return to hot mixture. Cook 1 minute more; remove from heat and add oysters. Spoon mixture into 6 individual baking shells or pour into a 1-quart oven-going serving dish. Toss bread crumbs with melted butter; sprinkle over top of mixture. Bake at 400° for 10 to 12 minutes. Makes 6 servings.

Treat the oyster lovers *in your family to Oyster Pudding for a light supper. Slices of American cheese are hidden in the center for a special surprise.*

STUFFING FOR GAME HENS

Save time when preparing a holiday meal— make oyster stuffing ahead and refrigerate until time to bake the Cornish game hens—

    2 cups corn bread crumbs
    4 cups soft bread cubes (4 slices)
 1½ teaspoons dried sage, crushed
    1 teaspoon salt
      Dash pepper
    1 10-ounce can frozen oysters, thawed
    1 tablespoon instant minced onion
   ¼ cup butter or margarine, melted
    4 1- to 1½-pound Cornish game hens
      Salad oil
      Butter or margarine, melted

Toss together corn bread crumbs, bread cubes, sage, salt, and pepper. Drain oysters, reserving liquid. Add onion to liquid. Chop oysters; add oysters, onion mixture, and ¼ cup melted butter to corn bread mixture. Toss to mix well. Chill. Salt insides of birds; truss each. Place, breast side up, in 13x9x2-inch baking pan. Rub with salad oil. Spoon stuffing around hens. Roast, loosely covered, at 400° for 1 hour. Uncover; roast 30 minutes longer, basting birds with melted butter or margarine.

To serve, arrange the roasted Cornish game hens on a large serving platter; spoon the oyster stuffing in center. Makes 4 servings.

OYSTER PUDDING

Spread one side of 6 slices white bread with softened butter or margarine. Cut into cubes. Place *half* the cubes in bottom of 11¾x7½x1¾-inch baking dish; top with 6 slices sharp process American cheese. Drain 1 pint shucked oysters, reserving liquid. Add enough milk to liquid to make 2½ cups. Arrange oysters over cheese slices. Top with remaining bread cubes. Blend together oyster-milk mixture, 2 beaten eggs, 1 teaspoon salt, and ¼ teaspoon pepper. Pour over ingredients in baking dish. Bake at 325° till knife inserted just off center comes out clean, about 1 to 1¼ hours. Serves 4 to 6.

OYSTER STUFFING

   ½ cup chopped celery
   ½ cup chopped onion
    1 bay leaf
   ¼ cup butter or margarine
    6 cups dry bread cubes
    1 tablespoon snipped parsley
    1 pint shucked oysters
    2 beaten eggs
    1 teaspoon poultry seasoning
      Milk

Cook celery, onion, and bay leaf in butter or margarine till vegetables are tender but not brown. Discard bay leaf. Add bread cubes and parsley to vegetable mixture; mix thoroughly. Drain oysters, reserving liquid. Chop oysters; add to bread mixture with eggs, poultry seasoning, 1 teaspoon salt, and dash pepper. Add milk to oyster liquid to make ⅓ cup. Add enough of this liquid to stuffing to moisten. Makes enough stuffing for a 10- to 12-pound turkey.

EASY OYSTER STUFFING

Thaw two 10-ounce cans frozen condensed oyster stew. Remove oysters and chop. Cook ½ cup chopped celery and ½ cup chopped onion in ¼ cup butter or margarine till tender but not brown. Add stew, oysters, one 7- or 8-ounce package herb-seasoned stuffing mix, and ¼ teaspoon ground sage; mix lightly. Makes 5 to 6 cups stuffing—enough for a 10-pound turkey or two 4- or 5-pound chickens. *Or* turn stuffing into a 1½-quart casserole. Cover and bake at 375° till heated through, 25 to 30 minutes.

OYSTER-MUSHROOM BAKE

12 oysters in shells
¼ cup chopped green onion
2 tablespoons butter or margarine
1 tablespoon all-purpose flour
½ teaspoon celery salt
Dash pepper
½ cup milk
1 3-ounce can chopped mushrooms,
   drained
1½ cups soft bread crumbs
2 tablespoons butter, melted

Shuck oysters. Chop oysters; wash shells well. Cook onion in 2 tablespoons butter till tender. Blend in flour, celery salt, and pepper. Add milk; cook and stir till thickened and bubbly. Add chopped oysters and mushrooms. Spoon mixture into oyster shells or 4 coquilles— individual baking shells. Toss bread crumbs and 2 tablespoons melted butter together; sprinkle over oysters. Bake at 400° till lightly browned, about 10 minutes. Makes 4 servings.

CLAM IN COQUILLES

1 pint shucked clams or 2
   7½-ounce cans minced clams
½ cup chopped celery
¼ cup chopped onion
2 tablespoons butter or margarine
1 tablespoon all-purpose flour
¾ teaspoon salt
¼ teaspoon dried thyme leaves, crushed
Dash bottled hot pepper sauce
1 beaten egg
1 cup soft bread crumbs (2 slices)
2 tablespoons snipped parlsey
1 tablespoon butter or margarine,
   melted

Drain clams. Coarsely chop whole clams. Cook celery and onion in the 2 tablespoons butter till tender but not brown. Blend in flour, salt, thyme, dash pepper, and hot pepper sauce. Stir a small amount of hot mixture into the egg; return to hot mixture. Add clams, *half* the bread crumbs, and parsley.

Spoon mixture into 4 or 5 buttered coquilles —individual baking shells. Combine remaining crumbs and the 1 tablespoon melted butter; sprinkle over clam mixture. Bake at 400° till browned, 10 minutes. Makes 4 or 5 servings.

CLAM HOT CAKES

1 7½-ounce can minced clams
   Milk
2 tablespoons finely chopped onion
2 tablespoons butter or margarine
1 cup sifted all-purpose flour
2 teaspoons baking powder
1 well-beaten egg
1 tablespoon snipped parsley
2 tablespoons butter or margarine
2 tablespoons all-purpose flour
¼ teaspoon salt
   Dash white pepper
1 cup milk
1 3-ounce can chopped mushrooms,
   drained

Drain clams, reserving liquid; add milk to equal ¾ cup. In skillet cook onion in 2 tablespoons butter till tender. Set aside. Sift together 1 cup flour, baking powder, and ½ teaspoon salt. Stir in egg, reserved liquid, clams, onion with butter, and parsley, just till moistened. Bake on a hot griddle, using about ¼ cup of batter for each of the hot cakes.

Meanwhile, melt 2 tablespoons butter in saucepan. Blend in 2 tablespoons flour, ¼ teaspoon salt, and pepper. Add 1 cup milk all at once. Cook, stirring constantly, till mixture is thickened and bubbly. Add mushrooms; heat through. Serve over hot cakes. Serves 4.

CLAMS PARMESAN

Roll clams in Parmesan cheese before frying—

48 large shucked clams
2 beaten eggs
2 tablespoons milk
½ cup fine saltine cracker crumbs
½ cup grated Parmesan cheese
½ teaspoon salt
   Dash pepper
   Shortening
   Lemon wedges

Dry clams with paper toweling. Combine beaten eggs and milk. Mix cracker crumbs, Parmesan cheese, salt, and pepper together. Dip clams in egg mixture, then roll in cracker mixture. Panfry on both sides in small amount of hot shortening about 4 to 5 minutes. Serve with lemon wedges. Makes 4 to 6 servings.

SPANISH PAELLA

    ¼ cup all-purpose flour
    1 2½- to 3-pound ready-to-cook
        broiler-fryer chicken, cut up
    ¼ cup olive or salad oil
    2 carrots, peeled and sliced lengthwise
    2 medium onions, peeled and quartered
    1 celery branch with leaves
    2 cups chicken broth
    1 clove garlic, minced
    ¼ cup chopped canned pimiento
    ¼ teaspoon ground oregano
    ¼ teaspoon ground saffron
    ⅔ cup uncooked long-grain rice
    1 9-ounce package frozen artichoke
        hearts, thawed
    12 ounces fresh or frozen shelled shrimp
    12 small clams in shells, washed

Combine flour, 1 teaspoon salt, and dash pepper; coat chicken with flour. In skillet brown chicken in hot oil for 20 minutes. Transfer to large kettle. Add next 9 ingredients and ½ teaspoon salt. Simmer, covered, 30 minutes. Add artichokes, shrimp, and clams; simmer, covered, 15 to 20 minutes longer. Makes 6 to 8 servings.

CLAM-MUSHROOM SPAGHETTI

In saucepan combine one 6-ounce can tomato paste; ¼ cup chopped onion; ¼ cup chopped green pepper; 1 clove garlic, crushed; ½ to ¾ teaspoon dried basil leaves, crushed; ½ teaspoon dried oregano leaves, crushed; ½ teaspoon salt; and ⅛ teaspoon pepper. Blend in 1 cup water. Drain two 7½-ounce cans minced clams and one 3-ounce can sliced mushrooms, reserving liquids. Add liquids to saucepan; set clams and mushrooms aside.

Simmer tomato mixture, uncovered, to desired thickness, about 45 to 50 minutes. Cook 8 ounces spaghetti; drain. Add clams and mushrooms to sauce; heat through. Serve sauce over spaghetti. Makes 4 servings.

A Spanish classic

← *Create Spanish Paella by cooking chicken, shrimp, clams in shells, artichoke hearts, and saffron rice together. This gourmet recipe is traditionally made in a two-handled casserole pan, called a paella.*

CLAMS IN PATTY SHELLS

    2 7½-ounce cans minced clams
      Milk
        • • •
    ¼ cup butter or margarine
    ¼ cup all-purpose flour
    ¼ teaspoon salt
    ⅛ teaspoon paprika
    1 teaspoon instant minced onion
    2 teaspoons lemon juice
    1 beaten egg yolk
    1 tablespoon snipped parsley
    6 patty shells

Drain clams, reserving liquid. Add enough milk to liquid to measure 2 cups; set aside. In saucepan melt butter; stir in flour, salt, and paprika. Add clam-milk mixture, onion, and lemon juice all at once. Cook, stirring constantly, till thickened and bubbly. Stir a small amount of hot sauce into egg yolk; return to saucepan. Cook and stir 1 minute. Add clams and parsley; heat through. Serve in patty shells. Serves 6.

SOUR CREAM-TOPPED CLAM PIE

    4 slices bacon
    ½ cup chopped onion
    ¼ cup all-purpose flour
    ¼ teaspoon salt
    ⅛ teaspoon pepper
      Clam liquid
    1 cup drained shucked small clams
        • • •
    2 beaten eggs
    2 tablespoons snipped parsley
    1 unbaked 8-inch pastry shell
    ¾ cup dairy sour cream
      Paprika

In skillet cook bacon till crisp; remove bacon, crumble, and set aside. Cook onion in 2 tablespoons drippings till tender. Stir in flour, salt, and pepper. Add enough water to clam liquid to equal ½ cup. Stir liquid and clams into flour in skillet. Cook till thickened, stirring constantly. Stir a small amount of hot sauce into eggs; return to skillet. Add parsley and crumbled bacon. Bake unpricked pastry shell at 400° for 7 to 8 minutes. Add clam mixture and bake 15 minutes longer. Spread sour cream over top; sprinkle with paprika. Bake till sour cream is set, 4 to 5 minutes. Makes 6 servings.

Menu

CLAMBAKE

Steamed Clams   Clam Liquid

Whole Lobster   Melted Butter

Grilled Chicken

Corn in Husks

Cold Watermelon

Beer   Coffee

One of the oldest and most colorful American traditions is the clambake. This feast can be cooked on the beach in much the same way as it was done by the Indians early in history. However, if you're an inlander, don't despair. The modern adaptation of the clambake in your backyard can be just as much fun.

To hold a traditional New England clambake, dig a pit on the beach. Build a roaring fire on rocks which line the shallow pit. Allow the fire to burn till the rocks are red hot. Then, rake the ashes to the sides and toss a layer of wet rockweed, about four inches thick, atop the hot rocks. Now, the pit is ready for long, slow cooking.

Place clams and lobsters on the steaming mass of rockweed. Layer precooked chicken and corn in husks, both wrapped in foil, atop the seafood. Place a thicker layer of rockweed atop the food to create steam for flavor. Cover all this with wet burlap bags or canvas. To hold in the heat, shovel sand on top of the bags. Allow several hours for the clambake to steam.

If you don't have access to a sandy beach, have a backyard clambake. Cooking the foods separately on a grill is the fastest and easiest method; however, this loses the flavor of rockweed. To retain this flavor, layer the foods in a large container the same as for beach clambakes. Or wrap individual servings of all the foods and rockweed in foil; grill over coals.

On the All-American roster

← *Feast on this modern, inland version of the clambake in your own backyard. Individual Clambake features the favorites of an authentic New England clambake —clams, lobster, chicken, and corn on the cob.*

Whichever method you use, be sure to have enough paper plates, napkins, and cups on hand. Plan about four plates per person—one for each item. Since most of the eating is done with the fingers, have plenty of large, sturdy paper napkins. Provide hot cups for the clam broth and melted butter, and have cold cups handy for the beverages.

With a party such as this, the entertainment does not need to be planned. General conversation, story-swapping, and singing (you might ask someone to bring their guitar) will develop naturally with good food and the informal atmosphere that has been created.

INDIVIDUAL CLAMBAKE

Seafoods have authentic flavor from rockweed—

48 soft-shelled clams in shells
8 whole live lobsters
4 2- to 2½-pound ready-to-cook broiler-fryer chickens, halved
½ cup butter or margarine, melted
8 whole ears of corn
Rockweed
1 pound butter, melted

Thoroughly wash clams in shells. Rinse off lobsters with salt water. For chickens, break joints of drumstick, hip, and wing so birds will stay flat. Brush chickens with the ½ cup melted butter; partially cook by broiling over *hot* coals, skin side down, for 5 minutes. Turn back husks of corn and strip off silk with a stiff brush. Lay husks back in place.

Tear off sixteen 3-foot lengths of 18-inch wide heavy foil. Place 1 sheet crosswise over a second sheet. Repeat making total of 8 sets. Lay a handful of rockweed in center of each set. Cut eight 18-inch squares cheesecloth; place 1 square atop rockweed.

For each package arrange the following: 6 live clams in shells, 1 live lobster, 1 precooked chicken half, and 1 ear of corn. Securely tie cheesecloth, opposite ends together. Seal the foil, opposite ends together, using the drugstore wrap. Place on grill, seam side up, over *hot* coals and cook for 45 minutes.

To test for doneness, the chicken drumstick should move up and down easily in socket. When the chicken is done, the clambake is ready. Serve with individual cups of hot, melted butter. Makes 8 servings.

LOBSTER WITH FRUIT STUFFING

  2 medium oranges
  2 cubs dry bread cubes (3 slices)
  ½ cup chopped, peeled apple
  3 tablespoons butter, melted
  2 1½-pound live lobsters
  ¼ cup butter, melted

Peel, section, and dice oranges, reserving ¼ cup juice. Toss together bread cubes, diced orange, reserved juice, apple, 3 tablespoons melted butter, and ¼ teaspoon salt.

Plunge live lobsters head first into enough boiling, salted water to cover. Cook 2 minutes. Remove from pan; place lobsters on backs on cutting board. Cut in half lengthwise: draw knife from head down to base of abdomen. Discard all organs in body section except brownish green liver and red coral roe (in females only). Remove black vein that runs down to tail. Crack large claws and spread body open. Fill each lobster cavity with stuffing. Place lobsters, shell side down, on baking sheet. Baste lobster with ¼ cup melted butter. Bake at 350° for 30 to 35 minutes, brushing with butter once or twice during baking. Baste with remaining butter just before serving. Serves 2.

LOBSTER WITH OYSTER STUFFING

Cook ¼ cup chopped celery, ¼ cup chopped onion, and 1 bay leaf in 2 tablespoons butter till tender. Discard bay leaf. Add 3 cups dry bread cubes and 1 tablespoon snipped parsley; mix. Drain ½ pint shucked oysters, reserving liquid; chop oysters. To bread mixture add oysters; 1 beaten egg; ½ teaspoon salt; ¼ teaspoon dried rosemary leaves, crushed; and dash pepper. Add milk to oyster liquid to make 3 tablespoons; add enough to stuffing to moisten.

Plunge four 1½-pound live lobsters head first into enough boiling, salted water to cover. Cook 2 minutes. Remove from pan; place lobsters on backs on cutting board. Cut in half lengthwise: draw sharp knife from head down to base of abdomen. Discard all organs in body section except brownish green liver and red coral roe. Remove black vein. Crack large claws and spread body open. Fill each lobster cavity with stuffing. Place, shell side down, on baking sheet. Baste with ¼ cup melted butter. Bake at 350° for 30 to 35 minutes; brush with butter once or twice during baking. Serves 4.

MUSHROOM-STUFFED LOBSTER

  2 live lobsters
  ½ cup butter or margarine, melted
  ¼ cup dry sherry
  2 tablespoons sliced green onion
  ¼ teaspoon salt
    Dash garlic powder
  1 6-ounce can sliced mushrooms, drained
  1 cup soft bread crumbs
  1 tablespoon butter, melted

Plunge live lobsters head first into enough boiling, salted water to cover. Bring to boiling; reduce heat and simmer 20 minutes. Remove at once. Place on backs on cutting board. Cut in half lengthwise: draw knife from head down to base of abdomen. Discard all organs in body section except brownish green liver and red coral roe (in females only). Remove black vein. Crack large claws. Remove meat from body and claws. Clean and reserve whole shells.

Coarsely chop the meat. Add the ½ cup melted butter, sherry, onion, salt, garlic powder, and dash pepper. Stir in mushrooms, roe, and liver. Stuff shells with mixture. Combine bread crumbs and 1 tablespoon butter. Sprinkle over stuffing. Place in shallow baking pan and bake at 350° for 30 to 35 minutes. Makes 2 servings.

LOBSTER Á LA THERMIDOR

  4 8-ounce frozen lobster tails
  3 tablespoons butter or margarine
  3 tablespoons all-purpose flour
  1 cup milk
  ¼ cup sauterne
  ¼ cup shredded process Swiss cheese
  2 tablespoons grated Parmesan cheese

Drop frozen lobster tails into boiling, salted water to cover. Return to boiling; simmer 10 minutes. Drain and remove meat from shells. Chop meat coarsely. Set meat and shells aside.

In saucepan melt butter; blend in flour and dash pepper. Add milk all at once. Cook quickly, stirring constantly, till mixture is thickened and bubbly. Add wine and Swiss cheese. Stir till cheese melts. Reserve ¼ cup sauce; mix remaining sauce and chopped lobster together. Spoon into shells. Spread reserved sauce atop and sprinkle with Parmesan cheese. Broil till the tops brown slightly, generally about 8 minutes. Makes 4 servings.

Cut lobster tails, *while partially frozen, through the hard top shell, then spread open, butterfly-style, to expose the meat for broiling and basting. This makes the Citrus-Buttered Lobster attractive and easier to eat.*

CITRUS-BUTTERED LOBSTER

    4 6- or 8-ounce frozen lobster tails
              • • •
¼ cup butter or margarine, melted
 2 teaspoons lemon juice
½ teaspoon grated orange peel
¼ teaspoon salt
    Dash ground ginger
    Dash paprika
    Lemon wedges

With a sharp, heavy knife, cut down through center of hard top shell of partially thawed lobster tails. Cut through meat, but not through under shell. Spread open, butterfly-style, so lobster meat is on top. Place tails on broiler pan, shell side down. Combine melted butter, lemon juice, orange peel, salt, ginger, and paprika. Brush over meat. Broil 4 inches from heat till meat loses its translucency and can be flaked easily when tested with a fork, about 17 to 20 minutes. Loosen meat from shell by inserting fork between shell and meat. Serve with lemon wedges. Makes 4 servings.

CURRIED LOBSTER

    6 4-ounce frozen lobster tails
              • • •
 2 tablespoons finely chopped onion
 3 tablespoons butter or margarine
 3 tablespoons all-purpose flour
¾ teaspoon salt
½ teaspoon curry powder
¼ teaspoon paprika
 2 cups milk
    Hot cooked rice

Drop frozen lobster tails into boiling, salted water to cover. Return to boiling; reduce heat and simmer 5 to 6 minutes. Drain; cut down both sides of lobster tail to remove thin underside membrane. Remove meat; cut into pieces.

In saucepan cook onion in butter till tender but not brown. Blend in flour, salt, curry, and paprika. Add milk all at once. Cook and stir till thickened and bubbly; cook 1 minute more. Stir in lobster; heat through. Serve over hot cooked rice with curry condiments—chutney, raisins, and coconut, if desired. Serves 4.

LOBSTER AND MUSHROOMS

>   3 tablespoons butter or margarine
>   5 ounces fresh mushrooms, sliced
>   (2½ cups)
>   1 tablespoon all-purpose flour
>   1 8-ounce can tomatoes, cut up
>   1 5-ounce can lobster, drained and
>   broken into chunks
>   2 teaspoons snipped chives
>   ¼ teaspoon salt
>   Hot cooked rice

Melt butter in skillet. Add mushrooms; sprinkle with flour and mix. Cover and cook over low heat till tender, about 8 minutes. Add tomatoes, lobster, chives, and salt; heat through. Serve over rice. Makes 4 servings.

CREAMED LOBSTER AND CLAMS

>   3 tablespoons sliced green onion
>   3 tablespoons butter or margarine
>   3 tablespoons all-purpose flour
>   ½ teaspoon salt
>   ¼ teaspoon paprika
>   1½ cups milk
>   3 tablespoons sauterne
>   1 7½-ounce can minced clams, drained
>   1 5-ounce can lobster, drained and
>   broken into large pieces
>   1 3-ounce can sliced mushrooms,
>   drained
>   Toast Cups

In saucepan or chafing dish cook onion in butter or margarine till tender but not brown. Blend in flour, salt, and paprika. Add milk all at once; cook, stirring constantly, till mixture is thickened and bubbly. Place over hot water if using chafing dish. Stir in wine, clams, lobster, and mushrooms. Heat through. Serve in warm toast cups. Makes 6 servings.

Toast Cups: Trim crusts from 6 slices white bread. Spread bread with softened butter or margarine. Carefully press each slice into an *ungreased* medium muffin cup. Toast at 350° till lightly browned, 15 to 20 minutes.

LOBSTER FRITTERS

Substitute bottled sweet and sour sauce for cheese sauce to add variety—

>   1 cup sifted all-purpose flour
>   2 teaspoons baking powder
>   ½ teaspoon salt
>   1 5-ounce can lobster, drained
>   and flaked
>   ⅔ cup milk
>   1 beaten egg
>   Shortening
>   2 tablespoons butter or margarine
>   2 tablespoons all-purpose flour
>   ¼ teaspoon salt
>   Dash white pepper
>   1 cup milk
>   ¼ cup sauterne
>   4 ounces process Swiss cheese,
>   shredded (1 cup)

Sift together 1 cup flour, baking powder, and ½ teaspoon salt. Combine lobster, ⅔ cup milk, and egg. Stir into flour mixture just till moistened. Drop from tablespoon into deep, hot fat (375°). Fry a few at a time till golden, 3 to 4 minutes. Drain on paper toweling.

Melt butter in saucepan; blend in 2 tablespoons flour, ¼ teaspoon salt, and white pepper. Add 1 cup milk and wine all at once. Cook and stir till mixture is thickened and bubbly. And cheese and stir till the cheese is melted. Pass cheese sauce with fritters. Serves 6.

LOBSTER SCALLOP

>   1 beaten egg
>   1 cup coarse saltine cracker crumbs
>   ¾ cup milk
>   2 teaspoons lemon juice
>   1½ teaspoons Worcestershire sauce
>   ¼ teaspoon salt
>   1 cup flaked cooked lobster or 1
>   5-ounce can lobster, drained and
>   flaked
>   ½ cup finely chopped celery
>   1 tablespoon butter or margarine

Combine beaten egg, cracker crumbs, milk, lemon juice, Worcestershire sauce, salt, and dash pepper. Fold in lobster and celery. Turn into 2½-cup baking dish. Dot with butter. Bake at 350° for 35 minutes. Serves 3 or 4.

CHESAPEAKE IMPERIAL CRAB

Savor the delicate flavor of crab accented by a rich sauce in this specialty from the Chesapeake Restaurant in Baltimore, Maryland—

½ cup mayonnaise or salad dressing
1 slightly beaten egg
½ cup finely chopped green pepper
1 tablespoon finely chopped canned
    pimiento
1 teaspoon dry mustard
½ teaspoon salt
⅛ teaspoon white pepper
1 pound fresh or frozen cooked lump
    crab meat or 2 7½-ounce cans crab
    meat, drained and cartilage removed
Mayonnaise or salad dressing
Paprika

Thoroughly combine mayonnaise, egg, green pepper, pimiento, dry mustard, salt, and pepper. Add crab meat; stir carefully to coat. Divide mixture between 4 cleaned crab shells or individual casseroles, heaping mixture lightly. Top with thin coating of mayonnaise; sprinkle with paprika. Bake at 350° for 15 minutes. Serve hot or chilled. Makes 4 servings.

CRAB CAKES

Mix these ahead and chill till dinner time—

2 eggs
2 tablespoons mayonnaise or salad
    dressing
1 tablespoon horseradish mustard
1 tablespoon snipped parsley
1 tablespoon lemon juice
1¼ cups fine saltine cracker crumbs
2 6-ounce packages frozen crab meat,
    thawed, flaked, cartilage removed
3 tablespoons salad oil

In bowl combine eggs, mayonnaise, mustard, parsley, lemon juice, ¼ teaspoon salt, and dash pepper. Add *1 cup* crumbs and crab; blend well. Using about ⅓ cup for each, shape into six ½-inch thick patties. Coat with remaining crumbs; chill at least 30 minutes.

Heat oil in skillet. Cook patties over medium heat till golden brown on both sides, 6 to 8 minutes. Drain and serve immediately with lemon wedges, if desired. Makes 6 servings.

CRACKED CRAB AND CURRY SAUCE

Pull off the small apron-shaped piece on bottom of 4 small, whole, cooked Dungeness crabs. Pull off top shell. Remove all spongy parts and rinse well. Rinse shell; scrub with brush. Break off front 2 claws and crack. Crack small claws. Cut body lengthwise through middle and cut through back between legs. Reassemble crabs, putting top shells back on. Arrange on bed of crushed ice. Mix together 1 cup mayonnaise, 2 teaspoons curry powder, ¼ teaspoon Worcestershire sauce, and few drops bottled hot pepper sauce. Serve with crabs. Provide picks to remove leg meat. Serves 4.

BARBECUED KING CRAB LEGS

¼ cup butter or margarine, melted
¼ cup snipped parsley
¼ cup lemon juice
1 tablespoon prepared mustard
2 pounds frozen king crab legs,
    thawed and shelled

Combine butter, parsley, lemon juice, mustard, and ¼ teaspoon salt. Brush the mixture on crab meat. Place crab legs on grill about 4 inches from *medium* coals. Brush with butter mixture and turn occasionally till heated through, about 5 to 8 minutes. Makes 6 servings.

Crack king crab legs *at the joints with a nutcracker and then push out the meat with the finger or a nutpick. Keep the meat in the largest pieces possible.*

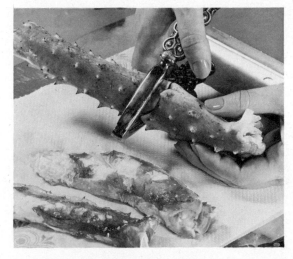

CRAB OR LOBSTER NEWBURG

    6 tablespoons butter
    2 tablespoons all-purpose flour
 1½ cups light cream
    3 beaten egg yolks
    1 7½-ounce can crab meat or 1 5-
        ounce can lobster, drained and
        broken into large pieces
    3 tablespoons dry white wine
    2 teaspoons lemon juice
      Pastry Petal Cups or toast points
      Paprika

Melt butter in saucepan; blend in flour. Add cream all at once. Cook, stirring constantly, till sauce thickens and bubbles. Stir small amount of hot mixture into egg yolks; return to hot mixture. Cook, stirring constantly, till thickened. Add crab or lobster; heat through. Add wine, lemon juice, and ¼ teaspoon salt. Serve in Pastry Petal Cups or over toast points. Sprinkle with paprika. Makes 4 or 5 servings.

Pastry Petal Cups: Prepare 1 stick piecrust mix according to package directions. Roll ⅛ inch thick; cut in 2¼-inch rounds. In each of 5 muffin cups, place one round in bottom and overlap 4 rounds on sides; press together. Prick. Bake at 450° for 10 to 12 minutes. Cool.

CRAB RAREBIT

    2 tablespoons chopped onion
    2 tablespoons chopped celery
    2 tablespoons butter or margarine
    2 tablespoons all-purpose flour
    ¼ teaspoon dry mustard
 1¼ cups milk
    1 teaspoon lemon juice
    4 ounces sharp process American
        cheese, shredded (1 cup)
    1 cup cooked crab meat or 1 7½-ounce
        can crab meat, drained, flaked, and
        cartilage removed
      Toast points or English muffins

Cook onion and celery in butter till tender but not brown. Stir in flour, dry mustard, and ⅛ teaspoon salt. Add milk all at once. Cook and stir till thickened and bubbly. Reduce heat; stir in lemon juice and cheese till melted. Fold in crab meat. Heat through, but do not boil. Serve at once over hot toast points or toasted English muffin halves. Makes 6 servings.

CRAB IN SOUR CREAM

    1 6-ounce package frozen crab meat
        or 1 7½-ounce can crab meat
    1 cup dairy sour cream
    2 tablespoons all-purpose flour
    1 beaten egg
    1 tablespoon chopped green onion
    1 teaspoon prepared horseradish
    ½ teaspoon paprika
    ¼ teaspoon salt
      Few drops bottled hot pepper sauce
      Hot cooked rice or 6 patty shells

Thaw frozen crab meat. Drain crab, remove cartilage, and cut into ½-inch pieces. In saucepan blend sour cream and flour; stir in egg. Add crab, onion, horseradish, paprika, salt, and hot pepper sauce. Cook mixture, stirring gently, till hot; *do not boil.* Serve over hot rice or in patty shells. Makes 3 or 4 servings.

CRAB SUPPER PIE

    4 ounces natural Swiss cheese,
        shredded (1 cup)
    1 unbaked 9-inch pastry shell
    1 7½-ounce can crab meat, drained,
        flaked, and cartilage removed
    2 green onions and tops, sliced
    3 beaten eggs
    1 cup light cream
    ½ teaspoon salt
    ½ teaspoon grated lemon peel
    ¼ teaspoon dry mustard
      Dash ground mace
    ¼ cup sliced almonds

Sprinkle cheese evenly over bottom of unbaked pastry shell. Top with crab meat and green onion. Combine eggs, cream, salt, lemon peel, dry mustard, and mace. Pour over crab meat. Top with almonds. Bake at 325° till set, about 45 minutes. Remove from oven and let stand 10 minutes before serving. Makes 6 servings.

Related to the quiche

Include Crab Supper Pie on the list of main dishes for → *elegant meals. It combines the basic quiche—a custard filled pastry—with delicate flakes of crab meat and sports a topping of slivered almonds.*

CAPE COD ROOM CRAB AU GRATIN

Plan a dinner party around this dish from the Cape Cod Room at the Drake Hotel in Chicago —

  1½ pounds fresh or frozen crab meat or
      3 7½-ounce cans crab meat
  ¼ cup chopped shallot or green onion
  ¼ cup butter or margarine
  1 cup light cream
     Salt
     Pepper
  ¼ cup grated Parmesan cheese

Thaw or drain crab meat. Remove cartilage; cut into chunks. Cook crab and shallots or onion in butter 5 minutes. Add cream, and salt and pepper to taste. Heat through. Turn into individual oven-going serving dishes; sprinkle Parmesan cheese over the top. Bake at 350° for 5 minutes. Makes 4 servings.

CRAB AND VEAL OSCAR

  1½ pounds veal tenderloin, well trimmed
  ¼ cup all-purpose flour
  ¾ teaspoon salt
     Dash pepper
  12 ounces fresh or frozen king crab legs,
      thawed and shelled (see page 99)
  2 tablespoons all-purpose flour
  1 well-beaten egg
  ½ cup soft bread crumbs
  ¼ cup butter or margarine
  ½ cup sauterne
  1 cup Béarnaise Sauce

Cut tenderloin into 8 pieces. Flatten slightly with a mallet. Combine the ¼ cup flour, salt and pepper; coat pieces of veal. Dip crab meat in the 2 tablespoons flour, then in beaten egg. Roll in bread crumbs. Preheat electric skillet to 300°. Fry veal in *2 tablespoons* of the butter till golden brown, about 10 minutes. Remove to warm platter. Swish sauterne in hot skillet; simmer 1 minute. Pour over veal. Place platter of veal, uncovered, in a slow oven to keep warm.

In another skillet fry crab in remaining 2 tablespoons butter till brown, about 5 minutes. Remove from heat; place in oven to keep warm. Warm the Béarnaise Sauce. Assemble by placing one heaping teaspoon sauce over each piece of veal; top with fried crab meat. Pass remaining Béarnaise Sauce. Makes 4 to 6 servings.

GRILLED ABALONE

  1 pound fresh or frozen abalone steaks
  ⅓ cup all-purpose flour
  1 teaspoon salt
  ¼ teaspoon pepper
  1 beaten egg
  1 tablespoon milk
  1½ cups fine saltine cracker crumbs
  ¼ cup butter or margarine

Thaw frozen abalone steaks. Combine flour, salt, and pepper. Combine egg and milk. Dip steaks in flour mixture and then in egg mixture. Coat each steak with cracker crumbs. Melt butter or margarine in skillet; cook steaks 1 minute on each side. *Do not overcook.* Drain on paper toweling Serve piping hot. Serves 4.

ORIENTAL ABALONE

  1 pound fresh or frozen abalone steaks
  1 chicken bouillon cube
  1 cup boiling water
        • • •
  1 5- or 6-ounce can water chestnuts,
      drained and sliced
  ½ cup sliced fresh mushrooms
  ½ cup bias-cut celery slices
  ⅓ cup diced green pepper
        • • •
  1 tablespoon soy sauce
  1 tablespoon lemon juice or
      dry white wine
  2 tablespoons cornstarch
     Dash ground ginger
     Hot cooked rice

Thaw frozen abalone; cut steaks into 1-inch strips. In saucepan dissolve bouillon cube in water. Add water chestnuts, mushrooms, celery, and green pepper. Cover and simmer 5 minutes. Blend soy sauce, lemon juice or wine, cornstarch, and ginger together. Add to mixture in saucepan and stir till thickened. Add the abalone strips and cook till tender, about 3 to 5 minutes. *Do not overcook.* Serve over fluffy hot cooked rice. Makes 4 servings.

FRIED SQUID

2 pounds fresh or frozen squid
1 slightly beaten egg
¼ cup milk
⅔ cup fine saltine cracker crumbs
¼ cup shortening

Thaw frozen squid. Clean and cut off head. Skin body portion, removing fins. Slit hollow body cavity; flatten and scrape clean with knife. Rinse well; pat dry. Combine egg and milk. Mix crumbs, ½ teaspoon salt, and ¼ teaspoon pepper. Dip squid into egg mixture; then coat with crumbs. Heat shortening in heavy skillet. Add squid and cook quickly till done, about 2 minutes per side. Makes 6 servings.

OVEN-FRIED FROG LEGS

2 pounds fresh or frozen frog legs
¼ cup butter or margarine, melted
⅔ cup fine saltine cracker crumbs

Thaw frozen frog legs. Secure frog legs at joints with string. Brush with melted butter or margarine; then roll in cracker crumbs.* Place in single layer on well-greased shallow baking pan. Bake at 375° till done, about 1 hour. Do not turn. Remove strings and serve with lemon wedges, if desired. Makes 6 servings.

*Or substitute one envelope seasoned coating mix for the cracker crumbs and omit the butter. Use mix according to package directions.

FROG LEGS WITH SAUCE

2 pounds fresh or frozen frog legs
½ cup milk
½ cup all-purpose flour
¾ cup butter or margarine
¼ cup slivered almonds
2 teaspoons lemon juice
¼ cup snipped parsley

Thaw frozen frog legs. Dip frog legs in milk, then in flour. In skillet brown frog legs in ½ cup butter for 10 to 15 minutes. If legs are large cook, covered, 15 minutes longer; remove to warm platter. Season with salt and pepper. Add remaining butter and almonds to skillet; brown lightly. Add lemon juice. Pour sauce over frog legs. Top with parsley. Makes 6 servings.

ESCARGOTS BOURGUIGNONNE

Discover how easily this gourmet dish is made —

½ cup butter or margarine, softened
1 tablespoon thinly sliced green onion
1 tablespoon snipped parsley
1 small clove garlic, minced
⅛ teaspoon salt
Dash pepper
1 can snails (12 snails — about 3 ounces)
2 teaspoons fine dry bread crumbs
¼ cup dry white wine
French bread

Combine butter or margarine, green onion, snipped parsley, minced garlic, salt, and dash pepper; blend together. Thoroughly drain snails. Rinse snails and 12 snail shells. Place a little of the green butter mixture in bottom of each snail shell. Add a snail and more butter mixture. Sprinkle opening of each shell lightly with bread crumbs. Place 6 filled shells on each of 2 snail dishes; pour 2 tablespoons wine in bottom of each dish. Bake at 400° for 8 minutes.

To eat, remove snail from shell with small fork, pouring liquid into the snail plate. Eat snail. Dip French bread in wine mixture in plate and eat. Makes 2 servings.

ESCARGOTS MONACO

¼ cup butter or margarine, softened
1 clove garlic, minced
12 large fresh mushroom crowns
2 cans snails (24 snails — about 6 ounces)
4 teaspoons grated Parmesan cheese
2 tablespoons snipped parsley

Combine butter or margarine and garlic; spread *half* the mixture in bottom of shallow oven-going serving dish. Dot mushroom crowns with remaining garlic butter; place in baking dish. Drain and rinse snails. Fill each mushroom with two snails; sprinkle with Parmesan and parsley. Broil 5 to 7 inches from heat till heated through, 5 to 6 minutes. Makes 4 servings.

SEAFOOD WITH WINE SAUCE

  French bread or hard rolls
1 12-ounce package frozen scallops,
  thawed
36 shucked mussels or oysters
1 beaten egg
¼ cup milk
1 cup fine saltine cracker crumbs
½ teaspoon salt
  Shortening

• • •

¾ cup sauterne
¼ cup water
2 tablespoons snipped parsley
½ teaspoon instant minced onion
¾ teaspoon salt
⅛ teaspoon white pepper
2 tablespoons butter or margarine
3 tablespoons all-purpose flour
1 cup milk
2 ounces process Swiss cheese,
  grated (½ cup)

Cut bread in bite-sized pieces, each having a crust on one side. Rinse scallops. Drain scallops and mussels or oysters; dry between paper toweling. Combine egg and the ¼ cup milk. Mix the cracker crumbs, ½ teaspoon salt, and dash pepper together. Dip seafoods into the egg mixture, then roll in the crumbs. Shake off excess crumbs. Fry in deep, hot fat (350°) till golden, 2 minutes for scallops and 3 minutes for mussels or oysters. Drain on paper toweling. Keep fried seafoods warm in slow oven.

Combine wine, water, parsley, instant onion, ¾ teaspoon salt, and ⅛ teaspoon white pepper. Let stand 15 to 20 minutes. Melt butter in saucepan; blend in flour. Add wine mixture and 1 cup milk all at once. Cook and stir till mixture is thickened and bubbly. Remove from heat. Add cheese, stirring till melted. Season with additional salt and pepper, if desired.

To serve, pour into candle warmer dish and keep hot. Spear bread and seafood with long forks; swirl in sauce. Makes 6 servings.

Seafood, fondue-style

← *Dipping fried scallops, fried oysters or mussels, and cubes of French bread into a fondue sauce changes a dinner into a party. Seafood with Wine Sauce provides a common activity plus a conversation piece.*

TERIYAKI SCALLOPS

1 pound fresh or frozen scallops
½ cup soy sauce
¼ cup dry sherry
2 tablespoons sugar
2 tablespoons salad oil
¾ teaspoon ground ginger
1 clove garlic, crushed

Thaw frozen scallops. Rinse and cut large scallops in half. Combine remaining ingredients; pour over scallops in shallow dish. Marinate 30 minutes at room temperature. Drain scallops, reserving marinade. Thread scallops on 4 skewers. Place on greased shallow baking pan. Bake at 450° for 15 minutes, turning and basting several times with marinade. Sprinkle with snipped parsley, if desired. Makes 4 servings.

SCALLOPS ELEGANT

1 pound fresh or frozen scallops
½ cup finely chopped celery
¼ cup chopped onion
1 small clove garlic, minced
2 tablespoons butter or margarine
¼ cup fine saltine cracker crumbs
1 tablespoon snipped parsley
1 tablespoon butter or margarine
1 tablespoon all-purpose flour
¼ teaspoon paprika
⅛ teaspoon salt
½ cup milk
2 tablespoons dry sherry
¼ cup shredded process Swiss cheese

Cook scallops; cut large scallops in half. In saucepan cook celery, onion, and garlic in 2 tablespoons butter till tender but not brown. Stir in scallops, cracker crumbs, and parsley. Turn into an 8-inch pie plate. Melt the 1 tablespoon butter in same saucepan. Blend in flour, paprika, and ⅛ teaspoon salt. Add milk all at once. Cook and stir till mixture is thickened and bubbly. Remove from heat; stir in sherry. Pour sauce over scallop mixture; sprinkle cheese atop. Bake at 425° for 15 minutes. Serves 4.

BUILD THE MAIN COURSE AROUND FISH

MINT-STUFFED STRIPED BASS

1 4-pound fresh or frozen dressed
    striped bass or other fish
3 cups dry bread cubes (4 slices)
1 teaspoon dried mint leaves, crushed
¼ teaspoon dried basil leaves, crushed
1 clove garlic, minced
3 tablespoons butter or margarine
2 teaspoons lemon juice
2 tablespoons salad oil
2 tablespoons lemon juice

Thaw frozen fish. Place in well-greased shallow baking pan. Combine bread cubes, mint, ½ teaspoon salt, basil, and dash pepper. In small saucepan cook garlic in butter 1 minute. Add to stuffing mixture with ¼ cup water and 2 teaspoons lemon juice; toss lightly. Stuff fish loosely with mixture. Combine salad oil and 2 tablespoons lemon juice. Brush fish with mixture. Bake at 350° for 50 to 60 minutes. Baste occasionally with oil mixture. Serves 8.

STUFFED TROUT

1 3-pound fresh or frozen dressed trout
2 cups dry bread cubes
⅓ cup finely chopped onion
⅓ cup dairy sour cream
¼ cup chopped dill pickle (optional)
½ teaspoon paprika
¼ cup salad oil

Thaw frozen fish. Sprinkle generously with salt and pepper. Place fish in well-greased shallow baking pan. Combine bread, onion, sour cream, pickle, paprika, ½ teaspoon salt, and ⅛ teaspoon pepper. Stuff fish loosely with mixture. Brush fish generously with oil; cover with foil. Bake at 350° for 45 to 60 minutes. Remove fish to serving platter. Makes 6 servings.

Almost any fish can be cooked by any method if allowances are made for the fat content of the fish during cooking.

CORN-STUFFED WHITEFISH

1 3-pound fresh or frozen dressed
    whitefish or other fish, boned
¼ cup chopped onion
3 tablespoons chopped green pepper
1 tablespoon butter or margarine
1 12-ounce can whole kernel corn,
    drained*
1 cup soft bread crumbs (1½ slices)
2 tablespoons chopped canned pimiento
⅛ teaspoon dried thyme leaves, crushed
2 tablespoons salad oil

Thaw frozen fish; dry fish. Sprinkle inside generously with salt. Place fish in well-greased shallow baking pan. In saucepan cook onion and green pepper in butter till tender. Stir in corn, crumbs, pimiento, ½ teaspoon salt, and thyme. Stuff fish loosely with mixture. Brush fish generously with oil; cover with foil. Bake at 350° till fish flakes easily when tested with a fork, 45 to 60 minutes. Remove to serving platter, using two spatulas. Serves 6.

*Or substitute one 12-ounce can vacuum-packed corn with peppers and omit the green pepper and pimiento from ingredient list.

PANFRIED SMELTS

Use 1 pound fresh or frozen smelts. Thaw if frozen. Rinse and wipe dry. Dip in ¼ cup milk, then in a mixture of ½ cup cornmeal and ½ teaspoon salt. In large skillet cook smelts in ¼ cup butter till done, about 5 minutes on each side. Sprinkle 2 tablespoons snipped parsley over fish; serve with lemon. Serves 2 or 3.

Indian summer feast

*Stuff a whole fish with an herb-seasoned mixture of →
corn, green pepper, and bits of pimiento. Be sure to
divide this colorful stuffing among the dinner plates
when carving Corn-Stuffed Whitefish.*

Menu

FISH FRY

Fried Mullet Parmesan

Corn on the Cob

Tossed Salad   Salad Dressing

French Bread   Butter

Ice Cream

Milk   Coffee

Stage a fish fry in your backyard. Whatever the size of your group, this menu adjusts to the amount needed. Plan on one ½-pound pan-dressed fish per person. Cook mullet in large skillets over the fire. Or select the recipe for Sesame Rainbow Trout and cook the fish in a broiler basket over coals.

To go along with the main feature, have several hot ears of corn for each person. Make a large bowl of tossed salad and have assorted salad dressings on hand. Then, heat loaves of French bread in foil. For the grand finale to this cookout feast, open freezers of homemade ice cream and scoop up generous servings.

FRIED MULLET PARMESAN

    6 fresh or frozen pan-dressed mullet or
       other fish (about ½ pound each)
½ cup all-purpose flour
⅛ teaspoon garlic salt
 1 beaten egg
¼ cup milk
 1 cup fine saltine cracker crumbs
¼ cup grated Parmesan cheese
 2 tablespoons snipped parsley
    Shortening

Thaw frozen fish. Dry fish thoroughly. Coat fish with a mixture of flour and garlic salt. Dip into a mixture of the egg and milk; then roll in a mixture of crumbs, cheese, and parsley. Heat small amount of shortening in a large skillet. Place fish in skillet in a single layer. Fry over medium heat till browned on one side, 4 to 5 minutes. Turn; fry till fish browns and flakes easily when tested with a fork, 4 to 5 minutes. Drain. Serves 6.

ORANGE-RICE STUFFED PERCH

    4 fresh or frozen pan-dressed perch or
       other pan-dressed fish (about ¾
       pound each)
½ cup chopped celery
 2 tablespoons butter or margarine
½ cup uncooked long-grain rice
¾ cup water
½ teaspoon grated orange peel
½ cup orange juice
 1 teaspoon lemon juice
½ teaspoon salt
 1 tablespoon snipped parsley
       • • •
 2 tablespoons butter or margarine,
       melted
 2 tablespoons orange juice

Thaw frozen fish. In small saucepan cook celery in 2 tablespoons butter till tender. Stir in rice, water, orange peel, ½ cup orange juice, lemon juice, and salt. Bring to boiling; cover and reduce heat. Simmer till rice is tender, 15 to 20 minutes. Stir in snipped parsley.

Sprinkle fish cavities with salt. Stuff *each* fish with about ½ cup orange-rice mixture. Tie or skewer closed and place in greased, shallow baking pan. Combine 2 tablespoons melted butter with 2 tablespoons orange juice. Brush over fish. Bake, uncovered, at 350° till fish flakes easily when tested with a fork, about 30 to 35 minutes. Baste with butter and orange juice mixture during baking. Makes 4 servings.

SMELTS IN BARBECUE SAUCE

    1 pound fresh or frozen smelts
    1 8-ounce can tomato sauce
½ cup chopped onion
 2 tablespoons brown sugar
 2 tablespoons vinegar
 1 tablespoon Worcestershire sauce
 1 tablespoon water
 2 teaspoons prepared mustard
¼ teaspoon salt

Thaw frozen smelts; clean, rinse and wipe dry. Combine all ingredients except smelts. Marinate smelts in tomato mixture, covered, in refrigerator several hours. In large skillet bring smelts and tomato mixture to boiling. Reduce heat and simmer, uncovered, till fish are done, 8 to 10 minutes. Makes 3 or 4 servings.

PLANKED FISH

1 3-pound fresh or frozen dressed fish
2 tablespoons salad oil
2 tablespoons lemon juice
4 cups hot mashed potatoes*
3 tablespoons butter or margarine, melted
2 beaten egg yolks
1 10-ounce package frozen peas, cooked and drained

Thaw frozen fish. Sprinkle cavity generously with salt and pepper. Place on seasoned plank or well-greased bake-and-serve platter. (To season plank, soak plank a few minutes in hot water. Dry. Brush with salad oil.) Combine the salad oil, lemon juice, 1 teaspoon salt, and dash pepper. Brush mixture over fish. Bake at 350° for 30 minutes.

Meanwhile, combine mashed potatoes, 1 *tablespoon* melted butter, egg yolks, and salt and pepper to taste; mix well. Using a pastry bag and large star tip, fill with potato mixture. Pipe potatoes on plank making a border around fish and a pocket for the peas. Drizzle remaining melted butter over the potatoes. Return plank to oven and bake till fish flakes easily when tested with a fork, about 15 to 30 minutes. Spoon hot peas into pocket. Serves 6.

*If using instant mashed potatoes, decrease milk in package directions by 2 tablespoons.

When going fishing *take a portable grill and the sauce mixed-up in a jar. Then, you're prepared to cook Sesame Rainbow Trout as soon as the fish are caught.*

Wrap foil *around the whole, stuffed fish before baking. Foil keeps Luau Fish Bake moist and makes it easy to move the fish from baking pan to serving dish.*

SESAME RAINBOW TROUT

Use four ½-pound fresh or frozen pan-dressed rainbow trout or other fish. Thaw frozen fish. Season generously with salt and pepper. Wrap tails with greased foil. Place in well-greased wire broiler basket. Combine ¼ cup salad oil, 2 tablespoons toasted sesame seed, 2 tablespoons lemon juice, ½ teaspoon salt, and dash pepper. Brush fish, inside and out, with the sesame mixture. Grill about 4 inches from *medium-hot* coals for 8 to 10 minutes. Repeat brushing. Turn and grill till fish test done, about 8 to 10 minutes longer. Remove foil. Serves 4.

LUAU FISH BAKE

Use one 2-pound fresh or frozen dressed trout or other fish, boned. Thaw frozen fish. Season fish cavity with salt. Brush with lemon juice. In small saucepan cook ¼ cup diced celery, ¼ cup chopped green pepper, and 2 tablespoons chopped onion in 3 tablespoons butter till tender. Toss with 1½ cups herb-seasoned stuffing mix and 3 tablespoons water.

Place fish on greased heavy foil; stuff cavity. Brush with ¼ cup bottled barbecue sauce. Seal foil. Place in shallow baking pan. Bake at 350° for 45 minutes. Turn back foil. Bake till fish tests done, about 15 minutes. Brush with ¼ cup bottled barbecue sauce. Serves 4.

CATFISH WITH TOMATO SAUCE

Another time, try pan-dressed trout—

3 fresh or frozen dressed catfish or
   other fish (about 1 pound each)
• • •
1 8-ounce can tomato sauce
2 tablespoons salad oil
1 teaspoon cheese-garlic salad dressing
   mix or Italian salad dressing mix
½ teaspoon salt
   Grated Parmesan cheese

Thaw frozen fish. Place in well-greased shallow baking pan. Combine tomato sauce, salad oil, dressing mix, and salt. Brush inside cavities with sauce; pour remaining sauce over and around fish. Sprinkle with Parmesan cheese. Bake at 350° till fish flakes easily when tested with a fork, about 40 to 45 minutes. Serves 6.

TROUT WITH SALAMI TOPPING

Salami adds unique flavor to fish—

4 fresh or frozen pan-dressed trout or
   other fish (about ½ pound each)
⅓ cup all-purpose flour
½ teaspoon paprika
¼ teaspoon salt
   Dash pepper
• • •
½ cup butter or margarine
4 ounces sliced salami
1 tablespoon lemon juice

Thaw frozen fish; dry with paper toweling. Combine flour, paprika, salt, and pepper. Roll fish in flour mixture. In a large heavy skillet melt the butter. Place fish in skillet in a single layer. Fry till browned on one side, 4 to 5 minutes. Turn carefully. Brown second side and cook till fish flakes easily when tested with a fork, about 4 to 5 minutes longer. Remove fish to platter; keep warm. Cut salami into thin strips; cook salami in butter in skillet for 1 to 2 minutes. Stir in lemon juice. Spoon over fish. Serves 4.

MIXED FISH FRY

3 fresh or frozen pan-dressed trout,
   perch, or whiting (½ pound each)
1 pound fresh or frozen haddock fillets
½ pound eel, cleaned
16 fresh or frozen jumbo shrimp in shells
½ cup all-purpose flour
1 teaspoon salt
⅛ teaspoon pepper
2 beaten eggs
1½ cups fine dry bread crumbs
   Shortening

Thaw frozen fish. Cut haddock into large chunks. Cut eel, crosswise, into 2-inch pieces. Shell shrimp, leaving last section and tail intact. Combine flour, salt, and pepper. Combine eggs and ¼ cup water. Dip seafoods into flour and then in egg mixture; roll in bread crumbs. Heat small amount of shortening in a large skillet. Place fish in skillet in a single layer. Fry on one side, 4 to 5 minutes. Turn and fry till brown and fish flakes easily when tested with a fork, about 4 to 5 minutes. Fry shrimp till done, about 3 to 5 minutes. Drain. Serves 8.

STEAMED CARP

1 3-pound fresh or frozen dressed
   carp
1 medium onion, sliced
2 sprigs parsley
1 bay leaf
3 whole peppercorns

Thaw frozen fish. Pour water into poacher or large skillet to depth of ½ inch. Add onion, parsley, bay leaf, peppercorns, and salt (use ½ teaspoon salt per cup of water). Bring to boiling. Place carp on greased rack; set into poacher. Cover and cook till fish flakes easily when tested with a fork, about 20 to 25 minutes. Drain; serve hot or cold with Horseradish Sauce (see page 154). Makes 6 servings.

Traditional Italian Christmas dinner

Feast on a fish dinner during the yuletide season or → any other time of the year. Use the fried, pan-dressed fish, shrimp, eel, and chunks of fillets in Mixed Fish Fry or substitute favorite fish that are in season.

DEVILED HADDOCK

2 pounds fresh or frozen haddock fillets
   or other fish fillets
2 tablespoons butter, melted
4 ounces natural Cheddar cheese,
   shredded (1 cup)
¼ cup chili sauce
1 teaspoon prepared mustard
½ teaspoon prepared horseradish
½ teaspoon Worcestershire sauce

Thaw frozen fish. Cut into 6 portions. Arrange fillets in a single layer on well-greased rack of broiler pan, tucking under any thin edges. Brush fillets with melted butter; sprinkle with salt and pepper. Broil 4 inches from heat till fish flakes easily when tested with a fork, 10 to 15 minutes; do not turn. Blend cheese, chili sauce, mustard, horseradish, and Worcestershire sauce; spread over fillets. Broil to melt the cheese, about 1 to 3 minutes longer. Serves 6.

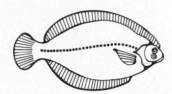

CHEESE-SAUCED STRIPED BASS

2 pounds fresh or frozen striped bass
   fillets or steaks or other fish
   fillets or steaks
¼ cup butter or margarine
¼ cup all-purpose flour
¼ teaspoon garlic salt
   Dash pepper
1½ cups milk
½ cup dry white wine
3 tablespoons grated Parmesan cheese
   Dash paprika

Thaw frozen fish. Cut into 6 portions. Place in shallow baking dish. In saucepan melt butter. Blend in flour, garlic salt, and dash pepper. Add milk and wine. Cook and stir till thickened and bubbly. Stir in *1 tablespoon* Parmesan cheese. Pour sauce over fish. Bake at 350° till fish flakes easily when tested with a fork, 20 to 25 minutes. Sprinkle remaining Parmesan cheese and paprika over top. Place under broiler just till cheese is browned and sauce is slightly bubbly, 1 minute. Makes 6 servings.

POMPANO—SCHULER STYLE

Present this elegant, yet simple, recipe as the entrée as it's served by Win Schuler's restaurant based in Marshall, Michigan—

4 fresh or frozen pompano fillets,
   skin removed
8 ounces fresh mushrooms
16 slices bacon, partially cooked and
   drained
¼ cup butter or margarine, melted
   Paprika

Thaw fish if frozen. Wash mushrooms with cold water and cut off the stem ends. Arrange *half* the bacon strips in a single layer in 11¾ x 7½ x 1¾-inch baking dish. Place the pompano on top of bacon; sprinkle with salt. Top with remaining bacon. Put mushrooms around sides of dish. Drizzle melted butter over fillets and mushrooms. Sprinkle with paprika. Bake at 350° till fish flakes easily when tested with a fork, about 20 minutes. Makes 4 servings.

BROILED BASS STEAKS

The seasoned sauce doubles as a marinade and basting sauce during cooking—

2 pounds fresh or frozen bass steaks or
   other fish steaks
   • • •
½ cup catsup
¼ cup salad oil
¼ cup lemon juice
1 teaspoon instant minced onion
1 teaspoon Worcestershire sauce
1 teaspoon prepared mustard
½ teaspoon garlic salt
¼ teaspoon salt

Thaw frozen steaks. Cut into 6 portions. Place fish in a single layer in shallow dish. Combine catsup, salad oil, lemon juice, onion, Worcestershire sauce, mustard, garlic salt, and salt. Pour sauce over fish and let stand 1 hour at room temperature, turning once or twice. Remove fish and reserve sauce.

Place fish in a single layer on greased rack of broiler pan. Broil about 4 inches from heat till fish flakes easily when tested with a fork, 10 to 15 minutes. Baste several times during broiling with reserved sauce. Serves 6.

DILLED SALMON STEAKS

4 fresh or frozen salmon steaks
2 tablespoons lemon juice
2 teaspoons instant minced onion
¼ cup dairy sour cream
1 teaspoon grated lemon peel
½ teaspoon dried dillweed

Thaw frozen fish. Place in greased baking dish. Combine lemon juice and onion; sprinkle over fish. Season with ½ teaspoon salt and dash pepper. Bake, uncovered, at 350° till fish flakes easily when tested with a fork, about 20 minutes. Remove from oven; spread sour cream over salmon. Sprinkle with lemon peel and dill. Bake 3 minutes longer. Serve with lemon wedges, if desired. Serves 4.

SESAME-TOPPED PERCH

Use 1 pound fresh or frozen perch fillets or other fish fillets. Thaw frozen fillets. Cut into 3 or 4 portions. Place in greased 11¾x7½x1¾-inch baking pan. Sprinkle with salt. Top with ½ cup crushed round sesame bread wafers. Drizzle 3 tablespoons melted butter atop. Bake at 350° till fish flakes easily when tested with a fork, about 20 minutes. Serves 3 or 4.

BAKED TURBOT FILLETS

2 pounds fresh or frozen skinned turbot
    fillets
1 tablespoon salad oil
1 10½-ounce can condensed cream of
    mushroom soup
1 cup dairy sour cream
3 tablespoons milk
6 slices bacon, crisp-cooked and
    crumbled
3 cups hot cooked rice
¼ cup snipped parsley

Thaw frozen fish. Cut into 6 portions. Place in greased 11¾x7½x1¾-inch baking dish. Brush with oil; sprinkle with ½ teaspoon salt. Bake at 350° till fish flakes easily when tested with a fork, about 20 minutes. Meanwhile, heat soup in small saucepan over low heat. Stir in sour cream, milk, and bacon; heat. Combine rice and parsley. Place fillets atop rice. Pour sauce over all. Makes 6 servings.

Accenting salmon's flavor *with a frosting of sour cream and a dash of dill gives Dilled Salmon Steaks a gourmet flair with a minimum of effort on your part.*

ROLLED FLOUNDER FILLETS

4 fresh or frozen flounder fillets or
    other fish fillets (about 1½ pounds)
2 ounces process Swiss cheese, cut in
    4 strips
½ cup chicken broth
1 tablespoon lemon juice
    Paprika
2 tablespoons all-purpose flour
½ cup cold milk
1 beaten egg
2 tablespoons sliced almonds, toasted

Thaw frozen fish. Skin fillets. Season fish with salt and pepper. Place a Swiss cheese strip on each fillet. Roll the fillet around cheese. Fasten with wooden picks or tie securely. Place rolled fillets in shallow baking pan.

Combine chicken broth and lemon juice; pour over fish. Sprinkle fish with paprika. Bake, covered, at 350° till fish flakes easily when tested with a fork, 20 to 25 minutes. Transfer fish to warm platter. Pour sauce from baking pan into small saucepan. Thoroughly blend flour and cold milk. Stir into liquid in saucepan; cook and stir till mixture is thickened and bubbly. Stir a small amount of hot mixture into egg; return to hot mixture. Cook and stir 1 minute longer. Spoon some sauce over fish. Sprinkle with toasted almonds. Pass remaining sauce. Makes 4 servings.

Keep a package of seasoned coating mix *made especially for fish on hand and some frozen steaks so you will be prepared to serve Crumb-Crowned Halibut on short notice. Trim the cooked fish with olive and lemon kabobs.*

CRUMB-CROWNED HALIBUT

  1½ **pounds fresh or frozen halibut steaks**
      or other fish steaks
   3 **tablespoons butter or margarine,**
      melted
   1 **2-ounce package seasoned coating**
      mix for fish
      Lemon wedges
      Pimiento-stuffed olives

Thaw frozen fish. Place on rack of broiler pan or in greased baking pan. Brush with 1 *tablespoon* melted butter or margarine. Sprinkle with a little salt and pepper. Broil 5 inches from heat till fish is almost done, about 10 minutes. Brush again with 1 *tablespoon* melted butter. Stir remaining 1 tablespoon melted butter into seasoned coating mix; spread on fish. Return to broiler till brown, about 5 minutes. Spear lemon wedges and olives on picks. Use to garnish steaks. Makes 4 servings.

SOLE WITH GRAPES

   1 **pound fresh or frozen sole**
      fillets or other fish fillets
   1 **cup sauterne**
  ½ **cup light cream**
   2 **teaspoons cornstarch**
  ¼ **teaspoon salt**
  ½ **cup seedless green grapes, halved**

Thaw frozen fish. Cut into 3 or 4 portions. Place fillets in greased 10-inch skillet. Add wine. Bring to boiling; reduce heat and simmer, covered, till fish flakes easily when tested with a fork, 4 to 8 minutes. Carefully remove fish to platter; sprinkle with salt. Keep the fish warm in a slow oven. Strain the wine.

Return ⅓ cup wine to skillet. Blend together light cream, cornstarch, and salt. Stir into wine in skillet; cook and stir till thickened and bubbly. Add grapes; heat through. Spoon sauce over fillets. Makes 3 or 4 servings.

FISH AND CHIPS

This typically English pair — fried fish and potatoes — is pictured on page 80 —

> 1 pound fresh or frozen fish fillets
> 1 pound potatoes, peeled (3 potatoes)
> Shortening
> ¼ cup all-purpose flour
> ½ teaspoon salt
> 1 egg yolk
> 2 tablespoons water
> 1 tablespoon salad oil
> 1 stiffly beaten egg white
> ¼ cup all-purpose flour

Thaw frozen fish. Cut into 3 or 4 portions. Cut potatoes into uniform strips, slightly larger than for french fries. Fry potatoes in deep, hot fat (375°) till golden brown, about 7 to 8 minutes. Remove, drain, and keep warm.

Combine ¼ cup flour and salt. Make well in center; add egg yolk, water, and oil. Stir till batter is smooth. Fold in egg white. Dip fish in ¼ cup flour, then into batter. Fry in deep, hot fat (375°) till golden brown, about 1½ minutes on each side. Sprinkle fish and chips with salt. To serve, sprinkle fish with vinegar, if desired. Makes 3 or 4 servings.

CURRIED SCROD

> 1½ pounds fresh or frozen scrod
>   fillets (young haddock or cod)
> ½ cup chopped onion
> 2 tablespoons butter or margarine
>   • • •
> 1 to 1½ teaspoons curry powder
> 2 tablespoons all-purpose flour
> ¾ teaspoon salt
> 1 cup milk
> 2 tablespoons chopped canned pimiento
> 3 cups hot cooked rice

Thaw frozen fillets. Cut into 4 or 5 portions. Place fillets in 11¾x7½x1¾-inch baking dish. Cook onion in butter till tender but not brown. Stir in curry powder; heat 1 minute. Blend in flour and salt. Add milk all at once. Cook and stir till thickened and bubbly. Stir in pimiento. Pour over fish. Bake, uncovered, at 350° till fish flakes when tested with a fork, about 25 minutes. Spoon sauce over fish once or twice during baking. Serve with hot rice. Makes 4 or 5 servings.

POMPANO EN PAPILLOTE

This famous entrée is pictured on page 2 —

> 6 fresh or frozen pompano fillets
>   or other fish fillets
> 3 cups water
> 1 teaspoon salt
> 2 lemon slices
> 1 bay leaf
> ⅛ teaspoon dried thyme leaves, crushed
>   • • •
> Parchment paper
>   • • •
> ½ cup finely chopped onion
> 1 clove garlic, minced
> 2 tablespoons butter or margarine
> 3 tablespoons all-purpose flour
> ¼ teaspoon salt
>   • • •
> 2 slightly beaten egg yolks
> 2 tablespoons dry white wine
>   (optional)
> 1 7½-ounce can crab meat, drained,
>   flaked, and cartilage removed
> 4 ounces shelled shrimp, cooked and
>   chopped (⅔ cup)
> 1 3-ounce can sliced mushrooms, drained

Thaw frozen fish. Bring water, 1 teaspoon salt, lemon, bay leaf, and thyme to boiling. Add fish and poach till fish flakes easily when tested with a fork, about 15 minutes. Remove fish, reserving stock. Cut 6 pieces parchment or brown paper into heart shapes, about 9x12 inches each. Place one fillet on half of each parchment heart.

Strain stock, reserving 1½ cups. In saucepan cook onion and garlic in butter till tender. Blend in flour and ¼ teaspoon salt. Add reserved stock. Cook and stir till thickened and bubbly. Gradually stir small amount of hot mixture into beaten egg yolks; return to hot mixture. Cook and stir over low heat till mixture bubbles. Stir in wine, if desired. Stir in crab, chopped shrimp, and the drained, sliced mushrooms; heat the mixture thoroughly.

Spoon about ½ cup sauce over each fillet. Fold other half of each paper heart over fillet to form individual cases. Seal, starting at top of heart, by turning edges up and folding, twisting tip of heart to hold case closed. Place cases in shallow baking pan. Bake at 400° for 10 to 15 minutes. Cut cases open with large X cut on top; fold back each segment. Transfer paper cases to dinner plates. Makes 6 servings.

LEMON-STUFFED FISH FILLETS

  2 16-ounce packages frozen fish fillets
½ cup finely chopped celery
¼ cup chopped onion
  3 tablespoons butter or margarine
  4 cups dry bread cubes
½ teaspoon grated lemon peel
  4 teaspoons lemon juice
  1 tablespoon snipped parsley
  1 tablespoon butter, melted

Partially thaw fish; slice each block in half horizontally, making 4 rectangular pieces. Place 2 pieces in greased 13x9x2-inch baking pan. Cook celery and onion in 3 tablespoons butter till crisp-tender. Pour over bread. Add lemon peel and juice, parsley, ½ teaspoon salt, and dash pepper; toss together. Spoon half the stuffing mixture on each fillet in pan.

Top with remaining two pieces fish; brush with 1 tablespoon butter. Sprinkle with salt and paprika, if desired. Bake, covered, at 350° till fish flakes easily when tested with a fork, about 20 to 25 minutes. Makes 6 servings.

HAWAIIAN MAHIMAHI FILLETS

1½ pounds fresh or frozen mahimahi
      fillets or other fish fillets
  1 8¾-ounce can pineapple slices
  1 tablespoon soy sauce
¼ teaspoon salt
¼ cup chopped macadamia nuts

Thaw frozen fish. Remove skin and cut into 4 portions. Drain pineapple, reserving ½ cup syrup. Combine reserved syrup with soy sauce, salt, and dash pepper. Place fish in a single layer in shallow dish. Pour syrup mixture over fish. Let stand at room temperature about 30 minutes, turning once. Remove fish from sauce; reserve sauce for basting fish during cooking.

Place fish on greased rack of broiler pan and broil 4 inches from heat till fish flakes easily when tested with a fork, about 10 minutes. Brush occasionally with sauce. During last few minutes of broiling, place pineapple slices on broiler pan. Brush with pineapple sauce and heat through. Sprinkle nuts atop fish and pineapple slices. Makes 4 servings.

Discover a different way *to complement the flavor of fish with citrus fruit. Add tangy lemon juice and zesty, grated lemon peel to a bread stuffing, then sandwich this stuffing between fillets for Lemon-Stuffed Fish Fillets.*

BLUE CHEESE-SAUCED FISH

2 12-ounce packages frozen halibut
   steaks or other fish steaks
1 10-ounce can frozen condensed cream
   of shrimp soup, thawed
2 teaspoons lemon juice
½ cup dairy sour cream
⅓ cup crumbled blue cheese

Partially thaw fish. Cut into 4 or 5 portions. Place in 11x7x1½-inch baking pan. In saucepan combine soup and lemon juice; heat till bubbly. Blend in sour cream and cheese; cook over low heat till heated. Pour over fish. Bake, uncovered, at 375° till fish flakes when tested with a fork, about 30 minutes. Serves 4 or 5.

BUFFALO FISH STEAKS

1 pound fresh or frozen buffalo fish
   steaks or other fish steaks
1 10¾-ounce can condensed tomato soup
2 tablespoons snipped parsley
¼ teaspoon dried basil leaves, crushed
6 thin lemon slices

Thaw frozen steaks. Cut into 3 or 4 portions. Sprinkle fish with salt and pepper. Place steaks in well-greased 10x6x1¾-inch baking dish. Combine soup, parsley, and basil. Pour soup over fish; top with lemon slices. Bake at 350° till fish flakes easily when tested with a fork, 20 to 25 minutes. Serves 3 or 4.

BROILED SALMON EPICUREAN

2 pounds fresh or frozen salmon or
   halibut steaks
¼ cup salad oil
2 tablespoons lemon juice
½ teaspoon dried rosemary leaves,
   crushed

Thaw frozen fish. Combine remaining ingredients; shake well. Let stand at room temperature 1 hour; strain. Cut fish into 6 portions. Dip into oil mixture; sprinkle with salt and pepper. Place in a greased wire broiler basket. Grill over *medium-hot* coals about 5 to 8 minutes. Baste and turn. Brush other side; broil till fish flakes easily when tested with a fork, about 5 to 8 minutes longer. Makes 6 servings.

SAUCY CHEESE-COATED PERCH

1 pound fresh or frozen perch fillets
   or other fish fillets
¼ cup all-purpose flour
1 beaten egg
1 teaspoon salt
   Dash pepper
¼ cup fine dry bread crumbs
¼ cup grated Parmesan cheese
¼ cup shortening
1 8-ounce can tomato sauce
½ teaspoon sugar
½ teaspoon dried basil leaves, crushed

Thaw frozen fillets. Cut into 4 portions. Coat fish with flour. Dip into a mixture of egg, salt, and pepper; then dip into a mixture of bread crumbs and cheese. In skillet fry fish slowly in hot shortening till browned on one side, 4 to 5 minutes. Turn and brown other side till fish flakes easily when tested with a fork, about 4 to 5 minutes longer.

Meanwhile, combine tomato sauce, ¼ cup water, sugar, and basil in a saucepan. Simmer 10 minutes. Serve with fish. Makes 4 servings.

HAKE KABOBS

2 pounds fresh or frozen hake fillets or
   other fish fillets
1 8-ounce can peeled, small, whole,
   stewed onions, drained
1 green pepper, cut in 1-inch squares
¼ cup Italian salad dressing
¼ cup salad oil
½ teaspoon salt
3 firm tomatoes

Thaw frozen fillets. Remove skin from fish and cut into strips 1 inch wide and 4 inches long. Roll fillets, starting at narrow end; thread on long skewers with the onions and green pepper. Combine the Italian salad dressing, oil, and salt. Place kabobs on well-greased rack of broiler pan. Brush with dressing mixture and broil about 3 inches from heat for 4 to 6 minutes. Turn kabobs carefully and brush again. Broil till fish flakes easily when tested with a fork, 4 to 6 minutes longer.

Cut tomatoes into sixths and place on separate skewer. Brush with marinade and broil with fish during last 2 to 3 minutes of cooking time. Makes 6 servings.

CHARCOALED HALIBUT STEAKS

Grill steaks as pictured on the cover —

Use 5 or 6 fresh or frozen halibut steaks. Thaw frozen steaks. Combine ¼ cup melted butter or margarine, 1 teaspoon salt, and ⅛ teaspoon pepper. Place fish on greased grill or in well-greased wire broiler basket. Brush with butter. Grill over *medium-hot* coals for 5 to 8 minutes. Turn and baste with remaining butter. Grill till fish flakes easily when tested with a fork, 5 to 8 minutes. Sprinkle with paprika. Serve with Cucumber Sauce (see page 156), if desired. Makes 5 or 6 servings.

BARBECUED BASS STEAKS

Use 2 pounds fresh or frozen bass steaks. Thaw frozen fish. Cut into 6 portions. Place in single layer in shallow dish. Combine ⅓ cup salad oil with 1 tablespoon *each* toasted sesame seed, lemon juice, wine vinegar, and soy sauce. Add ½ teaspoon salt. Pour over fish. Marinate 30 minutes at room temperature; turn once. Remove fish; reserve marinade.

Place fish in well-greased wire broiler basket. Grill over *medium-hot* coals for 10 minutes. Turn and baste with marinade. Grill till fish flakes easily when tested with a fork, 5 to 8 minutes longer. Makes 6 servings.

Marinate bass steaks *in a delectable sauce of vinegar, soy sauce, and lemon juice. Use the sauce also to baste Barbecued Bass Steaks during the cooking.*

┌─────────────────────────────────┐

Menu

DIETER'S SPECIAL
Pineapple-Perch Fillets
Tomato Stuffed with Green Beans
Tossed Salad   Low-Calorie Dressing
Bread Sticks
Tapioca Pudding
Iced Tea   Coffee

└─────────────────────────────────┘

Watching your calories and enjoying good food is not always an easy combination. However, because fish is noted for being low in calories, planning menus around fish, such as this one, helps to achieve both goals.

Featuring Pineapple-Perch Fillets as an entrée will account for only 150 calories per serving. With this, serve whole tomatoes, scooped out and stuffed with a chilled mixture of seasoned green beans and mushrooms. Accompany with a crisp tossed salad with low-calorie dressing and pass bread sticks. Finish the meal with tapioca pudding made with skim milk.

When you serve imaginative menus containing fish and low-calorie foods, both dieters and non-dieters will be able to eat the same foods and enjoy their meal, too.

PINEAPPLE-PERCH FILLETS

  1 pound fresh or frozen perch fillets
  ½ cup pineapple juice
  1 tablespoon lime juice
  2 teaspoons Worcestershire sauce
  ½ teaspoon salt

Thaw frozen fish. Cut into 4 portions. Place in shallow dish. Combine pineapple juice, lime juice, Worcestershire sauce, salt, and dash pepper. Pour over fish. Marinate fish in refrigerator 1 hour, turning once.

Drain, reserving marinade. Place fillets on greased rack of broiler pan. Broil 4 inches from heat till fish flakes easily when tested with a fork , 10 to 12 minutes. Brush occasionally with marinade. Heat remaining marinade and spoon over fish before serving. Trim with lime twists, if desired. Makes 4 servings.

DEVILED BASS FILLETS

Cut 2 pounds fresh striped bass fillets into 6 portions. Place on greased rack of broiler pan. Combine ¼ cup chili sauce, 3 tablespoons melted butter, 2 tablespoons snipped chives, 1 tablespoon prepared mustard, ½ teaspoon salt, and dash bottled hot pepper sauce. Brush sauce over fish. Broil about 4 inches from heat till fish flakes easily when tested with a fork, 10 to 15 minutes. Brush fish occasionally with the sauce. Makes 6 servings.

GRILLED SALMON STEAKS

**6 fresh or frozen salmon steaks or
    other fish steaks**
½ cup salad oil
¼ cup snipped parsley
¼ cup lemon juice
2 tablespoons grated onion
½ teaspoon dry mustard
¼ teaspoon salt

Thaw frozen fish. Place fish in shallow dish. Combine oil, parsley, lemon juice, onion, mustard, salt, and dash pepper. Pour over fish. Let stand at room temperature 2 hours, turning occasionally. (Or marinate in refrigerator 4 to 6 hours.) Drain, reserving marinade.

Place fish in well-greased wire broiler basket. Grill over *medium-hot* coals till lightly browned, 5 to 8 minutes. Baste with marinade and turn. Brush again with marinade; grill till fish flakes easily when tested with a fork, 5 to 8 minutes longer. Makes 6 servings.

SNAPPER WITH COCONUT

Use 2 pounds fresh or frozen red snapper fillets or other fish fillets. Thaw frozen fillets. Cut into 6 portions. Place in shallow dish. Combine ½ cup salad oil, ¼ cup lime juice, and 1 teaspoon salt. Pour mixture over fish. Marinate at room temperature 1 hour, turning once. Drain, reserving the oil-lime juice marinade.

Place fillets on well-greased rack of broiler pan. Broil about 4 inches from heat till fish flakes easily when tested with a fork, 10 to 15 minutes. Brush occasionally with reserved marinade. Remove to warm serving platter. Sprinkle ¼ cup toasted coconut over fillets. Serve with lime wedges. Makes 6 servings.

Grill fillets *over a portable barbecue in the backyard or beside the lake. Hot coals give Grilled Pike Fillets additional flavor, plus an alluring aroma.*

GRILLED PIKE FILLETS

Cut 2 pounds fresh pike fillets into 6 portions. Place in shallow dish. Combine ½ cup salad oil, ¼ cup lemon juice, 2 tablespoons snipped parsley, 1 teaspoon salt, ½ teaspoon Worcestershire sauce, and dash bottled hot pepper sauce. Pour over fish. Marinate at room temperature 1 hour, turning once. Drain, reserving marinade. Place fish in well-greased wire broiler basket. Sprinkle with salt. Grill over *medium-hot* coals for 5 to 8 minutes. Baste with marinade. Turn; grill till fish flakes easily when tested with a fork, 5 to 8 minutes longer. Sprinkle with paprika. Makes 6 servings.

FILLETS AMANDINE

Cut 1½ pounds fresh or frozen fish fillets into 4 portions. Thaw frozen fish. Place in greased baking pan. Combine 2 tablespoons melted butter and 1 tablespoon lemon juice. Brush on fish. Sprinkle with ¾ teaspoon salt and dash pepper. Bake, uncovered, at 350° till fish flakes when tested with a fork, 15 to 20 minutes. Melt 1 tablespoon butter in skillet. Brown ¼ cup sliced almonds in butter till golden, stirring constantly. Remove nuts; sprinkle over fish. Stir 1 tablespoon lemon juice and 2 teaspoons snipped parsley into melted butter in skillet; heat. Drizzle over fish. Makes 6 servings.

SALMON BALLS IN CAPER SAUCE

1 16-ounce can salmon
1 cup soft bread crumbs (2 slices)
2 eggs
2 tablespoons snipped parsley
1 tablespoon grated onion
½ teaspoon salt
½ teaspoon grated lemon peel
2 teaspoons lemon juice
½ cup sauterne
2 tablespoons butter, softened
2 tablespoons all-purpose flour
½ cup light cream
1 tablespoon snipped parsley
1 tablespoon capers, drained

Drain salmon, reserving liquid. Remove bones and skin from salmon; flake meat into bowl. Add bread crumbs, eggs, 2 tablespoons parsley, onion, salt, lemon peel, lemon juice, and dash pepper; mix well. Shape into 8 balls and place in medium skillet. Combine sauterne and reserved salmon liquid; add enough water to make 2 cups liquid. Pour over salmon balls. Heat to boiling; reduce heat. Cover and simmer 10 minutes. Remove balls to serving dish.

Combine butter and flour; stir into hot liquid. Cook and stir over high heat till mixture is thickened and bubbly. Stir in cream, 1 tablespoon parsley, and capers. Heat to boiling. Serve over salmon balls. Makes 4 servings.

Simmer salmon balls *in a sauterne mixture. Then, use this liquid to make a creamy sauce that is poured over the balls for Salmon Balls in Caper Sauce.*

FISH SHANTY BAKED FISH

Treat family or guests with an entrée from Smith Bros. Fish Shanty Restaurant located in Port Washington, Wisconsin —

2 pounds fresh or frozen whitefish
    fillets or other fish fillets
½ cup chopped celery
¼ cup chopped onion
¼ cup butter or margarine
9 cups crumbled stale rolls
1 beaten egg
1 tablespoon snipped parlsey
1 teaspoon salt
½ teaspoon poultry seasoning
    Dash pepper
    Cream Sauce
    Snipped parsley or paprika

Thaw frozen fillets. Cook celery and onion in butter till tender. Combine with rolls, egg, parsley, salt, poultry seasoning, and pepper. Add enough water to moisten, about ¾ cup. Mix.

Place fillets, skin side down, in single layer in a greased 11¾x7½x1¾-inch baking dish; sprinkle with salt. Cover fillets with dressing mixture. Bake at 350° till fish flakes easily when tested with a fork, 35 to 40 minutes. Cut into squares to serve. Spoon hot Cream Sauce over top and garnish with snipped parsley or paprika. Serves 8.

Cream Sauce: In medium saucepan cook 2 tablespoons chopped green pepper in ¼ cup butter or margarine till tender. Blend in ¼ cup all-purpose flour. Add 2 cups milk; cook and stir till thickened and bubbly. Add 1 tablespoon chopped canned pimiento and a few drops yellow food coloring. Blend a small amount of sauce into one 10½-ounce can condensed cream of mushroom soup; return mixture to saucepan. Heat through. Serve over baked fish and dressing.

CODFISH BALLS

Soak 8 ounces salt cod in water 12 hours. Dice. Cook 3 cups diced, peeled potatoes and cod in boiling water till potatoes are tender; drain. Beat with electric mixer. Add 1 beaten egg, 2 tablespoons butter, and ¼ teaspoon pepper; beat. Drop by heaping tablespoons into deep, hot fat (375°). Fry till golden, 2 to 3 minutes; turn once. Drain. Makes 30.

TURBOT WITH DILLED SAUCE

Use 2 pounds fresh or frozen turbot fillets or other fish fillets. Thaw frozen fish. Cut into 6 portions. Place in a greased skillet. Add 2 cups boiling water; 2 tablespoons lemon juice; 1 clove garlic, minced; and 1 teaspoon salt. Cover and simmer till fish flakes easily when tested with fork, 5 to 10 minutes.

Meanwhile, place 3 egg yolks, 2 tablespoons lemon juice, and ¼ teaspoon dried dillweed in blender container. Cover; quickly turn blender on and off. Heat ½ cup butter till melted and almost boiling. Turn blender on high speed. Slowly pour in butter, blending till thick and fluffy, about 30 seconds. Hold over warm, *not hot*, water till ready to serve. Carefully remove fish to platter; pour some hot sauce over fish. Pass remaining sauce. Serves 6.

Serve patties as a main dish *or as a sandwich perched atop toasted buns. Either way, the lemony cheese sauce adds a crowning touch to Seattle Salmon Patties.*

SALMON CROQUETTES

    1 16-ounce can salmon
    3 tablespoons butter or margarine
    ¼ cup all-purpose flour
    ½ cup milk
    1 tablespoon snipped parsley
    2 teaspoons lemon juice
    1 teaspoon grated onion
      Dash paprika
      Dash ground nutmeg
    1 cup fine dry bread crumbs
    1 beaten egg
    2 tablespoons water
    1 8- or 10-ounce package frozen peas
      with cream sauce

Drain salmon, reserving ½ cup liquid. Remove bones and skin; flake meat. Melt butter in saucepan. Blend in flour. Add milk and reserved liquid. Cook and stir till thickened and bubbly. Cook and stir 1 minute longer. Add next 5 ingredients, ¼ teaspoon salt, and dash pepper. Stir in salmon; chill.

With wet hands, shape salmon mixture into 8 balls, using about ¼ cup for each. Roll in crumbs. Shape balls into cones, handling lightly so crumbs remain on outside. Dip into mixture of beaten egg and water; roll in crumbs again.

Fry a few at a time in deep, hot fat (350°) till brown and hot, about 2½ to 3 minutes. Drain on paper toweling. Prepare peas with cream sauce according to package directions; spoon over croquettes or pass as a sauce. Serves 4.

SEATTLE SALMON PATTIES

Complement salmon with a creamy sauce—

    1 16-ounce can salmon
    ½ cup chopped onion
    2 tablespoons butter or margarine
    ⅔ cup fine dry bread crumbs
    2 beaten eggs
    ¼ cup snipped parsley
    1 teaspoon dry mustard
    3 tablespoons shortening
      Lemon-Cheese Sauce

Drain salmon, reserving ⅓ cup liquid. Remove bones and skin from salmon; flake meat. Cook onion in butter till tender. Add reserved liquid, ⅓ cup crumbs, eggs, parsley, mustard, and salmon; mix well. Shape into 6 patties; roll in remaining crumbs. In skillet melt shortening. Cook patties over medium heat till browned. Carefully turn; brown other side. Serve with Lemon-Cheese Sauce. Serves 6.

Lemon-Cheese Sauce: Melt 2 tablespoons butter in a saucepan; blend in 2 tablespoons all-purpose flour, ½ teaspoon salt, and dash pepper. Add 1 cup milk all at once; cook and stir till thickened and bubbly. Stir a small amount of hot mixture into 2 beaten egg yolks. Return to hot mixture. Add ½ cup shredded sharp process American cheese and 2 tablespoons lemon juice. Stir to melt cheese.

FRIED SHAD ROE

Rinse 2 pairs fresh shad roe.* In saucepan combine 2 cups water, 1 teaspoon salt, and 1 tablespoon vinegar. Bring to boiling. Add shad roe. Cover and simmer till done, 5 to 10 minutes; drain. Cut into serving-sized pieces. Dip into a mixture of 1 beaten egg and 1 tablespoon lemon juice; roll in ½ cup fine saltine cracker crumbs. Fry in ¼ cup butter till browned, turning carefully. Sprinkle the shad roe with paprika, if desired. Makes 4 servings.

*Or substitute one 7½-ounce can shad roe and omit precooking roe in salted water.

KULEBIAKA

Wrap salmon mixture with a pastry crust—

    2 tablespoons chopped onion
    3 tablespoons butter or margarine
 2¼ cups sifted all-purpose flour
    ¼ teaspoon dried dillweed
    1 cup milk
    2 tablespoons dry white wine
    1 16-ounce can red salmon, drained and
        flaked
    2 cups cooked rice
    1 3-ounce can sliced mushrooms, drained
    2 tablespoons snipped parsley
  ⅔ cup shortening
    1 beaten egg

In saucepan cook onion in butter till tender. Blend in ¼ *cup* flour, ½ teaspoon salt, and dillweed. Add milk. Cook and stir till thickened and bubbly; cook 1 minute more. Stir in wine, salmon, rice, mushrooms, and parsley. Sift together 2 cups flour and ½ teaspoon salt; cut in shortening till mixture resembles coarse crumbs. Gradually add ⅓ to ½ cup cold water, tossing with fork till moistened. Form into ball.

Roll dough between 2 pieces of waxed paper to a 20x10-inch rectangle. Remove top piece of paper. Mound salmon mixture lengthwise down center third of rectangle. Fold one side of dough over salmon; peel paper back. Repeat with second side of dough. Moisten edges with water; seal. Fold ends up; moisten and seal. Lifting paper, transfer to large greased baking sheet, seam side down. Peel off paper. Form into horseshoe shape; brush with egg. Prick top with fork. Bake at 400° for 25 to 30 minutes. Makes 6 to 8 servings.

LUTEFISK SPECIAL

    8 small potatoes, peeled
    2 cups boiling water
    1 teaspoon salt
    1 pound lutefisk, cut in serving-sized
        pieces
              • • •
    3 tablespoons butter or margarine
    2 tablespoons all-purpose flour
    ½ teaspoon salt
    ½ teaspoon dry mustard
 1¼ cups milk
    ½ cup butter or margarine, melted

Cook peeled potatoes in boiling, salted water till tender, about 25 to 35 minutes. Meanwhile, in saucepan bring 2 cups water and 1 teaspoon salt to boiling. Add lutefisk. Cover and simmer till fish is tender, about 15 minutes. Melt 3 tablespoons butter in saucepan. Blend in flour, salt, and mustard. Add milk. Cook quickly, stirring constantly, till thickened and bubbly. Serve sauce over potatoes and melted butter with lutefisk. Makes 4 servings.

SALMON LOAF

    1 16-ounce can salmon, drained and
        flaked
    2 cups soft bread crumbs
    1 tablespoon chopped onion
    1 tablespoon butter or margarine,
        melted
    ½ teaspoon salt
    ½ cup milk
    1 beaten egg
      Piquant Sauce

In a bowl combine salmon, crumbs, chopped onion, butter, and salt. Combine milk and egg; add to salmon mixture and mix thoroughly. Shape into a loaf on a greased shallow baking pan or in 7½x3¾x2¼-inch loaf pan. Bake at 350° for 35 to 40 minutes. Serve with Piquant Sauce or creamed peas, if desired. Serves 3 or 4.

Piquant Sauce: In saucepan cook 2 tablespoons chopped green onion in 3 tablespoons butter or margarine till tender but not brown. Blend in 2 tablespoons all-purpose flour, ½ teaspoon dry mustard, ½ teaspoon salt, and dash pepper. Add 1¼ cups milk and 1 teaspoon Worcestershire sauce all at once. Cook, stirring constantly, till sauce is thickened and bubbly.

FRIED FISH CAKES

Cook fish by steaming or poaching—

½ cup chopped onion
2 tablespoons butter or margarine
1 pound pollock fillets or other fish fillets, cooked and flaked
⅓ cup fine dry bread crumbs
2 beaten eggs
⅛ teaspoon lemon peel
1 tablespoon lemon juice
1 teaspoon salt
⅛ teaspoon ground ginger
Dash pepper

• • •

¼ cup all-purpose flour
⅛ teaspoon cayenne pepper
3 tablespoons butter or margarine

In skillet cook onion in 2 tablespoons butter till tender but not brown. Combine cooked onion, fish, crumbs, eggs, lemon peel, lemon juice, salt, ginger, and pepper. Mix well until mixture holds together and can be shaped. Chill 1 hour. Shape into 8 flat cakes. Combine flour and cayenne pepper. Coat fish cakes with flour mixture. In skillet brown cakes in 3 tablespoons butter till golden brown on both sides. Serves 4.

TUNA TURNOVERS

1 6½- or 7-ounce can tuna, drained and flaked
1 hard-cooked egg, chopped
¼ cup chopped celery
¼ cup mayonnaise or salad dressing
2 tablespoons coarsely chopped pecans
2 packages refrigerated crescent rolls (16 rolls)
4 ounces natural Cheddar cheese, shredded (1 cup)

Combine tuna, egg, celery, mayonnaise or salad dressing, and pecans. Remove rolls from packages; form eight 6x3½-inch rectangles by sealing perforated edges of 2 rolls. Sprinkle *1 tablespoon* cheese over half of each rectangle. Top with about ¼ cup tuna mixture and another tablespoon cheese. Fold other half of rectangle over filling; seal edges with tines of fork. Place on ungreased baking sheet. Bake at 425° till golden brown, about 15 minutes. Serve turnovers hot. Makes 8 servings.

GEFILTE FISH

½ pound fresh or frozen pike fillets
½ pound fresh or frozen whitefish fillets
½ pound fresh or frozen carp fillets

• • •

6 cups water
2 medium carrots, peeled and sliced
2 medium onions, chopped
1 tablespoon salt
⅛ teaspoon pepper

• • •

2 eggs
2 tablespoons ice water
2 tablespoons matzo meal or cracker meal
½ teaspoon salt
Dash pepper
Prepared horseradish
Pickles

Thaw frozen fish. In large saucepan combine 6 cups water, *half* the carrots, *half* the onions, 1 tablespoon salt, and ⅛ teaspoon pepper. Bring to boiling. Simmer, covered, 30 minutes. Finely grind fish and remaining vegetables. Place in large mixer bowl; add egg, ice water, meal, ½ teaspoon salt, and dash pepper. Beat at high speed till fluffy. Shape into balls or fingers, using 3 tablespoons for each. Place in broth. Cover. Simmer 20 minutes. Drain; serve hot or cold with horseradish and pickles. Serves 6.

Use crescent rolls *from refrigerated packages for the dough in Tuna Turnovers. Top the rolls with filling, fold in half, and seal edges with a fork.*

SPANISH-STYLE SALT COD

1 pound salt cod or other salt fish
1 cup chopped onion
½ cup chopped green pepper
2 cloves garlic, minced
3 tablespoons salad oil
2 tablespoons all-purpose flour

• • •

1 16-ounce can tomatoes, cut up
2 bay leaves
¼ teaspoon dried thyme leaves, crushed
Hot cooked rice

Soak cod in water 12 hours; rinse. Simmer in water till tender, about 15 minutes. Drain. Remove bones and skin; flake into large pieces. In skillet cook onion, pepper, and garlic in oil till tender. Stir in flour; cook till lightly browned. Add tomatoes, ¼ cup water, bay leaves, and thyme. Simmer, covered, 30 minutes, stirring occasionally. Remove bay leaves. Add cod; heat through. Serve over rice. Serves 6.

CREAMED FINNAN HADDIE

12 ounces smoked haddock fillets
2 tablespoons butter or margarine
2 tablespoons all-purpose flour
Dash pepper
1⅓ cups light cream
Patty shells or toast points

Poach or steam fillets (see page 16); skin and flake fish. In saucepan melt butter; stir in flour and pepper. Add cream all at once. Cook and stir till thickened and bubbly. Add flaked fish; heat through. Spoon into patty shells or over toast points. Garnish with sieved hard-cooked egg yolk, if desired. Makes 4 servings.

CURRIED TUNA OVER BISCUITS

In saucepan cook 2 tablespoons chopped green pepper and 1 tablespoon chopped onion in 1 tablespoon butter till tender. Stir in one 10½-ounce can condensed cream of celery soup, ⅓ cup mayonnaise or salad dressing, ⅓ cup milk, and ¼ to ½ teaspoon curry powder. Drain one 9¼-ounce can tuna; break into large chunks and fold into mixture. Cook, stirring occasionally, till heated through. Serve over hot biscuits split in half. Serves 6.

SWEET AND SOUR TUNA

1 8¾-ounce can pineapple tidbits
2 tablespoons brown sugar
4 teaspoons cornstarch
2 tablespoons vinegar
2 teaspoons soy sauce
¼ teaspoon salt
1 vegetable bouillon cube
1 9¼-ounce can tuna, drained
½ cup green pepper strips
Chow mein noodles or hot cooked rice

Drain pineapple, reserving syrup. Add water to syrup to equal 1 cup. In saucepan combine brown sugar and cornstarch; blend in reserved syrup, vinegar, soy sauce, salt, and crumbled bouillon cube. Cook and stir over medium heat till thickened and bubbly. Stir in pineapple, tuna, and green pepper. Cook over low heat till vegetables are crisp-tender and tuna is heated through, about 2 to 3 minutes. Serve over warmed noodles or rice. Serves 4.

ITALIAN FISH PORTIONS

¼ cup chopped onion
½ clove garlic, minced
1 tablespoon salad oil
1 16-ounce can tomatoes, cut up
1 6-ounce can tomato paste
¾ teaspoon dried oregano leaves, crushed
½ teaspoon sugar
½ teaspoon salt
⅛ teaspoon pepper

• • •

8 frozen, fried, breaded fish portions
¼ cup shredded Cheddar cheese

In saucepan cook onion and garlic in oil till tender. Stir in tomatoes, tomato paste, oregano, sugar, salt, and pepper. Simmer, covered, 20 minutes. Meanwhile, cook fish according to package directions. To serve, spoon hot sauce over fish. Sprinkle with cheese. Serves 8.

Dress up fish portions

*Perk up your family's interest and appetites by adding →
a foreign flair to dinner. Italian Fish Portions as the
main dish, a tossed salad with Italian dressing, bread
sticks, and tortoni dessert make a great menu.*

SPINACH-TOPPED FISH

1 10-ounce package frozen chopped
   spinach
1 3-ounce package cream cheese, cubed
¼ teaspoon onion salt

• • •

8 frozen breaded fish portions
2 tablespoons butter or margarine,
   melted
   Salt and pepper
   Dash ground nutmeg

Cook frozen spinach according to package
directions; drain thoroughly. Stir cream cheese
and onion salt into hot spinach; mix well. Place
frozen fish portions on greased baking sheet.
Drizzle with melted butter and sprinkle with
salt and pepper. Bake at 450° for 15 minutes.
Top with hot spinach and sprinkle with nutmeg.
Bake 2 to 3 minutes. Makes 4 servings.

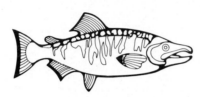

HAWAIIAN FISH PORTIONS

8 frozen breaded fish portions
2 tablespoons chopped green onion
2 tablespoons chopped green pepper
2 tablespoons butter or margarine
¼ cup brown sugar
1 tablespoon cornstarch
¼ teaspoon ground ginger

• • •

1 8½-ounce can pineapple tidbits
2 tablespoons vinegar
1 tablespoon soy sauce
½ cup cherry tomato halves

Cook fish portions according to package directions. Meanwhile, in small saucepan cook
onion and green pepper in butter till tender but
not brown. Combine brown sugar, cornstarch,
and ginger. Add to cooked vegetables in skillet.
   Drain pineapple tidbits, reserving syrup. Stir
pineapple syrup, vinegar, and soy sauce into
vegetable mixture. Cook and stir till thickened
and bubbly. Add the pineapple tidbits and
cherry tomato halves. Heat through. Serve over
cooked fish portions. Makes 4 servings.

DILLED FISH STICKS

20 frozen, fried, breaded fish sticks
¼ cup butter or margarine, melted
2 tablespoons lemon juice
½ teaspoon dried dillweed

Place fish sticks in ungreased shallow baking
pan. Combine melted butter or margarine,
lemon juice, and dillweed; brush over top of
frozen sticks. Bake according to package directions. Remove to serving platter. Serves 4 or 5.

SOUR CREAM-TOPPED FISH

4 frozen, breaded fish portions
2 tablespoons butter, melted
½ cup dairy sour cream
1 tablespoon snipped parsley
1½ teaspoons vinegar
1 teaspoon anchovy paste
1 teaspoon instant minced onion
4 tomato slices

Place fish portions in a greased shallow baking
pan. Brush with the melted butter and bake at
450° for 15 minutes. Meanwhile, combine the
sour cream, parsley, vinegar, anchovy paste,
and instant minced onion. Remove baked fish
portions from oven. Top each fish portion with a
tomato slice and spoon sour cream mixture
atop. Return to oven till topping is hot, about
5 minutes longer. Makes 4 servings.

PICKLE-TOPPED FISH PORTIONS

4 frozen, fried, breaded fish portions
¼ cup mayonnaise or salad dressing
1 beaten egg yolk
3 tablespoons finely chopped dill pickle
1 tablespoon finely chopped onion
½ teaspoon prepared mustard
⅛ teaspoon salt
   Dash pepper
1 stiffly beaten egg white

Place fish portions in a greased, shallow 10x6x
1¾-inch baking dish. Combine mayonnaise,
egg yolk, chopped dill pickle, onion, mustard,
salt, and pepper. Fold in egg white. Pour mixture over fish portions. Bake at 400° till fish
flakes easily when tested with a fork, about 15
to 20 minutes. Makes 3 or 4 servings.

MEXICAN FISH PORTIONS

12 frozen, fried, breaded fish portions
12 tortillas (frozen or canned)
   Shortening

• • •

1½ cups finely shredded lettuce
12 thin tomato slices
  6 ounces natural Cheddar cheese,
     shredded (1½ cups)
   Taco sauce

Cook fish portions according to package directions. Meanwhile, heat ¼ inch shortening in skillet. Fry tortillas till lightly browned. Drain on paper toweling. Place cooked fish portion on tortilla; top with lettuce, tomato slice, and shredded Cheddar cheese. Serve with bottled taco sauce. Makes 6 servings.

FISH WITH MUSTARD BUTTER

20 frozen, fried, breaded fish sticks
¼ cup butter or margarine, softened
2 teaspoons prepared mustard
½ teaspoon lemon juice
3 drops bottled hot pepper sauce
⅛ teaspoon garlic salt

Place fish sticks in a single layer in shallow baking pan. Combine butter, mustard, lemon juice, hot pepper sauce, and garlic salt. Spread sticks with butter mixture. Broil according to package directions. Serves 4 or 5.

FISH À LA GOLDENROD

8 frozen, breaded fish portions
1 10½-ounce can condensed cream of
    celery soup
¼ cup milk
   Few drops bottled hot pepper sauce
2 drops yellow food coloring (optional)
3 hard-cooked eggs
   Parsley

Cook fish portions according to package directions. Combine soup, milk, pepper sauce, and yellow food coloring, if desired. Heat thoroughly, stirring occasionally. Chop *1* egg and add to sauce. Slice remaining 2 eggs. Place egg slices on top of fish. Pour sauce over. Trim with snipped parsley. Makes 4 servings.

QUICK ITALIAN FISH BAKE

8 frozen, fried, breaded fish portions
1 8-ounce can spaghetti sauce with
    mushrooms
2 tablespoons water
½ teaspoon dried thyme leaves, crushed
2 tablespoons grated Parmesan cheese

Arrange frozen fish portions in greased 13½x-8¾x1¾-inch baking dish. Combine spaghetti sauce, water, and thyme; spread over fish portions. Bake fish at 400° for 15 minutes. Sprinkle with cheese; return to oven for 5 minutes more. Pass additional grated Parmesan cheese, if desired. Makes 8 servings.

FISH PORTION PUFF

12 frozen breaded fish portions
3 tablespoons butter or margarine,
    melted
¼ cup mayonnaise or salad dressing
2 beaten egg yolks
1 package green onion dip mix
1 tablespoon snipped parsley
2 stiffly beaten egg whites

Place frozen fish portions on greased baking sheet. Drizzle melted butter over portions. Broil about 4 inches from heat for 12 to 15 minutes. Meanwhile, combine mayonnaise or salad dressing, egg yolks, dip mix, and parsley; mix thoroughly. Fold in stiffly beaten egg whites. Top each cooked fish portion with about 2 tablespoons mayonnaise mixture. Broil 5 inches from heat till golden brown, about 1 minute. Serve immediately. Serves 6.

LEMON-TOPPED FISH PORTIONS

8 frozen, fried, breaded fish portions
3 tablespoons butter, melted
¼ teaspoon grated lemon peel
2 tablespoons lemon juice
¼ cup coarsely chopped salted peanuts

Place fish portions in a greased, shallow baking pan or on broiler pan. Combine butter, lemon peel, and lemon juice; drizzle over fish portions. Broil according to package directions. Sprinkle each portion with nuts. Broil about 1 minute longer. Makes 4 servings.

128

SERVE A ONE-DISH MEAL

CRAB-SOUFFLÉ BAKE

    3 tablespoons butter or margarine
    3 tablespoons all-purpose flour
    1 teaspoon salt
    1 cup milk
    3 eggs, separated
    1 7½-ounce can crab meat, drained,
        finely flaked, and cartilage removed
    1 3-ounce can chopped mushrooms,
        drained

In saucepan melt butter; blend in flour, salt, and dash pepper. Add milk. Cook quickly, stirring constantly, till thickened and bubbly. Remove from heat. Beat egg yolks till thick and lemon-colored. Slowly add sauce mixture to egg yolks, stirring constantly. Stir in crab meat and mushrooms. Beat egg whites till stiff peaks form. Fold into crab mixture. Turn into *ungreased* 1-quart soufflé dish. Bake at 325° till knife inserted comes out clean, 60 minutes. Serve immediately. Serves 4 or 5.

CRAB-FONDUE CASSEROLE

    1 tablespoon sliced green onion
    2 tablespoons butter or margarine
    2 tablespoons all-purpose flour
    ½ teaspoon salt
    ¼ teaspoon dry mustard
    1½ cups milk
    1 7½-ounce can crab meat, drained,
        flaked, and cartilage removed
    5 slices white bread
    1 cup soft bread crumbs
    2 tablespoons butter or margarine,
        melted

In saucepan cook onion in 2 tablespoons butter till tender but not brown. Blend in flour, ½ teaspoon salt, and mustard. Add milk; cook and stir till thickened and bubbly. Add crab. Remove crusts from sliced bread; cut bread into ½-inch cubes. Fold into crab mixture. Turn into 1-quart casserole. Combine bread crumbs and melted butter. Sprinkle atop casserole. Bake at 350° till heated through and topping is lightly browned, 35 to 40 minutes. Serves 4.

CRAB-LOBSTER CASSEROLE

    12 ounces frozen king crab legs, thawed
        and shelled or 1 6-ounce package
        frozen crab meat, thawed
    1 5-ounce can lobster, drained
    1 cup chopped celery
    ⅔ cup mayonnaise or salad dressing
    ¼ cup milk
    ¼ cup chopped onion
    1 teaspoon Worcestershire sauce
    1½ cups soft bread crumbs
    1 cup soft bread crumbs
    2 tablespoons butter or margarine,
        melted

Cut crab and lobster into pieces. Combine seafood with next 6 ingredients, ½ teaspoon salt, and dash pepper. Spoon into 1-quart casserole or 4 individual baking shells. Combine 1 cup crumbs and melted butter; sprinkle around edge of casserole. Bake, uncovered, at 350° till heated through, 30 to 35 minutes for casserole and 20 to 25 minutes for shells. Serves 4.

CRAB AND EGGS

Melt 2 tablespoons butter or margarine in saucepan. Blend in 2 tablespoons all-purpose flour, ¼ teaspoon salt, and dash pepper. Add 1 cup milk, all at once. Cook quickly, stirring constantly, till thickened and bubbly. Remove from heat. Stir in one 7½-ounce can crab meat, drained, flaked, and cartilage removed.

Combine 6 beaten eggs and ¼ cup milk; stir into crab mixture. Melt 2 tablespoons butter in 10-inch skillet. Pour in egg mixture. As mixture begins to set, lift and fold over with spatula. Cook eggs till done but still glossy, about 5 minutes. Serve immediately. Serves 6.

Elegant seafood casserole

Combine crab and lobster for a dish that's perfect for → *entertaining. Mix Crab-Lobster Casserole early and chill till dinner. However, do plan to allow some extra time for heating when the mixture is cold.*

SHRIMP AND CRAB AU GRATIN

Bring individual servings, piping hot, to the table as it's done at Massa's Restaurant in Houston, Texas —

  2 tablespoons butter or margarine
  3 tablespoons all-purpose flour
  1 tablespoon chicken-flavored gravy
     base
  2 cups milk
  5 ounces process American cheese,
     shredded (1¼ cups)
  8 ounces fresh or frozen cooked lump
     crab meat, or 1 7½-ounce can crab
     meat, drained and cartilage removed
  8 ounces fresh or frozen shelled
     shrimp, cooked
     Paprika
     Toast points

In saucepan melt butter; blend in flour and chicken base. Add milk. Cook and stir till thickened and bubbly. Add *1 cup* of the cheese; stir to melt. Tint with a few drops of yellow food coloring. Cut crab meat into pieces; add crab and shrimp to creamed mixture. Pour into four 8-ounce casserole dishes, top with remaining cheese, and sprinkle with paprika. Bake at 350° till hot, 10 to 15 minutes. Serve with toast points. Makes 4 servings.

SAUCY SHRIMP SQUARES

Combine 3 well-beaten eggs and 1½ cups milk. Stir in 3 cups soft bread crumbs; two 4½-ounce cans shrimp, drained; 2 tablespoons snipped parsley; 2 tablespoons finely chopped onion; 1 tablespoon lemon juice; ¼ teaspoon salt; and dash pepper. Turn into greased 10x6x1¾-inch baking dish. Bake at 350° for 35 to 40 minutes. Cut into 6 servings; serve with Sauce.

Sauce: Melt 1 tablespoon butter in saucepan. Stir in 1 tablespoon all-purpose flour and ¼ teaspoon salt. Add 1½ cups milk. Cook, stirring constantly, till thickened. Remove from heat; add 4 ounces sharp process American cheese, shredded (1 cup). Stir till melted.

JAPANESE TEMPURA

     Uncooked shelled shrimp
     Assorted fresh vegetables such as
        asparagus spears, parsley, sweet
        potatoes, spinach, mushrooms, and
        green beans
     Salad oil
  1 cup sifted all-purpose flour
  1 cup ice water
  1 slightly beaten egg
  2 tablespoons salad oil
  ½ teaspoon sugar
     Tempura Condiments

Wash and dry shrimp and vegetables well. Slice or cut vegetables into strips, if necessary. Fill skillet half full with salad oil; heat to 360° to 365°. To make batter combine flour, next 4 ingredients, and ½ teaspoon salt; beat just till moistened (a few lumps should remain). Stir in one or two ice cubes. Use at once. Dip shrimp and vegetables in cold batter. Fry in hot oil till light brown; drain.

Serve with Tempura Condiments: 1. grated fresh gingerroot; 2. equal parts grated turnip and radish, combined; and 3. ½ cup prepared mustard mixed with 3 tablespoons soy sauce.

HAM AND SHRIMP IN RICE RING

Combine ham and shrimp for delicious flavor —

  ¼ cup chopped onion
  ¼ cup chopped celery
  ¼ cup butter or margarine
  ¼ cup all-purpose flour
  2 cups milk
  ½ teaspoon prepared horseradish
  1½ cups chopped fully cooked ham
  10 ounces shelled shrimp, cooked
  3 cups hot cooked rice
  ¼ cup snipped parsley

In saucepan cook onion and celery in butter till tender but not brown. Blend in flour, ½ teaspoon salt, and dash pepper. Add milk all at once. Cook, stirring constantly, till mixture is thickened and bubbly. Stir in horseradish; add ham and cooked shrimp. Heat through.

Combine rice and parsley. Press rice lightly into greased 5½-cup ring mold. Unmold at once on platter. Place bowl in center of ring; fill with ham and shrimp mixture. Serves 6.

SHRIMP-STUFFED PEPPERS

6 medium green peppers
3 tablespoons butter or margarine
3 tablespoons all-purpose flour
1 teaspoon seasoned salt
⅛ teaspoon dried basil leaves, crushed
2 cups milk
¼ teaspoon Worcestershire sauce
½ cup chopped celery
1 pound fresh or frozen shelled shrimp
3 ounces macaroni, cooked
2 ounces Cheddar cheese, shredded
       (½ cup)

Cut off tops of green peppers; remove seeds and membrane. Scallop edges. Precook peppers in boiling, salted water 5 minutes; drain. (For crisp peppers, omit precooking.) Melt butter in skillet; blend in flour, salt, and basil. Add milk and Worcestershire sauce all at once; add celery. Cook, stirring constantly, till thickened and bubbly. Cook shrimp in boiling, salted water 1 to 3 minutes; drain and dice. Add shrimp and macaroni to sauce.

Lightly salt inside of peppers. Fill with shrimp mixture; stand upright in 10x6x1¾-inch baking dish. Bake, uncovered, at 350° for 20 to 25 minutes. Sprinkle with cheese. Continue baking till cheese melts. Makes 6 servings.

SHRIMP-NOODLE NEWBURG

1 10-ounce can frozen condensed cream
     of shrimp soup
1 6-ounce can evaporated milk
2 ounces natural Cheddar cheese,
     shredded (½ cup)
⅓ cup mayonnaise or salad dressing
¼ cup dry sherry
1 4½-ounce can shrimp, drained
4 ounces medium noodles, cooked
     and drained
½ cup broken potato chips

In saucepan combine soup and evaporated milk; heat to boiling, stirring occasionally. Remove from heat. Add cheese, mayonnaise, and ¼ teaspoon salt; stir till cheese melts. Blend in sherry. Add shrimp and cooked noodles; mix well. Turn into 1½-quart casserole. Bake, covered, at 350° for 25 minutes. Uncover; wreathe with broken potato chips. Return to oven; bake 5 minutes longer. Makes 4 to 6 servings.

SHRIMP IN SPANISH RICE

1½ pounds fresh or frozen shelled shrimp
1 28-ounce can tomatoes, cut up
¾ cup uncooked long-grain rice
½ cup chopped onion
¼ cup chopped green pepper
¾ teaspoon chili powder
½ teaspoon sugar
5 green pepper rings

Thaw frozen shrimp. In 2-quart casserole combine tomatoes, rice, onion, chopped green pepper, 1½ teaspoons salt, chili powder, sugar, and dash pepper. Cover and bake at 350° for 1 hour, stirring occasionally. Stir in shrimp and arrange green pepper rings on top. Cover and continue baking till shrimp and rice are cooked, about 30 minutes. Makes 6 to 8 servings.

SHRIMP AND EGGPLANT

8 ounces shelled shrimp, cooked
½ cup chopped onion
2 tablespoons chopped green pepper
1 large clove garlic, minced
¼ cup butter or margarine
1 medium eggplant
1 8-ounce can tomatoes, diced
1 teaspoon salt
¼ teaspoon ground thyme
    Dash pepper
1½ cups cooked rice
2 tablespoons butter or margarine
1½ cups soft bread crumbs

Split cooked shrimp lengthwise; set aside. In skillet cook onion, green pepper, and garlic in ¼ cup butter till tender but not brown. Peel eggplant and cut into ½-inch cubes; add to mixture in skillet with tomatoes, salt, thyme, and pepper. Cover and simmer till eggplant is tender, about 10 minutes. Stir in shrimp and rice. Spoon mixture into 4 individual casseroles. Melt 2 tablespoons butter; stir in bread crumbs. Sprinkle over shrimp-eggplant mixture. Bake at 400° till lightly browned, about 10 to 15 minutes. Makes 4 servings.

Use coquilles for individual servings *French Shrimp in Shells. These individual baking shells are made-to-order for cooking and serving seafoods. Inexpensive ones are available in department and variety stores.*

FRENCH SHRIMP IN SHELLS

Garnish with sprigs of parsley and lemon wedges sprinkled lightly with paprika—

Cook 1 pound shelled shrimp; drain. In saucepan melt ¼ cup butter or margarine. Stir in 3 tablespoons all-purpose flour. Add 1½ cups milk all at once; cook and stir till thickened and bubbly. Add shrimp, ¼ cup dry sherry, ½ teaspoon salt, dash pepper, and dash paprika. Pour into 5 coquilles—individual baking shells. Sprinkle each serving with 1 tablespoon grated Parmesan cheese. Broil 3 to 4 inches from heat till cheese browns. Makes 5 servings.

SAN FRANCISCO EGGS

Add crisp bacon and coffee for brunch—

Cook one 10-ounce package frozen chopped spinach according to package directions; drain well. Add dash ground nutmeg and dash pepper. Thaw one 10-ounce can frozen condensed cream of shrimp soup. Blend ¼ cup shrimp soup with 2 tablespoons milk. Mix remaining soup with spinach; heat through. Divide spinach mixture between 4 greased 1-cup baking dishes. Break an egg into each one. Spoon reserved soup-milk mixture over eggs. Bake at 350° till eggs are set, 15 to 20 minutes. Serves 4.

LOBSTER THERMIDOR BAKE

    4 frozen lobster tails (about 1 pound),
        cooked
    ⅓ cup chopped onion
    1 clove garlic, minced
    2 tablespoons butter or margarine
    1 10¾-ounce can condensed Cheddar
        cheese soup
    1 3-ounce can sliced mushrooms,
        drained
    ⅓ cup light cream
    ¼ cup dry sherry
    2 tablespoons snipped parsley
    1 10-ounce package frozen peas,
        cooked and drained
    2 tablespoons buttered soft bread
        crumbs

With a sharp knife, cut through lobster shell lengthwise. Remove meat from shells; cut meat into large pieces. In skillet cook onion and garlic in butter till tender but not brown. Stir in soup and mushrooms; gradually blend in cream, wine, and parsley. Add lobster pieces and peas. Cook, stirring occasionally, till heated through. Spoon into four 1-cup casseroles; top each with a wreath of crumbs. Bake at 350° for 25 to 30 minutes. Makes 4 servings.

LOBSTER-STUFFED POTATOES

    4 medium potatoes
    3 tablespoons butter or margarine
    ½ teaspoon salt
        Dash pepper
    6 to 8 tablespoons hot milk or
        light cream
    1 5-ounce can lobster, drained and
        flaked
    4 ounces sharp process American
        cheese, shredded (1 cup)
    2 tablespoons chopped green onion

Scrub potatoes, rub skins with shortening, and prick with fork. Bake at 375° till done, 70 to 80 minutes. Cut slice from top of each. Scoop out inside; reserve shells. Mash potatoes. Add butter, salt, pepper, and enough milk or cream to moisten. Beat till fluffy. Stir in lobster, ¾ *cup* cheese, and onion. Pile filling into potato shells. Bake 20 to 25 minutes longer. Sprinkle remaining cheese over tops of potatoes; bake 3 minutes more. Makes 4 servings.

LOBSTER-ASPARAGUS CASSEROLE

    1 10-ounce package frozen cut asparagus
    2 hard-cooked eggs, sliced
    1 cup dairy sour cream
    ¼ cup grated Parmesan cheese
    1 tablespoon milk
    1 teaspoon lemon juice
    ¼ teaspoon salt
        Dash bottled hot pepper sauce
    1 5-ounce can lobster, drained
        and flaked
    ¾ cup soft bread crumbs (1 slice)
    1 tablespoon butter or margarine,
        melted

Cook frozen asparagus according to package directions; drain. Arrange asparagus in 10x6x-1¾-inch baking dish. Arrange egg slices atop asparagus. Combine sour cream, Parmesan cheese, milk, lemon juice, salt, and hot pepper sauce; fold in lobster. Pour over eggs and asparagus. Combine bread crumbs and butter; sprinkle over casserole. Bake at 350° till heated through, 20 to 25 minutes. Serves 4.

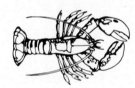

CLAM AND CORN CASSEROLE

    1¼ cups coarse saltine cracker crumbs
    1 cup milk
    2 well-beaten eggs
    1 8-ounce can whole kernel corn,
        drained
    1 7½-ounce can minced clams
    2 tablespoons finely chopped onion
    1 tablespoon finely chopped green
        pepper
    ½ teaspoon Worcestershire sauce
        Dash pepper
    2 ounces sharp process American
        cheese, shredded (½ cup)

Combine cracker crumbs, milk, and eggs. Stir in corn, *undrained* clams, onion, green pepper, Worcestershire sauce, and pepper. Turn into 1-quart casserole and bake at 350° till set, about 50 minutes. Sprinkle with shredded cheese and bake 5 minutes more. Makes 4 servings.

CLAM CASSEROLE

¾ cup sifted all-purpose flour
¼ cup shortening
2 to 3 tablespoons cold water
3 7½-ounce cans minced clams
½ cup chopped celery
½ cup chopped onion
¼ cup butter or margarine
1 cup milk
⅔ cup fine dry bread crumbs
2 beaten eggs
¼ teaspoon dried marjoram leaves,
    crushed
Milk

Sift flour and ¼ teaspoon salt together; cut in shortening with pastry blender till pieces are the size of small peas. Sprinkle *1 tablespoon* water over part of mixture; gently toss with fork. Push to side of bowl. Repeat till all is moistened. Form into ball. Flatten on lightly floured surface by pressing 3 times across in both directions. Roll from center to edge into 7-inch circle. Cut the pastry into 6 wedges.

Drain clams, reserving ½ cup liquid. Cook celery and onion in butter till tender but not brown. Stir in clam liquid, 1 cup milk, crumbs, eggs, ¾ teaspoon salt, marjoram, and ⅛ teaspoon pepper. Cook and stir till thickened and bubbly. Stir in clams; turn mixture into 1½-quart casserole. Arrange pastry wedges atop mixture. Brush with milk. Bake at 350° till pastry browns, 40 to 45 minutes. Serves 6.

JIFFY CLAM SKILLET

⅓ cup chopped onion
⅓ cup chopped green pepper
2 tablespoons butter or margarine
1 11-ounce can condensed bisque of
    tomato soup
1 to 2 teaspoons prepared horseradish
1 teaspoon Worcestershire sauce
1 7½-ounce can minced clams
2 cups hot cooked rice

Cook onion and green pepper in butter till tender but not brown. Add soup, horseradish, and Worcestershire sauce. Drain clams, reserving ¼ cup liquid. Stir reserved liquid into soup mixture. Cover and simmer 5 minutes. Add drained clams and heat through. Serve over hot cooked rice. Makes 4 servings.

BREAKFAST CLAM HASH

Listen to the praises when you serve this scrumptious dish for breakfast or a light supper—

3 medium potatoes, cooked, cooled,
    peeled, and shredded
1 7½-ounce can minced clams, drained
4 slices bacon, crisp-cooked and
    crumbled
1 beaten egg
2 tablespoons snipped chives
1 teaspoon salt
¼ teaspoon dry mustard
    Dash pepper
¼ cup butter or margarine

Combine all ingredients except butter or margarine. Melt butter in skillet; pat potato-clam mixture into skillet, leaving ½-inch space around edge. Brown 6 to 8 minutes over medium heat. Turn in large portions. Brown about 4 to 5 minutes longer. Makes 4 servings.

CLAM AND NOODLE CASSEROLE

Tuna casserole fans will like this, too—

1 10½-ounce can condensed cream of
    mushroom soup
¼ cup snipped parsley
¼ cup mayonnaise or salad dressing
1 teaspoon lemon juice
1 teaspoon grated onion
¼ teaspoon salt
    Dash pepper
2 7½-ounce cans minced clams
6 ounces narrow noodles, cooked and
    drained
1 cup crushed potato chips

Combine soup, parsley, mayonnaise, lemon juice, onion, salt, and pepper. Drain clams, reserving ½ cup liquid. Gradually blend reserved liquid into soup. Stir in drained clams and cooked noodles. Turn into 1½-quart casserole. Sprinkle crushed potato chips over top. Bake at 350° for 35 to 40 minutes. Serves 4.

SCALLOP CASSEROLE

1 pound fresh or frozen scallops
Instant mashed potatoes (enough for
4 servings)
6 ounces process American cheese,
shredded (1½ cups)
1 beaten egg
1 3-ounce can chopped mushrooms,
drained
2 tablespoons snipped chives
Dash pepper
2 tomatoes, sliced

Thaw frozen scallops. Cook scallops 1 minute in boiling, salted water. Drain; cut large scallops in half. Prepare potatoes according to package directions except *reduce water by ⅓ cup*. Combine the hot potatoes and *1 cup* cheese, stirring till cheese melts. Beat in egg. Add mushrooms, chives, dash pepper, and scallops. Turn into 10x6x1¾-inch baking dish. Arrange tomatoes atop potato mixture. Sprinkle with remaining cheese. Bake at 350° till heated through, 15 to 20 minutes. Makes 4 servings.

ORIENTAL SCALLOP SKILLET

1 pound fresh or frozen scallops
1 cup chicken broth
1 cup bias-cut celery slices
2 tablespoons sliced green onion
2 tablespoons cornstarch
2 tablespoons soy sauce
• • •
1 16-ounce can fancy mixed Chinese
vegetables, rinsed and drained
1 3-ounce can chopped mushrooms,
drained
¼ teaspoon salt
¼ cup toasted sliced almonds
Hot cooked rice or chow mein noodles

Thaw frozen scallops. Rinse scallops and drain. Cut large scallops in half. In saucepan combine scallops, chicken broth, celery, and green onion. Bring to boiling; reduce heat and simmer 3 to 4 minutes. Combine cornstarch and soy sauce; add to mixture in saucepan. Cook and stir till thickened and bubbly. Add Chinese vegetables, mushrooms, and salt; heat through. Stir in almonds. Serve over hot cooked rice or warmed chow mein noodles. Pass additional soy sauce, if desired. Makes 4 to 6 servings.

SCALLOPS TETRAZZINI

1 12-ounce package frozen scallops
½ teaspoon instant minced onion
1 cup water
2 tablespoons butter or margarine
2 tablespoons all-purpose flour
¼ teaspoon paprika
Dash dried oregano leaves, crushed
1 drop bottled hot pepper sauce
½ cup milk
1 slightly beaten egg
1 3-ounce can broiled, sliced mushrooms,
undrained
4 ounces spaghetti, cooked and drained
2 tablespoons grated Parmesan cheese

Thaw frozen scallops. Cut large scallops in half. In saucepan combine scallops, onion, ¼ teaspoon salt, and dash pepper. Add water. Cover; simmer 10 minutes. Drain, reserving ½ cup cooking liquid. Melt butter in saucepan. Blend in flour, paprika, oregano, dash salt, and hot pepper sauce. Add the reserved liquid and milk. Cook and stir till thickened and bubbly. Stir a small amount of hot mixture into the egg. Return to hot mixture; mix well.

Add mushrooms with liquid and scallops to sauce. Mix well. Spoon hot, cooked spaghetti into a 10x6x1¾-inch baking dish. Top with scallop mixture; sprinkle with grated Parmesan cheese. Broil about 5 minutes. Makes 4 servings.

HANGTOWN FRY

Beat together 6 eggs, ⅓ cup milk, and ½ teaspoon salt. Mix together ¼ cup all-purpose flour, ½ teaspoon salt, and dash pepper. Roll 12 medium-sized shucked oysters in the seasoned flour mixture till coated.

Melt 2 tablespoons butter or margarine in skillet. Cook oysters in butter till edges curl, about 1 minute on each side. Pour egg mixture into skillet with oysters. As egg mixture begins to set on bottom and sides, lift and fold over with wide spatula. Cook till eggs are cooked throughout, about 4 to 5 minutes. Remove from heat immediately. Makes 3 or 4 servings.

TUNA AND CORN BAKE

1 beaten egg
1 cup milk
1 17-ounce can cream-style corn
1 9¼-ounce can tuna, drained and flaked
½ cup fine saltine cracker crumbs
¼ cup chopped green onion
2 tablespoons butter or margarine
½ cup coarse saltine cracker crumbs

In saucepan combine egg and milk; add corn. Heat and stir till mixture bubbles. Stir in tuna, ½ cup fine cracker crumbs, onion, ½ teaspoon salt, and dash pepper. Turn into 1-quart casserole. Melt butter; toss with ½ cup coarse cracker crumbs. Sprinkle atop casserole. Bake at 350° for 20 minutes. Makes 4 servings.

TUNA-BROCCOLI CASSEROLE

2 10-ounce packages frozen chopped
    broccoli
6 tablespoons butter or margarine
½ cup all-purpose flour
1 teaspoon salt
3½ cups milk
⅓ cup grated Parmesan cheese
2 tablespoons lemon juice
¼ teaspoon dried dillweed
1 9¼-ounce can tuna, drained
1 package refrigerated biscuits
    (10 biscuits)

Cook broccoli according to package directions; drain. In saucepan melt butter or margarine over low heat; blend in flour and salt. Add milk all at once. Cook and stir till thickened and bubbly. Add Parmesan, lemon juice, and dillweed. Stir in broccoli and tuna.

Turn the tuna mixture into a 2-quart casserole. Bake at 375° for 30 minutes. Snip four refrigerated biscuits into quarters; arrange quarters around edge of hot casserole and bake 15 minutes longer. Makes 8 servings.

Featuring a built-in garnish

← *Snip refrigerated biscuits into quarters and arrange them around Tuna-Broccoli Casserole for a decorative trim. Dip the remaining biscuits in melted butter and cinnamon-sugar before baking for a sweet snack.*

TUNA SOUFFLÉ

¼ cup butter or margarine
¼ cup all-purpose flour
¼ teaspoon salt
1 cup milk
4 ounces sharp process American cheese,
    shredded (1 cup)
1 6½- or 7-ounce can tuna, drained
    and flaked
2 tablespoons chopped canned pimiento
4 eggs, separated

In saucepan melt butter; blend in flour and ¼ teaspoon salt. Add milk all at once; cook and stir till mixture is thickened and bubbly. Remove from heat. Add cheese, tuna, and pimiento; stir till cheese melts. Beat egg yolks till very thick and lemon-colored. Slowly add cheese mixture, stirring constantly; cool slightly. Wash beaters. Beat egg whites to stiff peaks. Gradually pour yolk mixture over whites, folding together well.

Pour into *ungreased* 1½-quart soufflé dish. For top hat that puffs, trace a circle through mixture 1 inch from edge and 1 inch deep. Bake at 300° till knife inserted off-center comes out clean, 65 to 70 minutes. Break apart into servings with two forks. Makes 4 servings.

TUNA-CHEESE PUFF

6 slices white bread
1 6½- or 7-ounce can tuna, drained
    and flaked
¼ cup mayonnaise or salad dressing
1 tablespoon chopped canned pimiento
2 teaspoons instant minced onion
• • •
2 beaten eggs
1½ cups milk
1 10¾-ounce can condensed
    Cheddar cheese soup

Cube *2 slices* of the bread and reserve; trim crusts from remaining 4 slices, if desired. Place the 4 slices bread in bottom of 8x8x2-inch baking dish. Combine tuna, mayonnaise, pimiento, and onion. Spread mixture over bread in pan. Sprinkle bread cubes atop tuna mixture. Combine beaten eggs and milk; pour over all. Cover and chill at least 1 hour. Stir soup and spoon over top. Bake, uncovered, at 325° till set, about 1 hour. Remove from oven and let stand 5 minutes before cutting. Serves 4.

TUNA PILAF

Gourmets will enjoy this one —

1 3-ounce can sliced mushrooms,
    drained
¼ cup finely chopped onion
¼ cup finely chopped celery
2 tablespoons finely chopped green
    pepper
2 tablespoons butter or margarine
    • • •
3 cups cooked rice
1 6½- or 7-ounce can tuna, drained
1 teaspoon Worcestershire sauce
½ teaspoon salt
⅛ teaspoon dried thyme leaves, crushed
    Dash pepper

In skillet cook mushrooms, onion, celery, and green pepper in butter till tender. Add rice, tuna, Worcestershire sauce, salt, thyme, and pepper; toss to mix. Reduce heat; cook and stir till heated through. Makes 4 servings.

TUNA-RICE MEDLEY

2 unpeeled medium apples, cored and
    chopped (2 cups)
1 cup chopped celery
½ cup chopped onion
¼ cup butter or margarine
1 10¾-ounce can condensed cream of
    vegetable soup
1 cup milk
2 6½- or 7-ounce cans tuna, drained
2 cups cooked rice
½ teaspoon salt
    Dash pepper
2 tablespoons butter or margarine,
    melted
1 cup crisp rice cereal squares,
    coarsely crumbled
½ teaspoon curry powder

In large saucepan cook apple, celery, and onion in ¼ cup butter till tender but not brown. Add soup; gradually stir in milk. Add tuna, rice, salt, and pepper; mix well. Turn into greased 2-quart casserole. Combine the 2 tablespoons melted butter, crushed cereal, and curry powder; sprinkle over top of casserole. Bake, uncovered, at 375° till heated through, 30 minutes. Makes 6 to 8 servings.

Divide Two-Way Tuna *among small baking dishes for individual servings. Add garnishes of lemon cartwheels, twists, or curls to each one for a final touch.*

TWO-WAY TUNA

Choose either curry or dill to flavor this individually baked casserole —

1 10-ounce package frozen chopped
    broccoli
¼ cup chopped onion
1 tablespoon butter or margarine
1 10½-ounce can condensed cream of
    mushroom soup
½ cup dairy sour cream
½ teaspoon curry powder or ½ teaspoon
    dried dillweed
1 6½- or 7-ounce can tuna, drained
    and flaked

Cook broccoli according to package directions; drain. In saucepan cook onion in butter till tender but not brown. Stir in soup, sour cream, and curry *or* dillweed. Fold in tuna and cooked broccoli. Turn into 4 individual casseroles. Bake at 375° till heated through, 20 to 25 minutes. Garnish tops of individual casseroles with lemon twists, if desired. Makes 4 servings.

TUNA-STUFFED SHELLS

    4 ounces conchiglioni (20 jumbo
        conch-shaped macaroni shells)
    1 6½- or 7-ounce can tuna, drained and
        flaked
    1 cup soft bread crumbs (1¼ slices)
    ¼ cup finely chopped onion
    1 beaten egg
    2 tablespoons snipped parsley
    1 teaspoon lemon juice
            • • •
    1 10¾-ounce can condensed cream of
        celery soup
    ½ cup milk
    2 tablespoons snipped parsley

Cook conchiglioni in boiling, salted water just till tender, about 15 to 20 minutes; drain. Rinse in cold water; drain. In bowl combine tuna, bread crumbs, onion, egg, 2 tablespoons parsley, and lemon juice. Fill each shell with 1 tablespoon tuna filling. Arrange stuffed shells in 11¾x7½x1¾-inch baking dish.

In saucepan heat together soup, milk, and 2 tablespoons parsley. Pour over shells. Sprinkle with paprika, if desired. Cover and bake at 350° for 20 minutes. Makes 5 servings.

TUNA-NOODLE CASSEROLE

    6 ounces medium noodles (3 cups)
    1 6½- or 7-ounce can tuna, drained
    1 cup sliced celery
    ½ cup mayonnaise or salad dressing
    ⅓ cup chopped onion
    ¼ cup chopped green pepper
    ¼ cup chopped canned pimiento
    ½ teaspoon salt
    1 10½-ounce can condensed cream of
        celery soup
    ½ cup milk
    4 ounces sharp process American
        cheese, shredded (1 cup)

Cook noodles according to package directions; drain. Combine noodles, tuna, celery, mayonnaise, onion, green pepper, pimiento, and salt. Blend soup and milk; heat through. Add American cheese to soup mixture; heat and stir till cheese melts. Add to noodle mixture. Turn into 2-quart casserole. If desired, top with ½ cup toasted slivered almonds. Bake, uncovered, at 425° for 20 minutes. Makes 6 servings.

FLORENTINE FILLETS

    1 pound fresh or frozen flounder
        fillets or other fish fillets
    1 10-ounce package frozen chopped
        spinach
    1 3½-ounce package process cheese
        spread with lobster or 1 3-ounce
        package cream cheese with
        pimiento, softened
    1 tablespoon butter or margarine
    4 teaspoons all-purpose flour
    ⅛ teaspoon salt
        Dash white pepper
    ¾ cup chicken broth
    1 tablespoon dry white wine
        Paprika

Thaw frozen fillets. Cook spinach according to package directions; drain thoroughly. Spread spinach in 1-quart casserole. Cut fillets into 4 portions; season with salt and pepper. Spread *half* the cheese atop fillets. Roll up each fillet and place on top of spinach.

In saucepan melt butter; blend in flour, salt, and white pepper. Add broth; cook and stir till mixture is thickened and bubbly. Remove from heat and gradually blend into remaining cheese; add wine. Pour sauce over fillets. Sprinkle with paprika. Bake, uncovered, at 350° for 20 to 25 minutes. Makes 4 servings.

POLYNESIAN FILLETS

    1 pound fresh or frozen pollock fillets
        or other fish fillets
    1 cup bias-cut celery slices
    ½ cup green pepper strips
    2 tablespoons butter or margarine
    1 16-ounce can bean sprouts, rinsed
        and drained
    3 tablespoons soy sauce
    1 tablespoon light molasses
    1 tablespoon cornstarch
    ½ cup cold water

Thaw frozen fillets. Poach fillets (see page 16). Remove fish to heated platter; keep warm.

In skillet cook celery and green pepper in butter till crisp-tender, about 2 to 3 minutes. Add bean sprouts, soy sauce, and molasses. Combine cornstarch and water; stir into skillet. Cook and stir till thickened and bubbly. Spoon bean sprout mixture over fillets. Serves 4.

Menu

POTLUCK SUPPER

Tuna Bake for Twelve

Succotash   Assorted Salads

Fruit Relishes

Toasted Bun Sticks

Cake   Brownies

Milk   Coffee

Do you want to have a party for a club, church group, neighborhood, or family reunion, yet think it's too much work for one person? Then try a potluck supper. Let each person select one or two dishes to bring. Bachelors and those who cannot bring a cooked dish can supply the paper plates and cups or beverages.

This type of party has many advantages. The work is divided, so no one has to furnish all the food or do all the cooking. The homemakers will enjoy sampling others' recipes. And everyone can join in the fun of sharing.

BISCUIT-CROWNED CASSEROLES

Cook 1 pound pollock fillets or other fish fillets; cut into chunks. Pour boiling water over one 10-ounce package frozen peas and carrots; drain. Cook ½ cup chopped onion in 6 tablespoons butter till tender but not brown. Blend in ½ cup all-purpose flour and 1 teaspoon salt. Stir in 3 cups chicken broth. Cook and stir till thickened and bubbly. Add fish, vegetables, and ¼ cup chopped canned pimiento; heat to boiling. Pour into 6 individual casseroles. Cut 6 refrigerated biscuits into quarters. Arrange 4 pieces atop each casserole while fish mixture is very hot. Bake at 450° till the biscuits are browned, about 10 minutes. Makes 6 servings.

Bring your own dish

← *Build a potluck supper around Tuna Bake for Twelve, succotash, relish, and toasted bun sticks. A variety of salads, desserts, and beverages for both adults and children will fit into the menu easily.*

TUNA BAKE FOR TWELVE

    8 ounces medium noodles (6 cups)
    8 tablespoons butter or margarine
    ½ cup milk
    ¼ cup all-purpose flour
    3 cups milk
    2 10½-ounce cans chicken gravy
    2 6½- or 7-ounce cans tuna, drained
        and broken into chunks
    ¼ cup chopped canned pimiento
    ½ cup fine dry bread crumbs
    2 ounces process American cheese,
        shredded (½ cup)

Cook noodles according to package directions; drain. Add *2 tablespoons* butter and ½ cup milk. In saucepan melt *4 tablespoons* butter; blend in flour, ½ teaspoon salt, and ⅛ teaspoon pepper. Add 3 cups milk. Cook and stir till thickened and bubbly. Stir in gravy, tuna, pimiento, and noodles. Spread in 13½x8¾x1¾-inch baking dish. Bake, covered, at 350° for 25 minutes. Melt *2 tablespoons* butter; toss with crumbs and cheese. Sprinkle on casserole. Bake till heated through, 10 minutes. Serves 12.

ANCHOVY PIZZA

Make pizza crusts by combining 1 cup sifted all-purpose flour and 1 package active dry yeast in mixer bowl. Add 1 cup hot water (120°), 1 tablespoon salad oil, and 1 teaspoon salt. Beat at low speed till blended. Beat at high speed 3 minutes. Gradually blend in 2½ cups sifted all-purpose flour. Turn onto floured surface and knead till smooth and elastic, about 12 minutes (will be firm). Place in lightly greased bowl; turn greased side up. Cover. Let rise in warm place till more than doubled, 1½ to 2 hours. Punch down; cover and let rest 10 minutes or cover and chill the dough till needed.

Cut dough in half. On lightly floured surface roll each into 12- or 14-inch circle. Place in two greased 12- or 14-inch pizza pans, forming rims. Brush with 2 tablespoons salad oil.

Combine two 8-ounce cans tomato sauce; ½ cup chopped onion; 2 to 3 teaspoons dried oregano leaves, crushed; dash pepper; and 1 clove garlic, crushed. Spread over dough circles. Drain two 2-ounce cans anchovy fillets; arrange on pizzas. Sprinkle 8 ounces mozzarella cheese, shredded (2 cups) over top. Bake at 425° for 20 to 25 minutes. Makes 2 pizzas.

Feature Salmon-Shrimp Casserole *at a dinner party. This one-dish meal includes two of the most popular seafoods, bright peas, a cheesy sauce, and even a biscuit topper for the bread. A crisp salad rounds out the menu.*

SALMON SCALLOP

    1 7¾-ounce can salmon
       Dash dried dillweed
    ½ cup fine saltine cracker crumbs
    2 teaspoons lemon juice
    ⅓ cup milk
    ¼ cup chopped celery
    1 tablespoon butter or margarine

Flake salmon (with liquid) into bowl, removing skin and bones. Stir in dash pepper, dillweed, crumbs, lemon juice, milk, and celery. Turn into a 2-cup casserole. Dot with butter. Bake at 350° for 35 minutes. Makes 2 servings.

FISH AND SCALLOPED POTATOES

Using one 5½-ounce package dry scalloped potato mix, place dry potatoes in a 2-quart casserole. Add ½ cup shredded process American cheese, 2 tablespoons snipped parsley, 1 tablespoon chopped canned pimiento, and 1 teaspoon instant minced onion. Sprinkle sauce mix from potato package over mixture. Pour 2 cups boiling water and 1¼ cups milk over top; stir till cheese melts. Add one 8-ounce package frozen, fried, breaded fish sticks, cut into thirds, and 2 hard-cooked eggs, coarsely chopped; mix. Cover; bake at 400° for 30 minutes. Uncover; bake 15 minutes. Serves 4 to 6.

SALMON-SHRIMP CASSEROLE

    2 tablespoons butter or margarine
    2 tablespoons all-purpose flour
    1 10-ounce can frozen condensed cream
        of shrimp soup, thawed
    1 cup milk
    2 ounces sharp process American cheese,
        shredded (½ cup)
    1 16-ounce can red salmon, drained,
        boned, and broken into large pieces
    ½ of a 10-ounce package frozen peas
    1 cup packaged biscuit mix

In saucepan melt butter; stir in flour. Add soup
and milk. Cook and stir till thickened and
bubbly. Remove from heat; add cheese, stirring
till melted. Gently stir in salmon and peas. Turn
into a 1-quart baking dish. Bake at 425° till
bubbly and heated through, about 30 minutes.
Prepare biscuit mix according to package
directions for drop biscuits. Spoon 10 biscuits
around edge of hot casserole. Bake till golden,
15 minutes longer. Makes 4 servings.

MACKEREL-CORN CASSEROLE

    2 chicken bouillon cubes
 1⅔ cups boiling water
    2 tablespoons chopped onion
    ¼ cup butter or margarine
    5 tablespoons all-purpose flour
       Dash pepper
    2 ounces process American cheese,
        shredded (½ cup)
    1 15-ounce can mackerel, drained,
        bones and skin removed, and flaked
    1 12-ounce can whole kernel corn,
        drained
    2 tablespoons chopped canned pimiento
  ¾ cup soft bread crumbs (1 slice)
    1 tablespoon butter or margarine,
        melted

Dissolve bouillon cubes in the boiling water;
set aside. Cook onion in ¼ cup butter till tender
but not brown. Blend in flour and pepper; add
bouillon all at once. Cook, stirring constantly,
till thickened and bubbly. Stir in cheese till
melted. Add flaked fish, corn, and pimiento.
Turn into a 1½-quart casserole. Toss bread
crumbs with melted butter. Sprinkle atop casserole. Bake at 350° till heated through, about 30
to 35 minutes. Makes 6 servings.

SALMON SUZETTE

       Crepes
    ¼ cup butter or margarine
    ¼ cup all-purpose flour
    2 cups milk
    1 16-ounce can salmon, drained, bones
        and skin removed, and flaked
    2 tablespoons snipped parsley
    4 ounces process American cheese,
        shredded (1 cup)
    ¼ cup milk

Crepes: In mixer bowl combine ⅔ cup sifted
all-purpose flour, 2 tablespoons sugar, 1½ cups
milk, 2 eggs, 2 egg yolks, 2 tablespoons melted
butter or margarine, and ⅛ teaspoon salt. Beat
till smooth. Lightly grease a 6-inch skillet; heat.
Remove from heat; add 2 tablespoons batter.
Rotate pan so batter spreads evenly over bottom.
Return to heat; brown on one side only. To
remove, invert pan over paper toweling. Repeat
with remaining batter, greasing pan occasionally. Makes 16 to 18 crepes.

  In saucepan melt butter. Add flour, ¼ teaspoon salt, and dash pepper. Add 2 cups milk.
Cook and stir till thickened and bubbly. Add
salmon and parsley to *half* the sauce; add
cheese and the ¼ cup milk to remaining sauce.
Spoon salmon mixture in center of crepes. Roll
up crepes and place in single layer in large
baking dish. Pour cheese sauce over. Bake at
325° till heated through, 20 minutes. Garnish
with toasted sliced almonds, if desired. Serves 8.

SMOKED SALMON AND MACARONI

    1 3⅔-ounce can sliced, smoked salmon
    1 15-ounce can macaroni and cheese
    1 3-ounce can chopped mushrooms,
        drained
    ¼ cup chopped green pepper
    1 teaspoon instant minced onion
    3 hard-cooked eggs, chopped
    2 tablespoons butter or margarine
 1½ cups soft bread crumbs

Rinse, drain, and cut salmon into small pieces.
Combine all ingredients except butter and
crumbs. Turn into a 1-quart casserole. Melt
butter; toss with crumbs. Sprinkle over casserole. Bake, uncovered, at 350° for 30 to 35
minutes. Garnish with green pepper rings or
hard-cooked egg slices, if desired. Serves 3 or 4.

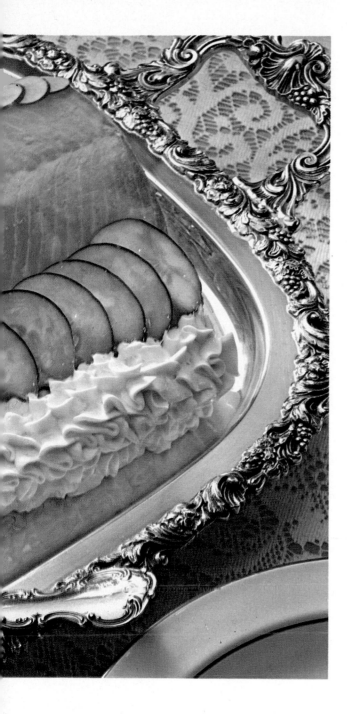

Finally, the meal is prepared and all that is needed are the finishing touches. How the dish is served can make a big difference, whether it is the garnish, the directions needed for eating the food, or the accompanying, tasty sauces.

Use your imagination to turn an everyday meal into something special —with the aid of garnishes. If possible, make the trims an edible part, such as the Glazed Salmon, decorated with cucumbers, radishes, and cream cheese. While lemon wedges are the most familiar additions, try your hand at cutting the lemon into different shapes. And there's no reason why limes and oranges can't be presented in the same way. You'll find many other garnishing ideas that should inspire you to create your own colorful trims.

When faced with one of these seafood beauties at the table, if you are a bit unsure of the proper way to eat some of the more complicated items, check this section before you begin. A little practice with these techniques and you'll be a pro in no time at all.

Looking for just the right sauce to complete the garnished dish is made easy when you see the assortment of hot and cold sauces that blend well with the delicate flavor of fish. Some can be made ahead of time, while others require a bit of last-minute preparation, such as Classic Hollandaise.

Find out for yourself just how easy it is to become a master saucier and an artist in your own kitchen. Then, try your hand at it.

Serving Helps

HOW TO GARNISH THE FINISHED DISH

The main reason for garnishing the finished sea-food dish, as with other foods, is to make the food look as appealing and appetizing as possible. By keeping garnishes uncomplicated, this goal is achieved with little effort.

Some fish dishes, particularly those that are poached or steamed, often need a spark of color. Garnishes add a lively note to the cooked dish—whether it is planned as part of the menu and is designed to be eaten, such as cream cheese piped around a glazed fish, or it is used primarily for ornamentation, such as parsley sprigs. Regardless of the reason for the garnish, there are some simple guidelines that should be followed in trimming plates.

Garnishes should be edible and compatible with the flavor of the dish, particularly if they are part of the planned menu. They should contrast the food in color and texture.

Simplicity is one of the key words when garnishing. Never use too much of a garnish. Some simple platter suggestions include a single arrangement slightly off-center or to the side; two unequally-sized arrangements; three or four identical arrangements, evenly spaced around the finished dish. For individual plates, however, use a small, colorful garnish.

Never let the food you are garnishing get cold, thus sacrificing the delicious flavor of the seafood just to have an attractive garnish. Also, do not give the impression that the garnish has been overly handled.

Simple kitchen tools will produce some very attractive garnishes. A paring knife and chopping knife are musts. Vegetable peelers, tiny cutters, sieves, scissors, wooden picks and skewers, and pastry bags should be included in your inventory of kitchen equipment.

With equipment at hand, you must decide what food you would like to use as the garnish. Fish and shellfish are delicious with most vegetables as well as citrus fruits. Lemons and limes are naturals with fish. Eggs, nuts, and mild cheeses are also compatible in flavor. Fish can be garnished with additional shellfish, such as a sauce with chunks of crab. And one cannot forget parsley, paprika, and other seasonings.

BUFFET GLAZED SALMON

This recipe is pictured on page 144—

1 3- to 4-pound dressed salmon
1 lemon, sliced
1½ cups chicken broth
**1 envelope unflavored gelatin
    (1 tablespoon)**
Sliced unpeeled cucumbers
Sliced radishes
**2 8-ounce packages cream cheese,
    softened**
2 tablespoons lemon juice
1 teaspoon onion salt
Milk

Salt inside of fish generously. Place on a well-greased 24-inch piece of heavy-duty foil on baking sheet. Place lemon slices inside and atop fish. Seal foil tightly; bake at 350° till fish flakes easily when tested with a fork, 45 to 60 minutes. Remove fish from foil; discard lemon. With sharp knife, carefully remove skin. Cover and chill fish thoroughly on a large serving platter.

In a small saucepan combine chicken broth and gelatin; dissolve over low heat. Chill till partially set. Spoon a small amount of gelatin glaze over fish. Place cucumber and radish slices on glaze atop fish in overlapping rows. Spoon remaining glaze over fish. Chill thoroughly. Remove any glaze from platter.

Combine cream cheese, lemon juice, and onion salt; thin with a little milk, if necessary. With a pastry tube, pipe a border around fish. Chill. Serve with mayonnaise and trim with additional lemon, cucumber, and salad greens, if desired. Makes about 24 buffet-sized servings.

Add the finishing touch

Try these garnishing ideas for dinner plates: a green →
onion cut in strips; lemon wedges dipped in snipped parsley with radish accordion and watercress; and cucumber slices folded around strips of pimiento.

Cucumbers, pickles, citrus fruits, vegetable and fruit kabobs, and eggs are all popular garnishes with seafood dishes. Arrange them attractively on the serving platter or place them atop a whole fish or on individual servings.

Cucumber baskets make attractive serving containers for mayonnaise, salad dressings, tartar sauce, or other cold sauces and can accompany a salad or other dish. To make the baskets, slice off a piece from one end of a large cucumber for the base so that the cucumber will sit flat. Then, cut off a small piece from the other end. Using knife, score lengthwise strips through peel, about ½ inch wide, around outside. Cut down every other strip to about two inches from base, making strips as thin as possible. Curl strips under and secure with wooden picks. Cut off top of cucumber leaving about a four-inch piece. Hollow out. Chill to crisp; remove picks. Fill with sauce.

Scored cucumbers are one of the easiest seafood garnishes. Run the tines of a fork lengthwise down an unpeeled cucumber, pressing to break through peel. Repeat around entire cucumber. Then, make slices by cutting straight across or on the bias. Overlap slices along the edge of the platter or place atop cooked fish.

Make *pickle fans* by slicing whole pickles lengthwise almost to stem end in very thin slices. Spread each fan and press uncut end of pickle so fan will hold its shape. Or cut pickle all the way through; arrange slices in fan shape.

Citrus garnishes — lemons, limes, and oranges — are good partners with seafood dishes. They add a tangy flavor and a colorful touch.

Dress-up everyday *lemon wedges* by dipping the edge in paprika or snipped parsley. Or make *cartwheels* by slicing the fruit ⅛ inch thick. Cut notches in the peel around the outside as desired. For *citrus twists,* slice fruit ⅛ inch thick. Make one cut to center of fruit slice and twist ends in opposite directions.

Use a cucumber basket filled with a sauce and topped with a sprig of parsley, rows of scored cucumber slices, and pickle fans to garnish seafood.

Include citrus garnishes when trimming fish — wedges dusted lightly with paprika, lemon cartwheels, perky lemon twists, citrus curls, and zigzag lemon or lime halves, ready for juicing.

To make *citrus curls,* cut a ⅛-inch citrus slice in half, cutting to, but not through, one edge of the peel. Remove the fruit from one half of the slice. Curl the peel. A simple way to make a *zigzag lemon or lime half* is to cut a thin slice off the bottom to make it sit flat. Cut fruit in half. Make a crosswise cut with knife at an angle; make the next cut at reverse angle. Remove V-shaped piece. Repeat across the fruit half.

Fruit and vegetable kabobs add interest to any seafood dinner plate. Use attractive metal skewers or bamboo skewers for threading various-sized pieces of fruit or vegetables. Some vegetable kabobs can be heated briefly under the broiler, while others may be served cold.

One tasty combination for a kabob includes cherry tomatoes, notched cucumber slices, and lemon wedges. Another kabob combination combines a mandarin orange segment, melon ball, and unpeeled apple wedge. A chunk of green pepper, a mushroom, and pineapple chunk make a combination that can be broiled.

Small, whole pickles, pitted olives, and carrot curls make colorful relish kabobs. To prepare *carrot curls,* rest a peeled carrot on cutting surface. Shave a thin, wide, lengthwise strip of carrot with vegetable peeler away from you. Roll up long slice; secure with wooden pick or skewer and plunge in ice water to crisp.

Other relish garnishes include radish roses and radish accordions. To make *radish roses,* cut root tip off radish, then cut 4 or 5 thin petals around radish, leaving a little red between petals. Chill in ice water till petals spread open like a flower. To make *radish accordions,* make crosswise cuts in long radishes, cutting partially through the radish in 8 narrow slices. Chill in ice water so slices will fan out.

Cranberry cutouts are another colorful garnish. Make them from jellied cranberry sauce. Cut slices about ¼ inch thick and use tiny cutters to make variously shaped pieces.

Hard-cooked eggs also add a special touch. Sieve egg yolk over sauces for a goldenrod effect. Or arrange sliced eggs in overlapping rows. Sprinkle egg wedges with finely snipped parsley or paprika. Or pipe deviled yolk mixture into egg white halves using a pastry tube.

Team vegetables and fruits to make colorful kabobs. Use fresh fruits in season, or substitute canned varieties when fresh are not available.

Slice or quarter hard-cooked eggs or pipe a deviled egg yolk mixture into hard-cooked egg white halves, using a pastry tube. Sprinkle with paprika.

HOW TO EAT FISH AND SHELLFISH

Bones: When you find bones in a serving of fish, try to remove as many as possible with a fork before putting the bite into your mouth. Remove any bones that accidentally remain in the bite with your thumb and forefinger after the bone is thoroughly cleaned in the mouth. Place the bone on the edge of the plate or on the bread and butter plate, if this plate is used in the place setting.

Clams: When eating hard-shell clams on the half shell, either raw or cooked, the muscle is sometimes already loosened from the shell. If not, steady clam with one hand and loosen muscle with a small, seafood fork.

To eat steamed soft-shell clams (steamers) from the shell, however, a different technique is used. (Discard any clams that have not popped open during cooking.) The entire shell can be picked up in the hands. If not fully opened during the cooking process, the first step would be to open the shell fully, bending it backward at the hinged part. This process should be done over a dish or plate since there will be some liquid in the shell. Then, holding the hinged clam shell in one hand, pull the clam free by grabbing the neck (long slender part). Pull off the black neck cover.

Eating steamed clams can be a very enjoyable experience. Pick up opened shells and pull out muscle by grabbing the long slender part of the clam.

Using the neck as a "handle," dip clams into a small cup of clam broth to remove any sand that might be present. Then, dip clams into an individual cup of melted butter and put the clam into your mouth. Place the shell to the side of the plate or put in a separate dish. At the end, you can drink the clam broth.

Crabs: Eating a whole, hard-shell crab is simplified when part of the work has been done in the kitchen. This includes pulling off the hard shell, removing the gills, spongy digestive organs, cartilage, and the triangular flap from the underside. It's also helpful to have the legs separated from the body and cracked.

All that's left for you to do when eating is to remove the meat from the claws, legs, and body with a nutpick or seafood fork and dip the meat into melted butter or cocktail sauce. A nutcracker may be necessary for additional cracking of the claws and legs. Often another plate or bowl is used for the discarded parts, or you can place shells to the edge of the dinner plate.

Soft-shell blue crabs are cleaned like the hard-shell crab, and the legs generally are broken off before cooking. The outer covering is edible, but it may be peeled back, if desired.

Finger bowls: It is almost a necessity to use a finger bowl or other type of moistened cloth after eating lobster or steamed clams. When using the finger bowl, only your finger tips should be dipped into the small bowl of warm water. Briefly dry your hands on a napkin which is left on the lap. Or a small packaged wet towel or moistened cloth, one for each individual, may be substituted for the finger bowl. A lemon or lime wedge may be squeezed into the water in the finger bowl for a refreshing touch.

Frogs Legs: If the leg bones of the frog are very small, they may be picked up with the fingers, gripping one end of the bone. The other end is put into the mouth and the meat is sucked off between closed lips. Otherwise, the meat may be cut from the bones with a knife and the meat is then eaten with a fork.

Lobsters: A whole lobster, like other types of shellfish, cannot be eaten very daintily. This is one type of food where it is necessary to use your fingers with dexterity. You can, however, rest assured that a whole lobster will never be served at a very formal meal.

The following drawings depict the steps for eating a whole lobster.

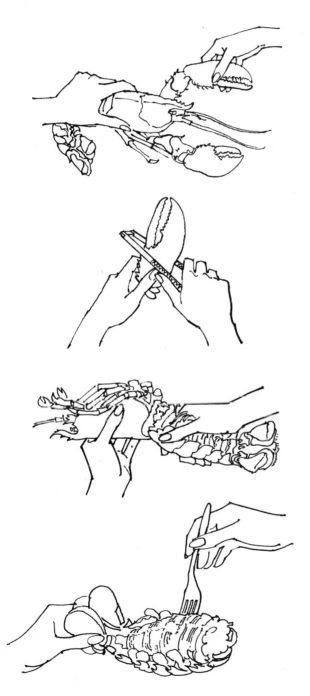

Begin eating a whole boiled or broiled lobster by grasping the body in one hand. With the other hand, twist off the two large claws of the cooked lobster.

Working with the large claws, use a nutcracker or some other utensil, such as a mallet, that will crack the claws. Remove meat with nutpick or seafood fork.

With the large claws removed, grasp the body and the tail with both hands. Arch the back of the lobster until it cracks. Then, separate tail from body.

Remove meat from tail by loosening it with a seafood fork. The meat is then cut into bite-sized pieces and eaten with the small seafood fork.

If desired, you can break off the small claws and place the end in your mouth. Gently and quietly suck out any meat that may be in these small claws.

Pick up the body section and crack it in half to expose the meat. Using a fork, remove and eat the meat, red coral roe, and brownish green liver.

Before you begin your lobster feast, whether it is a broiled, boiled, or baked stuffed lobster, don a king-sized plastic, cloth, or paper bib or napkin around your neck to protect clothing. A large napkin for the fingers should also be handy, as should a finger bowl or dampened cloth at the end of the meal. Nutcrackers and nutpicks or seafood forks are among the utensils you will need to eat the lobster.

As the meat is extracted from the shell with a fork, dip the meat into a small, individual container of melted butter or desired sauce.

Mussels: Steamed mussels can be eaten like steamed clams by dipping the meat from the mussel shell into melted butter after the meat has been removed from the shell.

When mussels in shells are cooked in a saucy mixture, the meat may be eaten, using a seafood fork or by picking up the mussel shell and silently sucking out both meat and sauce. Discard shells to a separate plate or container and eat remaining saucy mixture with a spoon.

Oysters: When eaten on the half shell, whether raw or cooked, the muscle of the oysters is sometimes loosened from the shell. Using a small seafood fork, the entire oyster is eaten in one bite, if possible. It is permissible to steady the shell with one hand, since it may be necessary to help free the oyster muscle from the shell. After the oyster is eaten, if desired, you can pick up the shell and drink the liquid that remains in the oyster shell.

When eating cooked oysters from the shell, place cupped side of oyster down on plate. Use

When eating oysters on the half shell, steady the shell with one hand while using the small seafood fork to remove the meat. Eat oyster in one bite.

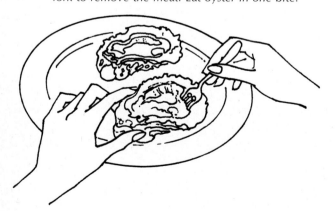

an oyster knife or other blunt knife to pry shell open along wide end of shell. Cut through muscle that holds shell closed. Remove top shell. Then, use a seafood fork to remove and eat meat. Fried oysters are also eaten with a fork.

Restaurant dining: It is perfectly proper to ask the waiter or waitress in restaurants to remove the head and bones when a whole fish is served. Or, if a whole lobster is ordered, you can ask to have the claws cracked. You may find that this has been taken care of before serving.

Seafood cocktails: Appetizers prepared with shrimp, lobster, crab, scallops, or other types of fish accompanied with a sauce are eaten with a seafood fork. When you are served shrimp that are larger than one bite, use a seafood fork to pick up the shrimp and bite off what you can eat. Then, if you have an individual serving of cocktail sauce, dip shrimp again in sauce. Avoid cutting up shrimp in the glass or on the plate on which cocktail is served.

Shrimp: If you are served shrimp with the shells left on, pick up the shrimp with your fingers, peel and clean them, then put the shrimp into your mouth with the fingers. Fried shrimp can also be picked up with the fingers if the shell on the tail is still intact. Using the tail as a "handle," dip the shrimp into a cocktail sauce first, then eat all of the shrimp, except the tail. When no tail shell is left on the shrimp, eat the fried shrimp with a fork.

Smelts: To eat, cut off heads and tails and discard these parts. Then open the fish and discard backbone and attached bones.

Snails: This delicacy is often called by its French name, *escargots*, and it is typically served on a metal or ovenproof plate having small, round indentations. The plate is designed to keep shells from sliding.

To eat snails, the shell is gripped with a hinged holder or napkin which protects the hands from the hot shells. Pick out the snail from the shell with a seafood fork or pick and then transfer it to the mouth. Snail should be eaten in one bite.

The garlicky mixture remaining in the shells may be consumed after the shells have been allowed to cool. It is proper to either drink the liquid from the shells or pour it onto the plate and soak up the mixture with French bread. The bread is then eaten with a fork.

Grasp snail shells with a hinged holder designed especially to hold the hot shells. Remove snail with a seafood fork and eat the snail in one bite.

Utensils: The most common piece of equipment used when eating fish or shellfish is the seafood fork. Other names that you might hear are cocktail or oyster fork. It can best be described as a small, two- or three-tined fork.

There are three places for this utensil in the table setting. It may be placed to the left of the other forks. Or it can be positioned to the farthest right of the plate, parallel to the knives, or it can be in a slanting position with the tines of the fork pointing upward in the bowl of the spoon placed at the right of the plate.

Other kitchen utensils that do double-duty at the dinner table are the nutcracker and the nutpick. The nutcracker is helpful when breaking crab or lobster claws. The nutpick is useful when removing the meat from small areas, such as from a snail shell or lobster claw.

Other specialty utensils are used for only one type of shellfish. For example, the hinged holder and special indented plate are made especially for eating snails. Another example is the oyster knife which is used primarily for opening oysters. It is a very strong, narrow-bladed knife having a blunt end perfect for prying shells open.

Whole fish: While fillets and steaks pose no eating problems, the whole fish may cause some puzzlement. It is proper to serve the fish either with or without the head. The following drawings show how to carve and remove the bones from many cooked, dressed fish.

Remove head and tail from cooked fish. Use a table knife to make a gentle lengthwise cut about one inch from upper edge, cutting into fish just to backbone.

Slide the table knife along top of backbone while gently lifting the top section away from backbone. Place top section on plate; repeat with bottom section.

Carefully slide the knife blade under the backbone while lifting it away from the cooked fish. Use a fork to assist this procedure. Discard the backbone.

Gently replace the two pieces that have been laid on the plate to their original position atop the fish. Head and tail may be replaced, if desired.

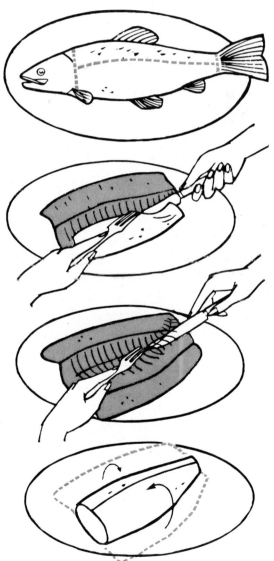

HOW TO MAKE TANTALIZING SAUCES

Choose one of these sauces to serve with a basic fish or shellfish recipe. You'll find that a sauce adds an important touch—it brings out flavor, enhances appearance, and varies the dish (try a different sauce each time).

CLASSIC HOLLANDAISE

>   4 egg yolks
>   ½ cup butter, cut in thirds
>   2 to 3 teaspoons lemon juice

Place egg yolks and ⅓ *of the butter* in top of double boiler. (Water in bottom pan should not touch top pan.) Cook over *hot, not boiling,* water till butter melts, stirring rapidly. Add ⅓ more of the butter and continue stirring. As mixture thickens and butter melts, add remaining butter, stirring constantly.

When butter is melted, remove pan from hot water; stir rapidly 2 minutes longer. Stir in lemon juice a teaspoon at a time; season with dash salt and dash white pepper. Heat again over hot water, stirring constantly till thickened, 2 to 3 minutes. Remove from heat at once. If sauce curdles, immediately beat in 1 or 2 tablespoons boiling water. Makes 1 cup.

TARTAR SAUCE

>   1 cup mayonnaise or salad dressing
>   3 tablespoons finely chopped dill
>   pickle
>   1 tablespoon snipped parsley
>   2 teaspoons chopped canned pimiento
>   1 teaspoon grated onion

Combine all ingredients; chill. Makes 1 cup.

HORSERADISH SAUCE

Combine 1 cup dairy sour cream, 3 tablespoons drained prepared horseradish, ¼ teaspoon salt, and dash paprika. Chill thoroughly.

JIFFY HOLLANDAISE

Combine ¼ cup dairy sour cream, ¼ cup mayonnaise, ½ teaspoon prepared mustard, and 1 teaspoon lemon juice. Cook and stir over low heat till heated through. Garnish with paprika and twist of lemon peel. Makes ½ cup.

EASY SEAFOOD SAUCE

>   ½ cup mayonnaise or salad dressing
>   3 tablespoons catsup
>   1 teaspoon prepared horseradish
>   ¼ teaspoon garlic salt
>   Snipped parsley

Combine mayonnaise, catsup, horseradish, and garlic salt; blend together. Chill thoroughly. Sprinkle with snipped parsley. Makes ¾ cup.

TARTAR SAUCE DELUXE

Blend together ½ cup dairy sour cream; ¼ cup mayonnaise or salad dressing; 1 hard-cooked egg, chopped; 2 tablespoons pickle relish; 2 tablespoons chopped green onion; and 2 tablespoons sauterne. Chill thoroughly. Garnish with sieved egg yolk and sliced green onion, if desired. Makes 1½ cups sauce.

CLARIFIED BUTTER

Melt butter over low heat without stirring; cool. Pour off oily top layer; discard bottom layer. Keep butter warm over candle warmer.

A sauce for every taste

Dressup fish and seafoods with a variety of sauces. → *Jiffy Hollandaise (top), Easy Seafood Sauce (middle), or Tartar Sauce Deluxe (bottom) adds flavor to fish, while Clarified Butter goes with lobster and crab.*

CUCUMBER SAUCE

Cut 1 medium unpeeled cucumber in half lengthwise; scoop out seeds. Shred enough to measure ½ cup; do not drain. Blend shredded cucumber with ½ cup dairy sour cream, ¼ cup mayonnaise or salad dressing, 1 tablespoon snipped chives, 2 teaspoons lemon juice, ¼ teaspoon salt, and dash white pepper. Chill.

DILL SAUCE

    ¼ **cup butter or margarine**
    ¼ **cup all-purpose flour**
    2 **cups strained fish broth**
    1 **tablespoon vinegar**
 1½ **tablespoons snipped fresh dillweed,**
        or 1½ teaspoons dried dillweed
    1 **teaspoon sugar**

In saucepan melt butter. Blend in flour. Add remaining ingredients. Cook and stir till thickened and bubbly. Serve hot. Makes 2 cups.

ALLEMANDE SAUCE

    2 **tablespoons butter or margarine**
    2 **tablespoons all-purpose flour**
    1 **cup chicken broth**
    ¼ **teaspoon salt**
      Dash white pepper
   ⅓ **cup light cream**
    1 **beaten egg yolk**
    1 **tablespoon lemon juice**
      Dash ground nutmeg

Melt butter in a saucepan; blend in flour. Add broth, salt, and white pepper. Cook and stir till thickened; add cream. Gradually stir about ½ *cup* of hot mixture into egg yolk; return to hot mixture. Cook and stir over low heat till thickened; remove from heat. Add lemon juice and nutmeg. Serve hot. Makes 1⅓ cups.

COCKTAIL SAUCE

Combine ¾ cup chili sauce, 2 tablespoons lemon juice, 1 to 2 tablespoons prepared horse-radish, 2 teaspoons Worcestershire sauce, ½ teaspoon grated onion, and few drops bottled hot pepper sauce. Season with salt to taste; chill thoroughly. Makes 1¼ cups.

MUSTARD SAUCE

    2 **tablespoons butter or margarine**
    2 **tablespoons all-purpose flour**
    ½ **teaspoon dry mustard**
 1¼ **cups milk**
    1 **teaspoon Dijon-style mustard**
    1 **teaspoon vinegar**

In saucepan melt butter. Blend in flour, dry mustard, ½ teaspoon salt, and dash white pepper. Add milk. Cook and stir till mixture is thickened and bubbly. Remove sauce from heat; stir in mustard and vinegar. For a more yellow sauce, add one or two drops yellow food coloring, if desired. Serve hot. Makes 1½ cups sauce.

BEER SAUCE

Combine 1 cup mayonnaise, ¼ cup catsup, ¼ cup beer, 1 tablespoon prepared mustard, 1 tablespoon lemon juice, and ½ teaspoon prepared horseradish. Chill. Makes 1½ cups.

BÉARNAISE SAUCE

In small saucepan combine 3 tablespoons tarragon vinegar; 1 teaspoon finely chopped shallots *or* green onion; 4 peppercorns, crushed; and Bouquet Garni of few tarragon and chervil leaves tied together. Simmer till liquid is reduced to half. Strain; add 1 tablespoon cold water.

Beat 4 egg yolks in top of double boiler (not over the water). Slowly add herb liquid. Have ½ cup butter at room temperature. Add a few tablespoons butter to egg yolks; place over *hot, not boiling* water. Cook and stir till butter melts and sauce starts to thicken. Continue adding butter and stirring till all has been used and sauce is smooth as thick cream.

Remove from heat. Salt to taste and add 1 teaspoon minced fresh tarragon or ¼ teaspoon dried tarragon leaves, crushed. Makes 1 cup.

LOUIS DRESSING

Whip ¼ cup whipping cream. Fold in 1 cup mayonnaise or salad dressing, ¼ cup chili sauce, ¼ cup chopped green pepper, 2 tablespoons sliced green onion with tops, and 1 teaspoon lemon juice. Season to taste with salt and pepper. Chill thoroughly. Serve over salads.

Almost any fish can be cooked by any method if allowances are made for the fat content of the fish during cooking.